OUT OF INDIA

OUT OF INDIA

THINGS I SAW, AND FAILED TO SEE, IN CERTAIN DAYS AND NIGHTS AT JEYPORE AND ELSEWHERE

RUDYARD KIPLING

GYAN

Published by

Gyan Publishing House
5, Ansari Road
Daryaganj, New Delhi-110002
Phone: 011-47034999, 9811692060
E-mail: books@gyanbooks.com

Distribution Network
gyanbooks.com
India, USA, Canada, UK, Australia

ISBN: 978-93-7169-202-1 (PB)

First Published, 1896

2nd Impression 2025

Printed at: Gyan Press, Delhi.

OUT OF INDIA
Author: RUDYARD KIPLING

OUT OF INDIA.

THINGS I SAW, AND FAILED TO SEE, IN CERTAIN DAYS AND NIGHTS AT JEYPORE AND ELSEWHERE.

BY

RUDYARD KIPLING

MDCCCXCVI

CONTENTS.

PART FIRST.

PART SECOND.

PART THIRD.

PART FOURTH.

OUT OF INDIA.

PART FIRST.

CHAPTER I.

AN ESCAPE FROM RIMMON—THE GLOBE TROTTER GOES TO JEYPORE—CERTAIN MORAL REFLECTIONS THEREON.

Except for those who, under compulsion of a sick certificate, are flying Bombaywards, it is good for every man to see some little of the great Indian Empire and the strange folk who move about it. It is good to escape for a time from the House of Rimmon—be it office or cutcherry—and to go abroad under no more exacting master than personal inclination, and with no more definite plan of travel than has the horse, escaped from pasture, free upon the country side. The first result of such freedon is extreme bewilderment, and the second reduces the freed to a state of mind which, for his sins, must be the normal portion of the Globe-Trotter—the man who "does" kingdoms in days and writes books upon them in weeks. And this desperate facility is not as strange as it seems. By the time that an Englishman has come by sea and rail *via* America, Japan, Singapore and Ceylon, to India, he can—these eyes have seen him do so—master in five minutes the intricacies of the *Indian Bradshaw*, and tell an old resident exactly how and where the trains run. Can we wonder that the intoxication of success in hasty assimilation should make him overbold, and that he should try to grasp—but a full account of the insolent Globe-Trotter must be reserved. He is worthy of a book. Given absolute freedom for a month, the mind, as I have said, fails to take in the situation and, after much debate, contents inself with following in old and well-beaten ways—paths that we in India have no time to tread, but must leave to the country cousin who wears his *pagri* tail fashion down his back, and says "cabman" to the driver of the ticca-ghari.

Now, Jeypore from the Anglo-Indian point of view is a station on the Rajputana-Malwa line, on the way to Bombay, where half an hour is allowed for dinner, and where there ought to be more protection from the sun than at present exists. Some few, more learned than the rest, know that garnets come from Jeypore, and here the limits of our wisdom are set. We do not, to quote the Calcutta shop-keeper, come out "for the good of our 'ealth," and what touring we accomplish is for the most part off the line of rail.

For these reasons, and because he wished to study our winter birds of passage, one of the few thousand Englishmen in India, on a date and in a place which have no concern with the story, sacrificed all his self-respect and became—at enormous personal inconvenience—a Globe-Trotter going to Jeypore, and leaving behind him for a little while all that old and well known life in which Commissioners and Deputy-Comissioners, Governors and Lieutenant-Governors, Aides-de-Camp, Colonels and their wives, Majors, Captains and Subalterns after their kind move and rule and govern and squabble and fight and sell each other's horses and tell wicked stories of their neighbors. But before he had fully settled into his part or accustomed himself to saying, "Please take out this luggage," to the coolies at the stations, he saw from the train the Taj wrapped in the mists of the morning.

There is a story of a Frenchman "who feared not God, nor regarded man," sailing to Egypt for the expressed purpose of scoffing at the Pyramids and —though this is hard to believe—at the great Napoleon who had warred under their shadow. It is on record that that blasphemous Gaul came to the Great Pyramid and wept through mingled reverence and contrition, for he sprang from an emotional race. To understand his feelings it is necessary to have read a great deal too much about the Taj, its design and proportions, to have seen execrable pictures of it at the Simla Fine Arts Exhibition, to have had its praises sung by superior and travelled friends till the brain loathed the repetition of the word, and then, sulky with want of sleep, heavy-eyed, unwashen and chilled, to come upon it suddenly. Under these circumstances everything, you will concede, is in favor of a cold, critical and not too impartial verdict: As the Englishman leaned out of the carriage he saw first an opal-tinted cloud on the horizon, and later certain towers. The mists lay on the ground, so that the splendor seemed to be floating free of the earth; and the mists rose in the background, so that at no time could everything be seen clearly. Then as the train sped forward, and the mists shifted and the sun shone upon the mists, the Taj took a hundred new shapes, each perfect and each beyond description. It was the Ivory Gate through which all good dreams come; it was the realization of the "glimmering halls of dawn" that Tennyson sings of; it was veritably the "aspiration fixed," the "sign made stone" of a lesser poet; and over and above concrete comparisons, it seemed the embodiment of all things pure, all things holy and all things unhappy. That was the mystery of the building. It may be that the mists wrought the witchery, and that the Taj seen in the dry sunlight is only as guide books say a noble structure. The Englishman could not tell, and has made a vow that he will never go nearer the spot for fear of breaking the charm of the unearthly pavilions.

It may be, too, that each must view the Taj for himself with his own eyes; working out his own interpretation of the sight. It is certain that no man can in cold blood and colder ink set down his impressions if he has been in the least moved.

To the one who watched and wondered that November morning the thing seemed full of sorrow —the sorrow of the man who built it for the woman he loved, and the sorrow of the workmen who died in the building—used up like cattle. And in the face of this sorrow the Taj flushed in the sunlight and was beautiful, after the beauty of a woman who has done no wrong.

Here the train ran in under the walls of Agra Fort, and another train—of thought incoherent as that written above—came to an end. Let those who scoff at overmuch enthusiasm look at the Taj and thenceforward be dumb. It is well on the threshold of a journey to be taught reverence and awe.

But there is no reverence in the Globe-Trotter : he is brazen. A Young Man from Manchester was travelling to Bombay in order—how the words hurt ! —to be home by Christmas. He had come through America, New Zealand and Australia, and finding that he had ten days to spare at Bombay, conceived the modest idea of "doing India." "I don't say that I've done it all ; but you may say that I've seen a good deal." Then he explained that he had been "much pleased" at Agra, "much pleased" at Delhi, and, last profanation, "very much pleased" at the Taj. Indeed he seemed to be going through life just then "much pleased" at everything. With rare and sparkling originality he remarked that India was a "big place," and that there were many things to buy. Verily, this Young Man must have been a delight to the Delhi boxwallahs. He had purchased shawls and embroidery "to the tune of" a certain number of rupees duly set forth, and he had purchased jewellery to another tune. These were gifts for friends at home, and he considered them "very Eastern." If silver filagree work modelled on Palais Royal patterns, or aniline blue scarves be "Eastern," he had succeeded in his heart's desire. For some inscrutable end it had been decreed that man shall take a delight in making his fellow-man miserable. The Englishman began to point out gravely the probable extent to which the Young Man from Manchester had been swindled, and the Young Man said: "By Jove. You don't say so. I hate being done. If there's anything I hate it's being done!"

He had been so happy in the "thought of getting home by Christmas," and so charmingly communicative as to the members of his family for whom such and such gifts were intended, that the Englishman cut short the record of fraud and soothed him by saying that he had not been so very badly "done" after all. This consideration was misplaced, for, his peace of mind restored, the Young Man from Manchester looked out of the window and, waving his hand over the Empire generally, said: "I say. Look here. All those wells are wrong, you know!" The wells were on the wheel and inclined plane system; but he objected to the incline, and said that it would be much better for the bullocks if they walked on level ground. Then light dawned upon him, and he said: "I suppose it's to exercise all their muscles. Y'know a canal horse is no use after he has been on the tow-path for some time. He can't walk anywhere but on the flat, y'know, and I suppose its just the same with bullocks." The spurs of the Aravalis, under which the train was running, had evidently suggested this brilliant idea which passed uncontradicted, for the Englishman was looking out of the window.

If one were bold enough to generalize after the manner of Globe-Trotters, it would be easy to build up a theory on the well incident to account for the apparent insanity of some of our cold weather visitors. Even the Young Man from Manchester could evolve a complete idea for the training of well-bullocks in the East at thirty-seconds' notice. How much the more could a cultivated observer from, let us say, an English constituency, blunder and pervert and mangle. We in this country have no time to work out the notion, which is worthy of the consideration of some leisurely Teuton intellect.

Envy may have prompted a too bitter judgment of the Young Man from Manchester ; for, as the train bore him from Jeypore to Ahmedabad, happy in " his getting home by Christmas," pleased as a child with his Delhi atrocities, pink-cheeked, whiskered and superbly self-confident, the Englishman whose home for the time was a dark bungaloathesome hotel, watched his departure regretfully ; for he knew exactly to what sort of genial, cheery British household, rich in untravelled kin, that Young Man was speeding. It is pleasant to play at Globe-Trotting ; but to enter fully into the spirit of the piece, one must also be going home for Christmas.

CHAPTER II.

RAJPUTANA, THE COCK-PIT OF INDIA—SOMETHING ABOUT THE HISTORY OF JEYPORE—THE GLOBE TROTTER SEES THE SIGHTS.

If any part of a land strewn with dead men's bones have a special claim to distinction, Rajputana, as the cock-pit of India, stands first. East of Suez men do not build towers on the tops of hills for the sake of the view, nor do they stripe the mountain sides with bastioned stone walls to keep in cattle. Since the beginning of time, if we are to credit the legends, there was fighting—heroic fighting—at the foot of the Aravalis, and beyond in the great deserts of sand penned by those kindly mountains from spreading over the heart of India. The "Thirty-six Royal Races" fought as royal races know how to do, Chohan with Rahtor, brother against brother, son against father. Later—but excerpts from the tangled tale of force, fraud, cunning, desperate love and more desperate revenge, crime worthy of demons and virtues fit for gods, may be found, by all who care to look, in the book of the man who loved the Rajputs and gave a life's labors in their behalf. From Delhi to Abu, and from the Indus to the Chambul, each yard of ground has witnessed slaughter, pillage and rapine. But, to-day, the capital of the State, that Dhola Rae, son of Soora Singh, hacked out more than nine hundred years ago with the sword from some weaker ruler's realm, is lighted with gas, and possesses many striking and English peculiarities which will be shown in their proper place.

Dhola Rae was killed in due time, and for nine hundred years Jeypore, torn by the intrigues of unruly princes and princelings, fought Asiatically.

When and how Jeypore became a feudatory of British power and in what manner we put a slur upon Rajput honor—punctilious as the honor of the Pathan—are matters of which the Globe-Trotter knows more than we do. He "reads up"—to quote his own words—a city before he comes to us, and, straightway going to another city, forgets, or, worse still, mixes what he has learnt—so that in the end he writes down the Rajput a Mahratta, says that Lahore is in the North-West Provinces and was once the capital of Sivaji, and piteously demands a "guide-book on all India, a thing that you can carry in your trunk y' know—that gives you plain descriptions of things without mixing you up." Here is a chance for a writer of discrimination and void of conscience!

But to return to Jeypore—a pink city set on the border of a blue lake, and surrounded by the low, red spurs of the Aravalis—a city to see and to puzzle over. There was once a ruler of the State, called Jey Singh, who lived in the days of Aurungzeb, and did him service with foot and horse. He must have been the Solomon of Rajputana, for through the forty-four years of his reign his "wisdom remained with him." He led armies, and when fighting was over, turned to literature; he intrigued desperately and successfully, but found time to gain a deep insight into astronomy, and, by what remains above ground now, we can tell that "whatsoever his eyes desired, he kept not from him." Knowing his own worth, he deserted the city of Amber founded by Dhola Rae among the hills, and, six miles further, in the open plain, bade one Vedyadhar, his architect, build a new city, as seldom Indian city was built before—with huge streets straight as an arrow, sixty yards broad, and cross-streets broad and straight. Many years afterwards the good people of America builded their towns after this pattern, but knowing nothing of Jey Singh, they took all the credit to themselves.

He built himself everything that pleased him, palaces and gardens and temples, and then died, and was buried under a white marble tomb on a hill overlooking the city. He was a traitor, if history speak truth, to his own kin, and he was an accomplished murderer, but he did his best to check infanticide; he reformed the Mahomedan calendar; he piled up a superb library and he made Jeypore a marvel.

Later on came a successor, educated and enlightened by all the lamps of British Progress, and converted the city of Jey Singh into a surprise—a big, bewildering, practical joke. He laid down sumptuous *trottoirs* of hewn stone, and central carriage drives, also of hewn stone, in the main street; he, that is to say, Colonel Jacob, the Superintending Engineer of the State, devised a water supply for the city and studded the ways with stand-pipes. He built gas works, set a-foot a School of Art, a Museum, all the things in fact which are necessary to Western municipal welfare and comfort, and saw that they were the best of their kind. How much Colonel Jacob has done, not only for the good of Jeypore city but for the good of the State at large, will never be known, because the officer in question is one of the not small class who resolutely refuse to talk about their own work. The result of the good work is that the old and the new, the rampantly raw and the sullenly old, stand cheek-by-jowl in startling contrast, Thus, the branded bull trips over the rails of a steel tramway which brings out the city rubbish ; the lacquered and painted *ruth*, behind the two little stag-like trotting bullocks, catches its primitive wheels in the cast-iron gas-lamp post with the brass nozzle a-top, and all Rajputana, gaily-clad, small-turbaned swaggering Rajputana, circulates along the magnificent pavements.

The fortress-crowned hills look down upon the strange medley. One of them bears on its flank in huge white letters the cherry inscript "Welcome !" This was made when the Prince of Wales visited Jeypore to shoot his first tiger ; but the average traveller of to-day may appropriate the message to himself, for Jeypore takes great care of strangers and shows them all courtesy. This, by the way, demoralizes the Globe-Trotter, whose first cry is : "Where can we get horses? Where can we get elephants? Who is the man to write to for all these things ?"

Thanks to the courtesy of the Maharaja, it is possible to see everything, but for the incurious who object to being driven through their sights, a journey down any one of the great main streets is a day's delightful occupation. The view is as unobstructed as that of the Champs Elysees ; but in place of the white-stone fronts of Paris, rises a long line of openwork screen-wall, the prevailing tone of which is pink, caramel-pink, but house-owners have unlimited license to decorate their tenements as they please. Jeypore, broadly considered, is Hindu, and her architecture of the riotous, many-arched type which even the Globe-Trotter after a short time learns to call Hindu. It is neither temperate nor noble, but it satisfies the general desire for something that "really looks Indian." A perverse taste for low company drew the Englishman from the pavement—to walk upon a real stone pavement is in itself a privilege—up a side-street where he assisted at a quail fight and found the low-caste Rajput a cheery and affable soul. The owner of the losing quail was a sowar in the Maharaja's army. He explained that his pay was six rupees a month paid bi-monthly. He was cut the cost of his khaki blouse, brown-leather accoutrements and jack-boots ; lance, saddle, sword and horse were given free. He refused to say for how many months in the year he was drilled, and said vaguely that his duties were mainly escort ones, and he had no fault to find with them. The defeat of his quail had vexed him, and he desired the Sahib to understand that the sowars of his Highness's army could rlde. A clumsy attempt at a compliment so fired his martial blood that he climbed into his saddle, and then and there insisted on showing off his horsemanship. The road was narrow, the lance was long, and the horse was a big one, but no one objected, and the Englishman sat him down on a doorstep and watched the fun. The horse seemed in some shadowy way familiar. His head was not the lean head of the Kathiawar, nor his crest the crest of the Marwarri, and his fore-legs did not seem to belong to the stony district. "Where did he come from?" The sowar pointed northward and said "from Amritsar," but he pronounced it "Armt-zar." Many horses had been bought at the spring fairs in the Punjab; they cost about Rs.200 each, perhaps more, the sowar could not say. Some came from Hissar and some from other places beyond Delhi. They were very good horses. "That horse there," he pointed to one a little distance down the street, "is the son of a big Sirkar horse—the kind that the Sirkar make for breeding horses—so high!" The owner of "that horse" swaggered up, jaw-bandaged and cat-moustached and bade the Englishman look at his mount; bought, of course, when a *butcha*. Both men together said that the Sahib had better examine the Maharaja Sahib's stable where there were hundreds of horses, huge as elephants or tiny as sheep.

To the stables the Englishman accordingly went, knowing beforehand what he would find, and wondering whether the Sirkar's "big horses" were meant to get mounts for Rajput sowars. The Maharaja's stables are royal in size and appointments. The enclosure round which they stand must be about half a mile long—it allows ample space for exercising, besides paddocks for the colts. The horses, about two hundred and fifty, are bedded in pure white sand—bad for the coat if they roll, but good for the feet—the pickets are of white marble, the heel-ropes in every case of good sound rope, and in every case the stables are exquisitely clean. Each stall contains above the manger, a curious little bunk for the syce who, if he uses the accommodation, must assuredly die once each hot weather.

A journey round the stables is saddening, for the attendants are very anxious to strip their charges, and the stripping shows so much. A few men in India are credited with the faculty of never forgetting a horse they have once seen, and of knowing the produce of every stallion they have met. The Englishman would have given something for their company at that hour. His knowledge of horseflesh was very limited ; but he felt certain that more than one or two of the sleek, perfectly groomed country-breds should have been justifying their existence in the ranks of the British cavalry, instead of eating their heads off on six seers of gram and one of *goor* per diem. But they had all been honestly bought and honestly paid for ; and there was nothing in the wide world to prevent His Highness, if he wished to do so, from sweeping up the pick and pride of all the horses in the Punjab. The attendants appeared to take a wicked delight in saying "eshtud-bred" very loudly and with unnecessary emphasis as they threw back the loin-cloth. Sometimes they were wrong, but in too many cases they were right.

The Englishman left the stables and the great central maidan, where a nervous Biluchi was being taught, by a perfect net-work of ropes, to "monkey-jump," and went out into the streets reflecting on the working of horse-breeding operations under the Government of India, and the advantages of having unlimted money wherewith to profit by other people's mistakes.

Then, as happened to the great Tartarin of Tarescon in Milianah, wild beasts began to roar, and a crowd of little boys laughed. The lions of Jeypore are tigers, caged in a public place for the sport of the people, who hiss at them and disturb their royal feelings. Two or three of the six great brutes are magnificent. All of them are short-tempered, and the bars of their captivity not too strong. A pariah-dog was furtively trying to scratch out a fragment of meat from between the bars of one of the cages, and the occupant tolerated him. Growing bolder, the starveling growled; the tiger struck at him with his paw and the dog fled howling with fear. When he returned, he brought two friends with him, and the trio mocked the captive from a distance.

It was not a pleasant sight and suggested Globe-Trotters—gentlemen who imagine that "more curricles" should come at their bidding, and on being undeceived become abusive.

CHAPTER III.

DOING AMBER—A CITY THAT WILL NEVER WAKE—THE MAHARAJA'S COTTON-PRESS.

And what shall be said of Amber, Queen of the Pass—the city that Jey Singh bade his people slough as snakes cast their skins. The Globe-Trotter will assure you that it must be "done" before anything else, and the Globe-Trotter is, for once, perfectly correct. Amber lies between six and seven miles from Jeypore among the "tumbled fragments of the hills," and is reachable by so prosaic a conveyance as a ticca-ghari, and so uncomfortable a one as an elephant. *He* is provided by the Maharaja, and the people who make India their prey, are apt to accept his services as a matter of course.

Rise very early in the morning, before the stars have gone out, and drive through the sleeping city till the pavement gives place to cactus and sand, and educational and enlightened institutions to mile upon mile of semi-decayed Hindu temples—brown and weather-beaten—running down to the shores of the great Man Sagar Lake, wherein are more ruined temples, palaces and fragments of causeways. The water-birds have their home in the half-submerged arcades and the *mugger* nuzzles the shafts of the pillars. It is a fitting prelude to the desolation of Amber. Beyond the Man Sagar the road of to-day climbs up-hill, and by its side runs the huge stone-causeway of yesterday—blocks sunk in concrete. Down this path the swords of Amber went out to kill. A triple wall rings the city, and, at the third gate, the road drops into the valley of Amber. In the half light of dawn, a great city sunk between hills and built round three sides of a lake is dimly visible, and one waits to catch the hum that should arise from it as the day breaks. The air in the valley is bitterly chill. With the growing light, Amber stands revealed, and the traveller sees that it is a city that will never wake. A few *meenas* live in huts at the end of the valley, but the temples, the shrines, the palaces and the tiers-on-tiers of houses are desolate. Trees grow in and split upon the walls, the windows are filled with brush wood, and the cactus chokes the street. The Englishman made his way up the side of the hill to the great palace that overlooks everything except the red fort of Jeighur, guardian of Amber. As the elephant swung up the steep roads paved with stone and built out on the sides of the hill, the Englishman looked into empty houses where the little grey squirrel sat and scratched its ears. The peacock walked upon the house-tops, and the blue pigeon roosted within. He passed under iron-studded gates whereof the hinges were eaten out with rust, and by walls plumed and crowned with grass, and under more gateways, till, at last, he reached the palace and came suddenly into a great quadrangle where two blinded, arrogant stallions, covered with red and gold trappings, screamed and neighed at each other from opposite ends of the vast space. For a little time these were the only visible living beings, and they were in perfect accord with the spirit of the spot. Afterwards certain workmen appeared, for it seems that the Maharaja keeps the old palace of his forefathers in good repair, but they were modern and mercenary, and with great difficulty were detached from the skirts of the traveller. A somewhat extensive experience of palace-seeing had taught him that it is best to see palaces alone, for the Oriental as a guide is undiscriminating and sets too great a store on corrugated iron-roofs and glazed drain-pipes.

So the Englishman went into this palace built of stone, bedded on stone, springing out of scarped rock, and reached by stone ways—nothing but stone. Presently, he stumbled across a little temple of Kali, a gem of marble tracery and inlay, very dark and, at that hour of the morning, very cold.

If, as Violet-le-Duc tells us to believe, a building reflects the character of its inhabitants, it must be impossible for one reared in an Eastern palace to think straightly or speak freely or—but here the annals of Rajputana contradict the theory—to act openly. The crampt and darkened rooms, the narrow smooth-walled passages with recesses where a man might wait for his enemy unseen, the maze of ascending and descending stairs leading nowhither, the ever present screens of marble tracery that may hide or reveal so much,—all these things breathe of plot and counter-plot, league and intrigue. In a living palace where the sightseer knows and feels that there are human beings everwhere, and that he is followed by scores of unseen eyes, the impression is almost unendurable. In a dead palace—a cemetery of loves and hatreds done with hundreds of years ago, and of plottings that had for their end—though the grey beards who plotted knew it not—the coming of the British tourist with guide-book and sun-hat—oppression gives place to simply impertinent curiosity. The Englishman wandered into all parts of the palace, for there was no one to stop him—not even the ghosts of the dead Ranis—through ivory-studded doors, into the women's quarters, where a stream of water once flowed over a chiselled marble channel. A creeper had set its hands upon the lattice there, and there was dust of old nests in one of the niches in the wall. Did the lady of light virtue who managed to become possessed of so great a portion of Jey Singhs library ever set her dainty feet in the trim garden of the Hall of Pleasure beyond the screen-work? Was it in the forty-pillared Hall of Audience that the order went forth that the Chief of Birjooghar was to be slain, and from what wall did the King look out when the horsemen clattered up the steep stone path to the palace, bearing on their saddle-bows the heads of the bravest of Rajore? There were questions innumerable to be asked in each court and keep and cell; aye, but the only answer was the cooing of the pigeons on the walls.

If a man desired beauty, there was enough and to spare in the palace; and of strength more than enough. By inlay and carved marble, by glass and color, the Kings who took their pleasure in that now desolate pile, made all that their eyes rested upon royal and superb. But any description of the artistic side of the palace, if it were not impossible, would be wearisome. The wise man will visit it when time and occasion serve, and will then, in some small measure, understand what must have been the riotous, sumptuous, murderous life to which our Governors, and Lieutenant-Governors, Commissioners and Deputy Commissioners, Colonels and Captains and the Subalterns after their kind, have put an end.

From the top of the palace you may read if you please the Book of Ezekiel written in stone upon the hill-side. Coming up, the Englishman had seen the city from below or on a level. He now looked into its very heart—the heart that had ceased to beat. There was no sound of men or cattle, or grind-stones in those pitiful streets—nothing but the cooing of the pigeons. At first it seemed that the palace was not ruined at all—that presently the women would come up on the house-tops and the bells would ring in the temples. But as he attempted to follow with his eye the turns of the streets, the Englishman saw that they died out in wood tangle and blocks of fallen stone, and that some of the houses were rent with great cracks, and pierced from roof to road with holes that let in the morning sun. The drip-stones of the eaves were gap-toothed, and the tracery of the screens had fallen out so that zenana-rooms lay shamelessly open to the day. On the outskirts of the city, the strong walled houses dwindled and sank down to mere stone-heaps and faint indications of plinth and wall, hard to trace against the background of stony soil. The shadow of the palace lay over two-thirds of the city and the trees deepened the shadow. "He who has bent him o'er the dead" *after* the hour of which Byron sings, knows that the features of the man become blunted as it were—the face begins to fade. The same hideous look lies on the face of the Queen of the Pass, and when once this is realized, the eye wonders that it could have ever believed in the life of her. She is the city "whose graves are set in the side of the pit, and her company is, round about her graves," sister of Pathros, Zoan and No.

Moved by a thoroughly insular instinct, the Englishman took up a piece of plaster and heaved it from the palace wall into the dark streets below. It bounded from a house-top to a window-ledge, and thence into a little square, and the sound of its fall was hollow and echoing, as the sound of a stone in a well. Then the silence closed up upon the sound, till in the far away courtyard below the roped stallions began screaming afresh. There may be desolation in the great Indian Desert to the westward, and there is desolation upon the open seas; but the desolation of Amber is beyond the loneliness either of land or sea. Men by the hundred thousand must have toiled at the walls that bound it, the temples and bastions that stud the walls, the fort that overlooks all, the canals that once lifted water to the palace, and the garden in the lake of the valley. Renan could describe it as it stands to-day, and Vereschaguin could paint it.

Arrived at this satisfactory conclusion, the Englishman went down through the palace and the scores of venomous and suggestive little rooms, to the elephant in the courtyard, and was taken back in due time to the Nineteenth Century in the shape of His Highness, the Maharajah's Cotton-Press, returning a profit of twenty-seven per cent., and fitted with two engines of fifty horse-power each, an hydraulic press, capable of exerting a pressure of three tons per square inch, and everything else to correspond. It stood under a neat corrugated iron roof close to the Jeypore Railway Station, and was in most perfect order, but somehow it did not taste well after Amber. There was aggressiveness about the engines and the smell of the raw cotton.

The modern side of Jeypore must not be mixed with the ancient.

CHAPTER IV.

THE HINDU TEMPLE OF MAHADEO—THE WORLD OF THE INNOCENTS ABROAD IS A TOUCHING AND UNSOPHISTICATED PLACE—READING ZOLA'S MOST ZOLAISTIC NOVELS—THE MAYO HOSPITAL AND THE MUSEUM.

From the Cotton-Press the Englishman wandered through the wide streets till he came into a Hindu temple—rich in marble stone and inlay, and a deep and tranquil silence, close to the Public Library of the State. The brazen bull was hung with flowers, and men were burning the evening incense before Mahadeo, while those who had prayed their prayer beat upon the bells hanging from the roof and passed out, secure in the knowledge that the god had heard them. If there be much religion, there is little reverence, as Westerns understand the term, in the services of the gods of the East. A tiny little maiden, child of a monstrously ugly priest, with one chalk-white eye, staggered across the marble pavement to the shrine and threw, with a gust of childish laughter, the blossoms she was carrying into the lap of the great Mahadeo himself. Then she made as though she would leap up to the bells and ran away, still laughing, into the shadow of the cells behind the shrine, while her father explained that she was but a baby and that Mahadeo would take no notice. The temple, he said, was specially favored by the Maharaja, and drew from lands an income of twenty thousand rupees a year. Thakoors and great men also gave gifts out of their benevolence; and there was nothing in the wide world to prevent an Englishman from following their example.

By this time, for Amber and the Cotton-Press had filled the hours, night was falling, and the priests unhooked the swinging jets and began to light up the impassive face of Mahadeo with gas! They used Taendstikker matches.

Full night brought the hotel and its curiously-composed human menagerie.

There is, if a work-a-day world will give credit, a society entirely outside, and unconnected with, that of the Station—a planet within a planet, where nobody knows anything about the Collector's wife, the Colonel's dinner-party, or what was really the matter with the Engineer. It is a curious, an insatiably curious, thing, and its literature is Newman's *Bradshaw*. Wandering "old arm-sellers" and others live upon it, and so do the garnetmen and the makers of ancient Rajput shields. The world of the innocents abroad is a touching and unsophisticated place, and its very atmosphere urges the Anglo-Indian unconsciously to extravagant mendacity. Can you wonder, then, that a guide of long-standing should in time grow to be an accomplished liar?

Into this world sometimes breaks the Anglo-Indian returned from leave, or a fugitive to the sea, and his presence is like that of a well-known landmark in the desert. The old arms-seller knows and avoids him, and he is detested by the jobber of gharis who calls every one "my lord" in English, and panders to the "glaring race anomaly" by saying that every carriage not under his control is rotten, my lord, having been used by natives." One of the privileges of playing at tourist is the brevet-rank of "Lord." *Hazur* is not to be compared with it.

At first, upon heaing the obsequious "Lord" of the natives, there comes a feeling of having duped some one, but this soon wears away, and the tourist grows accustomed to the appellation, much as a poor man does to a huge fortune suddenly acquired. In fact, he is, in the course of a few days, prone to regard it as his due in this region, and would mentally remark the omission of the sobriquet. Such is human nature.

There are many, and some very curious, methods of seeing India. One of these is buying English translations of the more Zolaistic of Zola's novels and reading them from breakfast to dinner-time in the verandah. Yet another, even simpler, is American in its conception. Take a Newman's *Bradshaw* and a blue pencil, and race up and down the length of the Empire, ticking off the names of the stations "done." To do this thoroughly, keep strictly to the railway buildings and form your conclusions through the carriage-windows. These eyes have seen both ways of working in full blast, and, on the whole, the first is the most commendable.

Let us consider now with due reverence the modern side of Jeypore. It is difficult to write of a nickel-plated civilization set down under the immemorial Aravalis in the first state of Rajputana. The red-grey hills seem to laugh at it, and the ever-shifting sand-dunes under the hills take no account of it, for they advance upon the bases of the monogrammed, coronet-crowned lamp-posts, and fill up the points of the natty tramways near the Waterworks, which are the out-posts of the civilization of Jeypore.

Escape from the city by the Railway Station till you meet the cactus and the mud-bank and the Maharaja's Cotton-Press. Pass between a tramway and a trough for wayfaring camels till your foot sinks ankle-deep in soft sand, and you come upon what seems to be the fringe of illimitable desert, mound upon mound of tussocks overgrown with plumed grass where the parrots sit and swing. Here, if you have kept to the road, you shall find a bund faced with stone, a great tank, and pumping machinery fine as the heart of a municipal engineer can desire—pure water, sound pipes and well-kept engines. If you belong to what is sarcastically styled an "able and intelligent municipality" under the British Raj, go down to the level of the tank, scoop up the water in your hands and drink, thinking meanwhile of the defects of the town whence you came. The experience will be a profitable one. There are statistics in connection with the Water-works figures relating to "three-throw-plungers," delivery and supply, which should be known to the professional reader. They would not interest the unprofessional who would learn his lesson among the thronged stand-pipes of the city.

While the Englishman was preparing in his mind a scathing rebuke for an erring municipality that he knew of, a camel swung across the sands, its driver's jaw and brow bound mummy fashion to guard against the dust. The man was evidently a stranger to the place, for he pulled up and asked the Englishman where the drinking troughs were. He was a gentleman and bore very patiently with the Englishman's absurd ignorance of his dialect. He had come from some village, with an unpronounceable name, thirty *kos* away, to see his brother's son who was sick in the big Hospital. While the camel was drinking the man talked, lying back on his mount. He knew nothing of Jeypore, except the names of certain

Englishmen in it, the men who, he said, had made the Water-works and built the Hospital for his brother's son's comfort.

And this is the curious feature of Jeypore; though happily the city is not unique in its peculiarity. When the late Maharaja ascended the throne, more than fifty years ago, it was his royal will and pleasure that Jeypore should advance. Whether he was prompted by love for his subjects, desire for praise, or the magnificent vanity with which Jey Singh must have been so largely dowered, are questions that concern nobody. In the latter years of his reign, he was supplied with Englishmen who made the State their father-land, and identified themselves with its progress as only Englishmen can. Behind them stood the Maharaja ready to spend money with a lavishness that no Supreme Goverment would dream of; and it would not be too much to say that the two made the State what it is. When Ram Singh died, Madho Singh, his successor, a conservative Hindu, forebore to interfere in any way with the work that was going forward. It is said in the city that he does not overburden himself with the cares of State, the driving power being mainly in the hands of a Bengali, who has everything but the name of Minister. Nor do the Englishmen, it is said in the city, mix themselves with the business of government; their business being wholly executive.

They can, according to the voice of the city, do what they please, and the voice of the city—not in the main roads but in the little side-alleys where the stall-less bull blocks the path—attests how well their pleasure has suited the pleasure of the people. In truth, to men of action few things could be more delightful than having a State of fifteen thousand square miles placed at their disposal, as it were, to leave their mark on. Unfortunately for the vagrant traveller, those who work hard for practical ends prefer not to talk about their doings, and he must, therefore, pick up what information he can at second-hand or in the city. The men at the stand-pipes explain that the Maharaja Sahib's father gave the order for the Water-works and that Yakub Sahib made them—not only in the city but out away in the district. "Did people grow more crops thereby?" Of course they did: were canals made to wash in only?" "How much more crops?" "Who knows? The Sahib had better go and ask some official." Increased irrigation means increase of revenue for the State somewhere, but the man who brought about the increase does not say so.

After a few days of amateur globe-trotting, a shamelessness great as that of the other loafer—the red-nosed man who hangs about compounds and is always on the eve of starting for Calcutta—possesses the masquerader; so that he feels equal to asking a Resident for a parcel-gilt howdah, or dropping into dinner with a Lieutenant-Governor. No man has a right to keep anything back from a Globe-Trotter, who is a mild, temperate, gentlemanly and unobtrusive seeker after truth. Therefore he who, without a word of enlightenment, sends the visitor into a city which he himself has beautified and adorned and made clean and wholesome, deserves unsparing exposure. And the city may be trusted to betray him. The *malli* in the Ram Newa's Gardens, Gardens—here the Englishman can speak from a fairly extensive experience—finer than any in India and fit to rank with the best in Paris—says that the Maharaja gave the order and Yakub Sahib made the Gardens. He also says that the Hospital just outside the Gardens was built by Yakub Sahib, and if the Sahib will go to the centre of the Gardens, he will find another big building, a Museum by the same hand.

But the Englishman went first to the Hospital, and found the out-patients beginning to arrive. A Hospital cannot tell lies about its own progress as a municipality can. Sick folk either come or lie in their own villages. In the case of the Mayo Hospital, they came, and the operation-book showed that they had been in the habit of coming. Doctors at issue with provincial and local administrations, Civil Surgeons who cannot get their indents complied with, ground-down and mutinous practitioners all India over, would do well to visit the Mayo Hospital, Jeypore. They might, in the exceeding bitterness of their envy, be able to point out some defects in its supplies, or its beds, or its splints, or in the absolute isolation of the women's quarters trom the men's.

Envy is a low and degrading passion, and should be striven against. From the Hospital the Englishman went to the Museum in the centre of the Gardens, and was eaten up by it, for Museums appealed to him. The casing of the jewel was in the first place superb—a wonder of carven white stone of the Indo-Saracenic style. It stood on a stone plinth, and was rich in stone-tracery, green marble columns from Ajmir, red marble, white marble colonnades, courts with fountains, richly-carved wooden doors, frescoes, inlay and color. The ornamentation of the the tombs of Delhi, the palaces of Agra and the walls of Amber, have been laid under contribution to supply the designs in bracket, arch and soffit ; and stone-masons from the Jeypore School of Art have woven into the work the best that their hands could produce. The building in essence if not in the fact of to-day, is the work of Free Masons. The men were allowed a certain scope in their choice of detail and the result . . . but it should be seen to be understood, as it stands in those Imperial Gardens. And, observe, the man who had designed it, who had superintended its erection, had said no word to indicate that there were such a thing in the place, or that every foot of it, from the domes of the roof to the cool green chunam dadoes and the carving of the rims of the fountains in the court-yard, was worth studying ! Round the arches of the great centre court are written in Sanskrit and Hindi, texts from the great Hindu writers of old bearing on the beauty of wisdom and the sanctity of knowledge.

In the central corridor are six great frescoes, each about nine feet by five, copies of illustrations in the Royal Folio of the *Razmnameh*, the *Mahabharata*, which Abkar caused to be done by the best artists of his day. The original is in the Museum, and he who can steal it, will find a purchaser at any price up to fifty thousand pounds.

CHAPTER V.

A COMPLETE DESCRIPTION OF THE WONDERFUL MUSEUM OF JEYPORE—THEN GO TO THE PALACE OF THE MAHARAJA—THE BRONZE HORSE AND THE YANTI SAMRAT, PRINCE OF DIALS— "ADSMIR."

Internally, there is, in all honesty, no limit to the luxury of the Jeypore Museum. It revels in "South Kensington" cases—of the approved pattern—that turn the beholder homesick, and South Kensington labels, whereon the description, measurements and price of each object, are fairly printed. These make savage one who knows how labelling is bungled in some of the Government Museums—those starved barns that are supposed to hold the economic exhibits, not of little States but of great Provinces.

The floors are of dark red chunam, overlaid with a discreet and silent matting; the doors, where they are not plate glass, are of carved wood, no two alike, hinged by sumptuous brass hinges on to marble jambs and opening without noise. On the carved marble pillars of each hall are fixed revolving cases of the S. K. M. pattern to show textile fabrics, gold lace and the like. In the recesses of the walls are more cases, and on the railing of the gallery that runs round each of the three great central rooms, are fixed low cases to hold natural history specimens and models of fruits and vegetables.

Hear this, Governments of India from the Punjab to Madras ! The doors come true to the jamb, the cases, which have been through a hot weather, are neither warped nor cracked, nor are there unseemly tallow-drops and flaws in the glasses. The maroon cloth, on or against which the exhibits are placed is of close texture, untouched by the moth, neither stained nor meagre nor sunfaded ; the revolving cases revolve freely and without rattling ; there is not a speck of dust from one end of the building to the other, because the menial staff are numerous enough to keep everything clean, and the Curator's office is a veritable office—not a shed or a bath-room, or a loose-box partitioned from the main building. These things are so because money has been spent on the Museum, and it is now a rebuke to all other Museums in India, from Calcutta downwards. Whether it is not too good to be buried away in a native State is a question which envious men may raise and answer as they choose. Not long ago, the editor of a Bombay paper passed through it, but having the interests of the Egocentric Presidency before his eyes, dwelt more upon the idea of the building than its structural beauties ; saying that Bombay, who professed a weakness for technical education should be ashamed of herself. And herein he was quite right.

The system of the Museum is complete in intention as are its appointments in design. At present there are some fifteen thousand objects of art, " surprising in themselves" as, Count Smaltork would say, a complete exposition of the arts, from enamels to pottery and from brass-ware to stone-carving, of the State of Jeypore. They are compared with similar arts of other lands. Thus a Damio's sword—a gem of lacquer-plated silk and stud-work—flanks the *tulwars* of Marwar and the *jezails* of Tonk; and reproductions of Persian and Russian brass-work stand side by side with the handicrafts of the pupils of the Jeypore School of Art. A photograph of His Highness the present Maharaja is set among the arms, which are the most prominent features of the first or metal-room. As the villagers enter, they salaam reverently to the photo, and then move on slowly, with an evidently intelligent interest in what they see.

Ruskin could describe the scene admirably—pointing out how reverence must precede the study of art, and how it is good for Englishmen and Rajputs alike to bow on occasion before Geisler's cap. They thumb the revolving cases of cloths do those rustics, and artlessly try to feel the texture through the protecting glass. The main object of the Museum is avowedly provincial—to show the craftsman of Jeypore the best that his predecessors could do, and to show him what foreign artists have done. In time—but the Curator of the Museum has many schemes which will assuredly bear fruit in time, and it would be unfair to divulge them. Let those who doubt the thoroughness of a Museum under one man's control, built, filled and endowed with royal generosity—an institution perfectly independent of the Government of India—go and exhaustively visit Dr. Hendley's charge at Jeypore. Like the man who made the building, he refuses to talk, and so the greater part of the work that he has in hand must be guessed at.

At one point, indeed, the Curator was taken off his guard. A huge map of the kingdom showed in green the portions that had been brought under irrigation, while blue circles marked the towns that owned dispensaries. "I want to bring every man in the State within twenty miles of a dispensary, and I've nearly done it," said he. Then he checked himself, and went off to food-grains in little bottles as being neutral and colorless things. Envy is forced to admit that the arrangement of the Museum—far too important a matter to be explained off-hand—is Continental in its character, and has a definite end and bearing—a trifle omitted by many institutions other than Museums. But—in fine, what can one say of a collection whose very labels are gilt-edged! Shameful extravagance? Nothing of the kind—only finish, perfectly in keeping with the rest of the fittings—a finish that we in *kutcha* India have failed to catch. That is all!

From the Museum go out through the city to the Maharaja's Palace—skillfully avoiding the man who would show you the Maharaja's European billiard-room, and wander through a wilderness of sunlit, sleepy courts, gay with paint and frescoes, till you reach an inner square, where smiling grey-bearded men squat at ease and play *chaupur*—just such a game as cost the Pandavs the fair Draupadi—with inlaid dice and gaily-lacquered pieces. These ancients are very polite and will press you to play, but give no heed to them, for *chaupur* is an expensive game—expensive as quail-fighting, when you have backed the wrong bird and the people are laughing at your inexperience. The Maharaja's Palace is arrogantly gay, overwhelmingly rich in candelabra, painted ceilings, gilt mirrors and other evidences of a too hastily assimilated civilization ; but, if the evidence of the ear can be trusted, the old, old game of intrigue goes on as merrily as of yore. A figure in saffron came out of a dark arch into the sunlight, almost falling into the arms of one in pink. "Where have you come from ?" "I have been to see ——" the name was unintelligible. "That is a lie : you have *not !*" Then, across the court, some one laughed a low, croaking laugh. The pink and saffron figures separated as though they had been shot, and disappeared into separate bolt-holes. It was a curious little incident, and might have meant a great deal or just nothing at all. It distracted the attention of the ancients bowed above the *chaupur* cloth.

In the Palace-gardens there is even a greater stillness than that about the courts, and here nothing of the West, unless a hypercritical soul might take exception to the lamp-posts. At the extreme end lies a lake-like tank swarming with *muggers*. It is reached through an opening under a block of zenana buildings. Remembering that all beasts by the palaces of Kings or the temples of priests in this country would answer to the name of "Brother," the Englishman cried with the voice of faith across the water, in a key as near as might be to the melodious howl of the "monkey faquir" on the top of Jakko. And the mysterious freemasonry did not fail. At the far end of the tank rose a ripple that grew and grew and grew like a thing in a nightmare, and became presently an aged *mugger*. As he neared the shore, there emerged, the green slime thick upon his eyelids, another beast, and the two together snapped at a cigar-butt—the only reward for their courtesy. Then, disgusted, they sank stern first with a gentle sigh. Now a *mugger's* sigh is the most suggestive sound in animal speech. It suggested first the zenana buildings overhead, the walled passes through the purple hills beyond, a horse that might clatter through the passes till he reached the Man Sagar Lake below the passes, and a boat that might row across the Man Sagar till it nosed the wall of the Palace-tank and then—then uprose the *mugger* with the filth upon his forehead and winked one horny eyelid—in truth he did!—and so supplied a fitting end to a foolish fiction of old days and things that might have been. But it must be unpleasant to live in a house whose base is washed by such a tank.

And so back as Pepys says, through the chunamed courts, and among the gentle sloping paths between the orange trees, up to an entrance of the palace, guarded by two rusty brown dogs from Kabul, each big as a man, and each requiring a man's charpoy to sleep upon. Very gay was the front of the palace, very brilliant were the glimpses of the damask-couched, gilded rooms within, and very, very civilized were the lamp-posts with Ram Singh's monogram, devised to look like V. R., at the bottom, and a coronet, as hath been shown, at the top. An unseen brass band among the orange bushes struck up the overture of the *Bronze Horse*. Those who know the music will see at once that that was the only tune which exactly and perfectly fitted the scene and its surroundings. It was a coincidence and a revelation.

In his time and when he was not fighting, Jey Singh, the second, who built the city, was a great astronomer—a royal Omar Khayyam, for he, like the tent-maker of Nishapur, reformed a calendar, and strove to wring their mysteries from the stars with instruments worthy of a king. But in the end he wrote that the goodness of the Almighty was above everything, and died ; leaving his observatory to decay without the palace-grounds.

From the *Bronze Horse* to the grass-grown enclosure that holds the Yantr Samrat, or Prince of Dials, is rather an abrupt passage. Jey Singh built him a dial with a gnomon some ninety feet high, to throw a shadow against the sun, and the gnomon stands to-day, though there is grass in the kiosque at the top and the flight of steps up the hypotenuse is worn. He built also a zodiacal dial—twelve dials upon one platform—to find the moment of true noon at any time of the year, and hollowed out of the earth place for two hemispherical cups, cut by belts of stone, for comparative observations.

He made cups for calculating eclipses, and a mural quadrant and many other strange things of stone and mortar, of which people hardly know the names and but very little of the uses. Once, said the keeper of two tiny elephants, *Indur* and *Har*, a *Sahib* came with the *Burra Lat Sahib*, and spent eight days in the enclosure of the great neglected observatory, seeing and writing things in a book. But *he* understood *Sanskrit*—the Sanskrit upon the faces of the dials, and the meaning of the gnoma and pointers. Now-a-days no one understands Sanskrit—not even the Pundits; but without doubt Jey Singh was a great man.

The hearer echoed the statement, though he knew nothing of astronomy, and of all the wonders in the observatory was only struck by the fact that the shadow of the Prince of Dials moved over its vast plate so quickly that it seemed as though Time, wrath at the insolence of Jey Singh, had loosed the Horses of the Sun and were sweeping everything—dainty Palace-gardens and ruinous instruments—into the darkness of eternal night. So he went away chased by the shadow on the dial, and returned to the hotel, where he found men who said—this must be a catch-word of Globe-Trotters—that they were "much pleased at" Amber. They further thought that "house-rent would be cheap in those parts," and sniggered over the witticism. There is a class of tourists, and a strangely large one, who individually never get farther than the "much pleased" state under any circumstances. It is assumed that they would be "much pleased" with the Sphinx of Egypt, and the Pyramids, but if they were capable of stronger appreciation of anything, however vast or sublime, none should ever know it. Whether they have no higher emotions, or whether they only regard the external indication of some loftier sentiment as an irreparable crime, is a mooted question in the mind of a stranger. This same class of tourists, it has also been observed, are usually free with hackneyed puns, vapid phrases, and alleged or bygone jokes. Jey Singh, in spite of a few discreditable *laches*, was a temperate and tolerant man; but he would have hanged those Globe-Trotters in their trunk-straps as high as the Yantr Samrat.

Next morning, in the grey dawn, the Englishman rose up and shook the sand of Jeypore from his feet, and went with Master Coryatt and Sir Thomas Roe to "Adsmir," wondering whether a year in Jeypore would be sufficient to exhaust its interest, and why he had not gone out to the tombs of the dead Kings and the passes of Gulta and the fort of Motee Dungri. But what he wondered at most—knowing how many men who have in any way been connected with the birth of an institution, do, to the end of their days, continue to drag forward and exhume their labors and the honors that did *not* come to them—was the work of the two men who, together for years past, have been pushing Jeypore along the stone-dressed paths of civilization, peace and comfort. "Servants of the Raj" they called themselves, and surely they have served the Raj past all praise. The pen and tact of a Wilfred Blunt are needed to fitly last their reticence. But the people in the city and the camel-driver from the sand-hills told of them. They themselves held their peace as to what they had done, and, when pressed, referred—crowning baseness—to reports. Printed ones!

CHAPTER VI.

FROM A CRIMINAL POINT OF VIEW AJIMIR IS NOT A PLEASANT PLACE—UDAIPUR DOES NOT APPROVE OF ENGLISHMEN.

Arrived at Ajmir, the Englishman fell among tents pitched under the shadow of a huge banian tree, and in them was a Punjabi. Now there is no brotherhood like the brotherhood of the Pauper Province; for it is even greater than the genial and unquestioning hospitality which in spite of the loafer and the Globe-Trotter, seems to exist throughout India. Ajmir being British territory, though the inhabitants are allowed to carry arms, is the headquarters of many of the banking firms who lend to the Native States. The complaint of the Setts to-day is that their trade is bad, because an unsympathetic Government induces Native States to make railways and become prosperous. "Look at Jodhpur!" said a gentleman whose possessions might be roughly estimated at anything between thirty and forty-five lakhs. "Time was when Jodhpur was always in debt—and not so long ago, either. Now, they've got a railroad and are carrying salt over it, and, as sure as I stand here, they have a *surplus!* What can we do?" Poor pauper! However, he makes a little profit on the fluctuations in the coinage of the States round him, for every small king seems to have the privilege of striking his own image and inflicting the Great Exchange Question on his subjects. It is a poor State that has not two seers and five different rupees.

From a criminal point of view, Ajmir is not a pleasant place. The Native States lie all round and about it, and portions of the district are ten miles off, Native State-locked on every side. Thus the criminal, who may be a burglarious Meena lusting for the money bags of the Setts, or a Peshawari down south on a cold weather tour, has his plan of campaign much simplified.

The Englishman made only a short stay in the town, hearing that there was to be a ceremony—*tamasha* covers a multitude of things—at the capital of His Highness the Maharana of Udaipur—a town some hundred and eighty miles south of Ajmir, not known to many people beyond Viceroys and their Staffs and the officials of the Rajputana Agency. So he took a Neemuch train in the very early morning and, with the Punjabi, went due south to Chitor, the point of departure for Udaipur. In time the Aravalis gave place to a dead, flat, stone-strewn plain, thick with dhak-jungle. Later the date-palm fraternized with the dhak, and low hills stood on either side of the line. To this succeeded a tract rich in pure white stones, the line was ballasted with it. Then came more low hills, each with a comb of splintered rock a-top, overlooking dhak-jungle and villages fenced with thorns—places that at once declared themselves tigerish. Last, the huge bulk of Chitor showed itself on the horizon. The train crossed the

Gumber River and halted almost in the shadow of the hills on which the old pride of Udaipur was set.

It is difficult to give an idea of the Chitor fortress; but the long line of brown wall springing out of bush-covered hill suggested at once those pictures, such as the *Graphic* publishes, of the *Inflexible* or the *Devastation*—gigantic men-of-war with a very low free-board ploughing through green sea. The hill on which the fort stands is ship-shaped and some miles long, and, from a distance, every inch appears to be scarped and guarded. But there was no time to see Chitor. The business of the day was to get, if possible, to Udaipur from Chitor Station, which was composed of one platform, one telegraph-room, a bench and several vicious dogs.

The State of Udaipur is as backward as Jeypore is advanced—if we judge it by the standard of civilization. It does not approve of the incursions of Englishmen, and, to do it justice, it thoroughly succeeds in conveying its silent sulkiness. Still, where there is one English Resident, one Doctor, one Engineer, one Settlement Officer and one Missionary, there must be a mail at least once a day. There was a mail. The Englishman, men said, might go by it if he liked, or he might not. Then, with a great sinking of the heart, he began to realize that his caste was of no value in the stony pastures of Mewar, among the swaggering gentlemen, who were so lavishly adorned with arms. There was a mail, the ghost of a tonga, with tattered side-cloths and patched roof, inconceivably filthy within and without, and it was Her Majesty's. There was another tonga—an *aram* tonga

—but the Englishman was not to have it. It was reserved for a Rajput Thakur who was going to Udripur with his "tail." The Thakur, in claret-colored velvet with a blue turban, a revolver—Army pattern—a sword, and five or six friends, also with swords, came by and endorsed the statement. Now, the mail tonga had a wheel which was destined to become the Wheel of Fate, and to lead to many curious things. Two diseased yellow ponies were extracted from a dung-hill and yoked to the tonga; and after due deliberation Her Majesty's mail started, the Thakur following.

In twelve hours, or thereabouts, the seventy miles between Chitor and Udaipur would be accomplished. Behind the tonga cantered an armed sowar. He was the guard. The Thakur's tonga came up with a rush, ran deliberately across the bows of the Englishman, chipped a pony, and passed on. One lives and learns. The Thakur seems to object to following the foreigner.

At the halting-stages, once in every six miles, that is to say, the ponies were carefully undressed and all their accoutrements fitted more or less accurately on to the backs of any ponies that might happen to be near; the released animals finding their way back to their stables alone and unguided. There were no *syces*, and the harness hung on by special dispensation of Providence. Still the ride over a good road, driven through a pitilessly stony country, had its charms for a while. At sunset the low hills turned to opal and wine-red and the brown dust flew up pure gold; for the tonga was running straight into the sinking sun. Now and again would pass a traveller on a camel, or a gang of *Bunjarras* with their pack-bullocks and their women ; and the sun touched the brasses of their swords and guns till the poor wretches seemed rich merchants come back from travelling with Sindbad.

On a rock on the right hand side, thirty-four great vultures were gathered over the carcass of a steer. And this was an evil omen. They made unseemly noises as the tonga passed, and a raven came out of a bush on the right and answered them. To crown all, one of the hide and skin castes sat on the left hand side of the road, cutting up some of the flesh that he had stolen from the vultures. Could a man desire three more inauspicious signs for a night's travel? Twilight came, and the hills were alive with strange noises, as the red moon, nearly at her full, rose over Chitor. To the low hills of the mad geological formation, the tumbled strata that seem to obey no law, succeeded level ground, the pasture lands of Mewar, cut by the Beruch and Wyan, streams running over smooth water-worn rock, and, as the heavy embankments and ample waterways showed, very lively in the rainy season.

In this region occurred the last and most inauspicious omen of all. Something had gone wrong with a crupper, a piece of blue and white punkah-cord. The Englishman pointed it out, and the driver, descending, danced on that lonely road an unholy dance, singing the while: "The *dumchi!* The *dumchi!* The *dumchi!*" in a shrill voice. Then he returned and drove on, while the Englishman wondered into what land of lunatics he was heading. At an average speed of six miles an hour, it is possible to see a great deal of the country; and, under brilliant moonlight, Mewar was desolately beautiful. There was no night traffic on the road, no one except the patient sowar, his shadow an inky blot on white, cantering twenty yards behind. Once the tonga strayed into a company of date-trees that fringed the path, and once rattled through a little town, and once the ponies shyed at what the driver said was a rock; but it jumped up in the moonlight and went away.

Then came a great blasted heath whereon nothing was more than six inches high—a wilderness covered with grass and low thorn; and here, as nearly as might be midway between Chitor and Udaipur, the Wheel of Fate, which had been for some time beating against the side of the tonga, came off, and Her Majesty's mails, two bags including parcels, collapsed on the wayside: while the Englishman repented him that he had neglected the omens of the vultures and the raven, the low caste man and the mad driver.

There was a consultation and an examination of the wheel, but the whole tonga was rotten, and the axle was smashed and the axle pins were bent and nearly red-hot. "It is nothing," said the driver, "the mail often does this. What is a wheel?" He took a big stone and began hammering the wheel proudly on the tire, to show that that at least was sound. A hasty court-martial revealed that there was absolutely not one single "breakdown tonga" on the whole road between Chitor and Udaipur.

Now this wilderness was so utterly waste that not even the barking of a dog or the sound of a night-fowl could be heard. Luckily the Thakur had, some twenty miles back, stepped out to smoke by the road-side, and his tonga had been passed meanwhile. The sowar was sent back to find that tonga and bring it on. He cantered into the haze of the moonlight and disappeared. Then said the driver: "Had there been no tonga behind us, I should have put the mails on a horse, because the Sirkar's dak cannot stop." The Englishman sat down upon the parcels-bag, for he felt that there was trouble coming.

The driver looked East and West and said: "I too will go and see if the tonga can be found, for the Sirkar's dak cannot stop. Meantime, oh, Sahib, do you take care of the mails—one bag and one bag of parcels." So he ran swiftly into the haze of the moonlight and was lost, and the Englishman was left alone in charge of Her Majesty's mails, two unhappy ponies and a lop-sided tonga. He lit fires, for the night was bitterly cold, and only mourned that he could not destroy the whole of the territories of His Highness the Maharana of Udaipur. But he managed to raise a very fine blaze, before he reflected that all this trouble was his own fault for wandering into Native States undesirous of Englishmen.

The ponies coughed dolorously from time to time, but they could not lift the weight of a dead silence that seemed to be crushing the earth. After an interval measurable by centuries, sowar, driver and Thakur's tonga reappeared; the latter full to the brim and bubbling over with humanity and bedding. "We will now," said the driver, not deigning to notice the Englishman who had been on guard over the mails, "put the Sirkar's dak into this tonga and go forward." Amiable heathen! He was going, he said so, to leave the Englishman to wait in the Sahara, for certainly thirty hours and perhaps forty-eight. Tongas are scarce on the Udaipur road. There are a few occasions in life when it is justifiable to delay Her Majesty's Mails. This was one of them. Seating himself upon the parcels-bag, the Englishman cried in what was intended to be a very terrible voice, but the silence soaked it up and left only a thin trickle of sound, that any one who touched the bags would be hit with a stick, several times, over the head. The bags were the only link between him and the civilization he had so rashly foregone. And there was a pause.

The Thakur put his head out of the tonga and spoke shrilly in Mewari. The Englishman replied in English-Urdu. The Thakur withdrew his head, and from certain grunts that followed seemed to be wakening his retainers. Then two men fell sleepily out of the tonga and walked into the night. "Come in," said the Thakur, "you and your baggage. My *banduq* is in that corner; be careful." The Englishman, taking a mail-bag in one hand for safety's sake—the wilderness inspires an Anglo-Indian Cockney with unreasoning fear—climbed into the tonga, which was then loaded far beyond Plimsoll mark, and the procession resumed its journey. Every one in the vehicle—it seemed as full as the railway carriage that held Alice. Through the Looking Glass—was *Sahib* and *Hazur*. Except the Englishman. He was simple *tum*, and a revolver, Army pattern, was printing every diamond in the chequer-work of its handle, into his right hip. When men desired him to move, they prodded him with the handles of *tulwars* till they had coiled him into an uneasy lump. Then they slept upon him, or cannoned against him as the tonga bumped. It was an *Aram* tonga, or tonga for ease. That was the bitterest thought of all.

In due season the harness began to break once every five minutes, and the driver vowed that the wheels would give way also.

After eight hours in one position, it is excessively difficult to walk, still more difficult to climb up an unknown road into a dak-bungalow ; but he who has sought sleep on an arsenal and under the bodies of burly Rajputs, can do it. The grey dawn brought Udaipur and a French bedstead. As the tonga jingled away, the Englishman heard the familiar crack of broken harness. So he was not the Jonah he had been taught to consider himself all through that night of penance !

A jackal sat in the verandah and howled him to sleep, wherein he dreamed that he had caught a Viceroy under the walls of Chitor and beaten him with a *tulwar* till he turned into a dak-pony whose near foreleg was perpetually coming off and who would say nothing but *um* when he was asked why he had not built a railway from Chitor to Udaipur.

What a distorted combination of a day's events and experiences is a first dream at Udaipur ?

CHAPTER VII.

ON THE VARIOUS USES OF LETHAL WEAPONS—SHOWING HOW THE ENGLISHMAN CAME TO THE CITY OF THE CHILDREN OF THE SUN—THE PADRE-SAHIB, THE GOOD MAN OF THE WILDERNESS.

It was worth a night's discomfort and revolver-bed to sleep upon—this city of the Suryavansi, hidden among the hills that encompass the great Pichola lake. Truly, the King who governs to-day is wise in his determination to have no railroad to his capital. His predecessor was more or less enlightened, and had he lived a few years longer, would have brought the iron horse through the Dobarri—the green gate which is the entrance of the Girwa or girdle of hills around Udaipur; and, with the train, would have come the tourist who would have scratched his name upon the Temple of Garuda and laughed horse-laughs upon the lake. Let us, therefore, be thankful that the capital of Mewar is hard to reach, and go abroad into a new and a strange land rejoicing.

Each man who has any claims to respectability walks armed, carrying his tulwar sheathed in his hand, or hung by a short sling of cotton passing over the shoulder, under his left armpit. His matchlock, or smooth-bore if he has one, is borne naked on the shoulder.

Now it is possible to carry any number of lethal weapons without being actually dangerous. An unhandy revolver, for instance, may be worn for years, and, at the end, accomplish nothing more noteworthy than the murder of its owner. But the Rajput's weapons are not meant for display. The Englishman caught a camel-driver who talked to him in Mewari, which is a heathenish dialect, something like Multani to listen to ; and the man, very gracefully and courteously, handed him his sword and matchlock, the latter a heavy stump-stock arrangement without pretence of sights. The blade was as sharp as a razor, and the gun in perfect working order. The coiled fuse on the stock was charred at the end, and the curled ram's-horn powder-horn opened as readily as a whisky-flask that is much handled. Unfortunately, ignorance of Mewari prevented conversation ; so the camel-driver resumed his accoutrements and jogged forward on his beast—a superb black one, with the short curled *hubshee* hair—while the Englishman went to the city, which is built on hills on the borders of the lake. By the way, everything in Udaipur is built on a hill. There is no level ground in the place, except the Durbar Gardens, of which more hereafter. Because color holds the eye more than form, the first thing noticeable was neither temple nor fort, but an ever-recurring picture, painted in the rudest form of native art, of a man on horseback armed with a lance, charging an elephant-of-war. As a rule, the elephant was depicted on one side the house-door and the rider on the other. There was no representation of an army behind. The figuresstood alone upon the whitewash on house and wall and gate, again and again and again. A highly intelligent priest grunted that it was a *tazwir*; a private of the Maharana's regular army suggested that it was a *hathi*; while a wheat-seller, his sword at his side, was equally certain that it was a Raja. Beyond that point, his knowledge did not go. The explanation of the picture is this. In the days when Raja Maun of Amber put his sword at Akbar's service and won for him great kingdoms, Akbar sent an army against Mewar, whose then ruler was Pertap Singh, most famous of all the princes of Mewar. Selim, Akbar's son, led the army of the Toork ; the Rajputs met them at the pass of Huldighat and fought till one-half of their band were slain. Once, in the press of battle, Pertap, on his great horse, "Chytak," came within striking distance of Selim's elephant, and slew the mahout, but Selim escaped, to become Jehangir afterwards, and the Rajputs were broken. That was three hundred years ago, and men have reduced the picture to a sort of diagram that the painter dashes in, in a few minutes, without, it would seem, knowing what he is commemorating. Elsewhere, the story is drawn in lines even more roughly.

Thinking of these things, the Englishman made shift to get to the city, and presently came to a tall gate, the gate of the Sun, on which the elephant-spikes, that he had seen rotted with rust at Amber, were new and pointed and effective. The City gates are said to be shut at night, and there is a story of a Viceroy's Guard-of-Honor which arrived before day-break, being compelled to crawl ignominiously man by man through a little wicket-gate, while the horses had to wait without till sunrise. But a civilized yearning for the utmost advantages of octroi, and not a fierce fear of robbery and wrong, is at the bottom of the continuance of this custom. The walls of the City are loopholed for musketry, but there seem to be no mounting for guns, and the moat without the walls is dry and gives cattle pasture. Coarse rubble in concrete faced with stone, makes the walls moderately strong.

Internally, the City is surprisingly clean, though with the exception of the main street, paved after the fashion of Jullundur, of which, men say, the pavement was put down in the time of Alexander and worn by myriads of naked feet into deep barrels and grooves. In the case of Udaipur, the feet of the passengers have worn the rock veins that crop out everywhere, smooth and shiny ; and in the rains the narrow gullies must spout like fire-hoses. The people have been untouched by cholera for four years, proof that Providence looks after those who do not look after themselves, for Neemuch Cantonment, a hundred miles away, suffered grievously last summer. "And what do you make in Udaipur?" "Swords," said the man in the shop, throwing down an armful of *tulwars, kuttars* and *khandas* on the stones. "Do you want any? Look here!" Hereat, he took up one of the commoner swords and flourished it in the sunshine. Then he bent it double, and, as it sprang straight, began to make it "speak." Arm-vendors in Udaipur are a genuine race, for they sell to people who really use their wares. The man in the shop was rude—distinctly so. His first flush of professional enthusiasm abated, he took stock of the Englishman and said calmly: "What do *you* want with a sword?" Then he picked up his goods and retreated, while certain small boys, who deserved a smacking, laughed riotously from the coping of a little temple hard by. Swords seem to be the sole manufacture of the place. At least, none of the inhabitants the Englishman spoke to could think of any other.

There is a certain amount of personal violence in and about the State, or else where would be the good of the weapons? There are occasionally dacoities more or less important; but these are not often heard of, and, indeed, there is no special reason why they should be dragged into the light of an unholy publicity, for the land governs itself in its own way, and is always in its own way, which is by no means ours, very happy. The Thakurs live, each in his own castle on some rock-faced hill, much as they lived in the days of Tod; though their chances of distinguishing themselves, except in the school, sowar and dispensary line, are strictly limited. Nominally, they pay *chutoond*, or a sixth of their revenues to the State, and are under feudal obligations to supply their Head with so many horsemen per thousand rupees; but whether the *chutoond* justifies its name and what is the exact extent of the "tail" leviable, they, and perhaps the Rajputana Agency, alone know. They are quiet, give no trouble except to the wild boar, and personally are magnificent men to look at. The Rajput shows his breeding in his hands and feet which are almost disproportionately small, and as well shaped as those of a woman. His stirrups and sword-handles are even more unusable by Westerns than those elsewhere in India, while the Bhil's knife-handle gives as large a grip as an English one. Now the little Bhil is an aborigine, which is humiliating to think of. His tongue, which may frequently be heard in the City, seems to possess some variant of the Zulu click; which gives it a weird and unearthly character. From the main gate of the City the Englishman climbed uphill towards the Palace and the Jugdesh Temple built by one Juggat Singh at the beginning of the last century. This building must be—but ignorance is a bad guide—Jain in character. From basement to the stone socket of the temple flag-staff, it is carved in high relief with elephants, men, gods and monsters in friezes of wearying profusion.

The management of the temple have daubed a large portion of the building with whitewash, for which their revenues should be "cut" for a year or two. The main shrine holds a large brazen image of Garuda, and, in the corners of the courtyard of the main pile, are shrines to Mahadeo, and the jovial, pot-bellied Ganesh. There is no repose in this architecture, and the entire effect is one of repulsion; for the clustered figures of man and brute seem always on the point of bursting into unclean, wriggling life.

But it may be that the builders of this form of house desired to put the fear of all their many gods into the hearts of the worshippers. From the temple whose steps are worn smooth by the feet of men, and whose courts are full of the faint smell of stale flowers and old incense, the Englishman went to the Palaces which crown the highest hill overlooking the City. Here, too, whitewash had been unsparingly applied, but the excuse was that the stately fronts and the pierced screens were built of a perishable stone which needed protection against the weather. One projecting window in the facade of the main palace had been treated with Minton tiles. Luckily it was too far up the wall for anything more than the color to be visible, and the pale blue against the pure white was effective.

A picture of Ganesh looks out over the main courtyard which is entered by a triple gate, and hard by is the place where the King's elephant's fight over a low masonry wall. In the side of the hill on which the Palaces stand, is built stabling for horses and elephants—proof that the architects of old must have understood their business thoroughly. The Palace is not a "show place," and, consequently, the Englishman did not see much of the interior. But he passed through open gardens with tanks and pavilions, very cool and restful, till he came suddenly upon the Pichola lake, and forgot altogether about the Palace. He found a sheet of steel-blue water, set in purple and grey hills, bound in, on one side, by marble bunds, the fair white walls of the Palace, and the grey, time-worn ones of the city ; and, on the other, fading away through the white of shallow water, and the soft green of weed, marsh, and rank-pastured river field, into the land.

To enjoy open water thoroughly, live for a certain number of years barred from anything better than the yearly swell and shrinkage of one of the Five Rivers, and then come upon two and a half miles of solid, restful lake, with a cool wind blowing off it and little waves spitting against the piers of a veritable, albeit hideously ugly, boat-house. On the faith of an exile from the Sea, you will not stay long among Palaces, be they never so lovely, or in little rooms panelled with Dutch tiles, be these never so rare and curious. And here follows digression. There is no life so good as the life of a loafer who travels by rail and road ; for all things and all people are kind to him. From the chill miseries of a dak-bungalow where they slew one hen with as much parade as the French guillotined Pranzini, to the well-ordered sumptuousness of the Residency, was a step bridged over by kindly and unqestioning hospitality. So it happened that the Englishman was not only able to go upon the lake in a soft-cushioned boat, with everything handsome about him, but might had he chosen, have killed wild-duck with which the lake swarms.

The mutter of water under a boat's nose was a pleasant thing to hear once more. Starting at the head of the lake, he found himself shut out from sight of the main sheet of water in a loch bounded by a sunk, broken bund to steer across which was a matter of some nicety. Beyond that lay a second pool, spanned by a narrow-arched bridge built, men said, long before the City of the Rising Sun, which is little more than three hundred years old. The bridge connects the City with Brahmapura—a white-walled enclosure filled with many Brahmins and ringing with the noise of their conches. Beyond the bridge, the body of the lake, with the City running down to it, comes into full view; and Providence has arranged for the benefit of such as delight in colors, that the Rajputni shall wear the most striking tints that she can buy in the bazaars, in order that she may beautify the ghâts where she comes to bathe.

The bathing-ledge at the foot of the City wall was lighted with women clad in raw vermillion, dull red, indigo and sky-blue, saffron and pink and turquoise; the water faithfully doubling everything. But the first impression was of the unreality of the sight, for the Englishman found himself thinking of the Simla Fine Arts Exhibition and the over-daring amateurs who had striven to reproduce scenes such as these. Then a woman rose up, and clasping her hands behind her head, looked at the passing boat, and the ripples spread out from her waist, in blinding white silver, far across the water. As a picture, a daringly insolent picture, it would have been superb.

The boat turned aside to shores where huge turtles were lying, and a stork had built her a nest, big as a haycock, in a withered tree, and a bevy of coots were flapping and gabbling in the weeds or between great leaves of the *Victoria Regia*—an "escope" from the Durbar Gardens. Here were, as Mandeville hath it, "all manner of strange fowle'"—divers and waders, after their kinds, king-fishers and snaky-necked birds of the cormorant family, but no duck. They had seen the guns in the boat and were flying to and fro in companies across the lake, or settling, wise birds, in the glare of the sun on the water. The lake was swarming with them, but they seemed to know exactly how far a twelve-bore would carry. Perhaps their knowledge had been gained from the Englishman at the Residency. Later, as the sun left the lake and the hills began to glow like opals, the boat made her way to the shallow side of the lake, through fields of watergrass and dead lotus-raffle that rose as high as the bows, and clung lovingly about the rudder, and parted with the noise of silk when it is torn. There she waited for the fall of twilight when the duck would come home to bed, and the Englishman sprawled upon the cushions in deep content and laziness, as he looked across to where two marble Palaces floated upon the waters, and saw all the glory and beauty of the City, and wondered whether Tod, in cocked hat and stiff stock, had ever come shooting among the reeds, and, if so, how in the world he had ever managed to bowl over. . . .

"Duck and drake, by Jove! Confiding beasts, weren't they. Hi! Lalla, jump out and get them!" It was a brutal thing, this double-barrelled murder perpetrated in the silence of the marsh when the lingly wild-duck came back from his wanderings with his mate at his side, but—but—the birds were very good to eat. After this, and many other rlaughters had been accomplished, the boat went back in the full dusk, down narrow water-lanes and across belts of weed, disturbing innumerable fowl on the road, till she reached open water and "the moon like a rick afire was rising over the dale," and it was not the "whit, whit, whit" of the nightingale, but the stately "*honk, honk*" of some wild geese, thanking their stars that these pestilent *shikaris* were going away.

If the Venetian owned the Pichola Sagar he might say with justice :—"See it and die." But it is better to live and go to dinner, and strike into a new life—that of the men who bear the hat-mark on their brow as plainly as the well-born native carries the *trisul* of Shiva.

They are of the same caste as the toilers on the Frontier—tough, bronzed men, with wrinkles at the corners of the eyes, gotten by looking across much sun-glare. When they would speak of horses they mention Arab ponies, and their talk, for the most part, drifts Bombaywards, or to Abu, which is their Simla. By these things the traveller may see that he is far away from the Presidency ; and will presently learn that he is in a land where the railway is an incident and not an indispensable luxury. Folk tell strange stories of drives in bullock-carts in the rains, of break-downs in nullahs fifty miles from everywhere, and of elephants that used to sink "for rest and refreshment" half-way across swollen streams. Every place here seems fifty miles from everywhere, and the "legs of a horse" are regarded as the only natural means of locomotion. Also, and this to the Indian Cockney, who is accustomed to the bleached or office man is curious, there are to be found many veritable "tiger-men"—not story-spinners but such as have, in their wanderings from Bikaneer to Indore dropped their tiger in the way of business. They are enthusiastic over princelings of little known fiefs, lords of austere estates perched on the tops of unthrifty hills, hard riders and good sportsmen. And five, six, yes fully nine hundred miles to the northward, lives the sister branch of the same caste—the men who swear by Pathan, Biluch and Brahui, with whom they have shot or broken bread.

There is a saying in Upper India that the more desolate the country the greater the certainty of finding a Padre-Sahib. The proverb seems to hold good in Udaipur, where the Scotch Presbyterian Mission have a post, and others at Todgarh to the north and elsewhere. To arrive, under Providence at the cure of souls through the curing of bodies certainly seems the rational method of conversion; and this is exactly what the Missions are doing. Their Padre in Udaipur is also an M. D., and of him a rather striking tale is told. Conceiving that the City could bear another hospital in addition to the State one, he took furlough, went home, and there, by crusade and preaching, raised sufficient money for the scheme, so that none might say that he was beholden to the State. Returning, he built his hospital, a very model of neatness and comfort, and, opening the operation-book, announced his readiness to see any one and every one who was sick. How the call was and is now responded to, the dry records of that book will show ; and the name of the Padre-Sahib is honored, as these ears have heard, throughout Udaipur and far around. The faith that sends a man into the wilderness, and the secular energy which enables him to cope with an ever-growing demand for medical aid, must, in time, find their reward. If patience and unwearying self-sacrifice carry any merit, they should do so soon. To-day the people are willing enough to be healed, and the general influence of the Padre-Sahib is very great. But beyond that . . . Still it was impossible to judge aright.

CHAPTER VIII.

"SAD STORIES OF THE DEATH OF KINGS"—HIS HIGHNESS PRIME MINISTER RAE PUNNA LAL IS A RACIAL ANOMALY.

In this land men tell "sad stories of the death of Kings" not easily found elsewhere ; and also speak of *sati*, which is generally supposed to be an "effete curiosity" as the Bengali said in a manner which makes it seem very near and vivid. Be pleased to listen to some of the tales, but with all the names cut out, because a King has just as much right to have his family affairs respected as has a British householder paying income tax.

Once upon a time, that is to say when the British power was well established in the land and there were railways, there was a King who lay dying for many days, and all, including the Englishmen about him, knew that his end was certain. But he had chosen to lie in an outer court or pleasure-house of his Palace; and with him were some twenty of his favorite wives. The place in which he lay was very near to the City; and there was a fear that his womenkind should, on his death, going mad with grief, cast off their veils and run out into the streets, uncovered before all men. In which case nothing, not even the power of the Press, and the locomotive, and the telegraph, and cheap education and enlightened municipal councils, could have saved them from *sati*, for they were the wives of a King. So the Political did his best to induce the dying man to go to the Fort of the City, a safe place close to the regular zenana, where all the women could be kept within walls. He said that the air was better in the Fort, but the King refused; and that he would recover in the Fort; but the King refused. After some days, the latter turned and said; *Why* are you so keen, Sahib, upon getting my old bones up to the Fort." Driven to his last defences, the Political said simply: "Well, Maharana Sahib, the place is close to the road you see, and . . ." The King saw and said: "Oh, *that's* it. I've been puzzling my brain for four days to find out what on earth you were driving at. I'll go to-night." "But there may be some difficulty," began the Political. "You think so," said the King. "If I only hold up my little finger, the women will obey me. Go now, and come back in five minutes, and all will be ready for departure." As a matter of fact, the Political withdrew for the space of fifteen minutes, and gave orders that the conveyances which he had kept in readiness day and night should be got ready. In fifteen minutes those twenty women, with their hand-maidens, were packed and ready for departure; and the King died later at the Fort, and nothing happened. Here the Englishman asked why a frantic woman must of necessity become *sati*, and felt properly abashed when he was told that she *must*. There was nothing else for her if she went out unveiled deliberately.

The rush-out forces the matter. And, indeed, if you consider the matter from a Rajput point of view it does.

Then followed a very grim tale of the death of another King; of the long vigil by his bedside, before he was taken off the bed to die upon the ground; of the shutting of a certain mysterious door behind the bed-head, which shutting was followed by a rustle of women's dress; of a walk on the top of the Palace, to escape the heated air of the sick room; and then, in the grey dawn, the wail upon wail breaking from the zenana as the news of the King's death went in. "I never wish to hear anything more horrible and awful in my life. You could see nothing. You could only hear the poor wretches," said the Political with a shiver.

The last resting-place of the Maharanas of Udaipur is at Ahar, a little village two miles east of the City. Here they go down in their robes of State, their horse following behind, and here the Political saw, after the death of a Maharana, the dancing girls dancing before the poor white ashes, the musicians playing among the cenotaphs, and the golden hookah, sword and water-vessel laid out for the naked soul doomed to hover twelve days round the funeral pyre, before it could depart on its journey towards a fresh birth in the endless circle of the Wheel of Fate. Once, in a neighboring State it is said, one of the dancing-girls stole a march in the next world's precedence and her lord's affections, upon the legitimate queens. The affair happened, by the way, after the Mutiny, and was accomplished with great pomp in the light of day. Subsequently those who might have stopped it but did not, were severely punished. The girl said that she had no one to look to but the dead man, and followed him, to use Tod's formula, "through the flames." It would be curious to know what is done now and again among these lonely hills in the walled holds of the Thakurs.

But to return from the burning-ground to modern Udaipur, as at present worked under the Maharana and his Prime Minister Rae Punna Lal, *C. I. E.* To begin with, His Highness is a racial anomaly in that, judged by the strictest European standard, he is a man of temperate life, the husband of one wife whom he married before he was chosen to the throne after the death of the Maharana Sujjun Singh in 1884. Sujjun Singh died childless and gave no hint of his desires as to succession and—omitting all the genealogical and political reasons which would drive a man mad—Futteh Singh was chosen, by the

Thakurs, from the Seorati Branch of the family which Sangram Singh II. founded. He is thus a younger son of a younger branch of a younger family, which lucid statement should suffice to explain everything. The man who could deliberately unravel the succession of any one of the Rajput States would be perfectly capable of clearing the politics of all the Frontier tribes from Jumrood to Quetta.

Roughly speaking, the Maharana and the Prime Minister—in whose family the office has been hereditary for many generations—divide the power of the State. They control, more or less, the Mahand Raj Sabha or Council of Direction and Revision. This is composed of many of the Rawats and Thakurs of the State, *and* the Poet Laureate who, under a less genial administration, would be presumably the Registrar. There are also District Officers, Officers of Customs, Superintendents of the Mint, Master of the Horses, and Supervisor of Doles, which last is pretty and touching. The State officers itself, and the Englishman's investigations failed to unearth any Bengalis. The Commandant of the State Army, about five thousand men of all arms, is a retired non-commissioned officer, a Mr. Lonergan ; who, as the medals on his breast attest, has "done the State some service," and now in his old age rejoices in the rank of Major-General, and teaches the Maharaja's guns to make uncommonly good practice. The Infantry are smart and well set up, while the Cavalry —rare thing in Native States—have a distinct notion of keeping their accoutrements clean. They are, further, well mounted on light wiry Mewar and Kathiawar horses. Incidentally, it may be mentioned that the Pathan comes down with his pickings from the Punjab to Udaipur, and finds a market there for animals that were much better employed in—but the complaint is a stale one. Let us see, later on, what the Jodhpur stables hold; and then formulate an indictment against the Government. So much for the indigenous administration of Udaipur. The one drawback in the present Maharaja, from the official point of view, is his want of education. He is a thoroughly good man, but was not brought up with a seat on the *guddee* before his eyes, consequently he is not an English-speaking man.

There is a story told of him, which is worth the repeating. An Englishman who flattered himself that he could speak the vernacular fairly well, paid him a visit and discoursed with a round mouth. The Maharana heard him politely, and turning to a satellite, demanded a translation; which was given. Then said the Maharana:—"Speak to him in *Angrezi*." The *Angrezi* spoken by the interpreter was the vernacular as the Sahibs speak it, and the Englishman, having ended his conference, departed abashed. But this backwardness is eminently suited to a place like Udaipur, and a "varnished" prince is not always a desirable thing. The curious and even startling simplicity of his life is worth preserving. Here is a specimen of one of his days. Rising at four—and the dawn can be bitterly chill—he bathes and prays after the custom of his race, and at six is ready to take in hand the first installment of the day's work which comes before him through his Prime Minister, and occupies him for three or four hours till the first meal of the day is ready. At two o'clock he attends the Mahand Raj Sabha, and works till five, retiring at a healthily primitive hour. He is said to have his hand fairly, firmly upon the reins of rule, and to know as much as most monarchs know of the way in which the revenues—about thirty lakhs—are disposed of. The Prime Minister's career has been a chequered and interesting one, including, *interalia* a dismissal from power (this was worked from behind the screen), and arrest and an attack with words which all but ended in his murder. He has not so much power as his predecessors had, for the reason that the present Maharaja allows little but tiger-shooting to distract him from the supervision of the State. His Highness, by the way, is a first-class shot and has bagged eighteen tigers already. He preserves his game carefully, and permission to kill tigers is not readily obtainable.

A curious instance of the old order giving place to the new is in process of evolution and deserves notice. The Prime Minister's son, Futteh Lal, a boy of twenty years old, has been educated at the Mayo College, Ajmir, and speaks and writes English. There are few native officials in the State who do this ; and the consequence is that the lad has won a very fair insight into State affairs, and knows generally what is going forward both in the Eastern and Western spheres of the little Court. In time he may qualify for direct administrative powers, and Udaipur will be added to the list of the States that are governed "English fash," as the irreverent Americans put it. What the end will be, after three generations of Princes and Dewans have been put through the mill of Rajkumar Colleges, those who live will learn.

More interesting is the question, For how long can the vitality of a people whose life was arms be suspended? Men in the North say that, by the favor of the Government, the Sikh Sirdars are rotting on their lands; and the Rajput Thakurs say of themselves that they are growing "rusty." The old, old problem forces itself on the most unreflective mind at every turn in the gay streets of Udaipur. A Frenchman might write: "Behold there the horse of the Rajput—foaming, panting, caracoling, but always fettered with his head so majestic upon his bosom so amply filled with a generous heart. He rages, but he does not advance. See there the destiny of the Rajput who bestrides him, and upon whose left flank bounds the sabre useless—the haberdashery of the ironmonger only. Pity the horse in reason, for that life there is his *raison d'etre.* Pity ten thousand times more the Rajput, for he has no *raison d'etre.* He is an anachronism in a blue turban."

The Gaul might be wrong, but Tod wrote things which seem to support this view, in the days when he wished to make "buffer-states" of the land he loved so well.

Let us visit the Durbar Gardens, where little naked Cupids are trampling upon fountains of fatted fish, all in bronze, where there are cypresses and red paths, and a deer-park full of all varieties of deer, besides two growling, fluffy little panther cubs, a black panther who is the Prince of Darkness and a gentleman, and a terrace-full of tigers, bears and Guzerat lions brought from the King of Oudh's sale.

On the best site in the Gardens is rising the Victoria Hall, the foundation-stone of which was laid by the Maharana on the 21st of June last. It is built after the designs of Mr. C. Thompson, Executive Engineer of the State, and will be in the Hindu-Saracenic style; having two fronts, west and north. In the former will be the principal entrance, approached by a flight of steps leading to a handsome porch of carved pillars supporting stone beams—the flat Hindu arch. To the left of the entrance hall will be a domed octagonal tower eighty feet high, holding the principal staircase leading to the upper rooms. A corridor on the right of the entrance will lead to the museum, and immediately behind the entrance hall is the reading-room, 42 by 24 feet, and beyond it the library and office. To the right of the reading-room will be an open courtyard with a fountain in the centre, and, beyond the courtyard, the museum—a great hall, one hundred feet long. Over the library and the entrance hall will be private apartments for the Maharana, approached by a private staircase.

The communication between the two upper rooms will be by a corridor running along the north front having a parapet of delicately cut pillars and cusped arches—the latter filled in with open tracery. Pity it is that the whole of this will have to be white-washed to protect the stone from the weather. Over the entrance-porch, and projecting from the upper room, will be a very elaborately cut balcony supported on handsome brackets. Facing the main entrance will be a marble statue, nine feet high, of the Queen, on a white marble pedestal ten feet high. The statue is now being made at home by Mr. Birch, *R. A.* The cost of the whole will be about Rs. 80,000. Now, it is a curious thing that the statue of Her Majesty will be put some eighty feet below the level of the great bund that holds in the Pichola lake. But the bund is a firm one and has stood for many years.

Another public building deserves notice, and that is the Walter Hospital for native women, the foundation-stone of which was laid by the Countess of Dufferin on that memorable occasion when the Viceroy, behind Artillery Horses, covered the seventy miles from Chitor to Udaipur in under six hours. The building by the same brain that designed the hall, will be ready for occupation in a month. It is in strict keeping with the canons of Hindu architecture externally, and has a high, well-ventilated waiting-room, out of which, to the right, are two wards for in-patients, and to the left a dispensary and consulting-room. Beyond these, again, is a third ward for in-patients. In a courtyard behind are a ward for low caste patients and the offices.

When all these buildings are completed, Udaipur will be dowered with three good hospitals, including the State's and the Padre's, and a first instalment of civilization.

The British civilization, by scientific legislation,

by peace and order, by the recognition of property in land, by education in the widest sense, by works of material improvement, such as these hospitals, and by the introduction of western ideas, is fast affecting the mind of nearly all the nationalities now existing in the empire.

CHAPTER IX.

SHOWING HOW THE ENGLISHMAN TRIED TO SHOOT PIGS AND CAME UPON "BAGHEERA," THE PANTHER.

Above the Durbar Gardens lie low hills, in which the Maharana keeps, very strictly guarded, his pig and his deer, and anything else that may find shelter in the low scrub or under the scattered boulders. These preserves are scientifically parcelled out with high, red-stone walls ; and, here and there, are dotted tiny shooting-boxes, in the first sense of the term—masonry sentry boxes, in which five or six men may sit at ease and shoot. It had been arranged to entertain the Englishmen who were gathered at the Residency to witness the investiture of the King with the G. C. S. I.—that there should be a little pig-drive in front of the Kala Odey or black shooting-box. The Rajput is a man and a brother, in respect that he will ride, shoot, eat pig, and drink strong waters like an Englishman. Of the pig-hunting he makes almost a religious duty, and of the wine-drinking no less. Read how desperately they used to ride in

Udaipur at the beginning of the century when Tod, always in his cocked hat to be sure, counted up the tale of accidents at the end of the day's sport.

There is something unfair in shooting pig; but each man who went out consoled himself with the thought that it was utterly impossible to ride the brutes up the almost perpendicular hillsides, or down rocky ravines, and that he individually would only go "just for the fun of the thing." Those who stayed behind made rude remarks on the subject of "pork butchers," and the dangers that attended shooting from a balcony. These were treated with a contempt they merited. There are ways and ways of slaying pig—from the orthodox method which begins with "*The Boar—the Boar—the mighty Boar!*" overnight, and ends with a shaky bridle-hand next morn, to the sober and solitary pot-shot at dawn, from a railway embankment running through river marsh; but the perfect way is this. Get a large, four-horse break, and drive till you meet an unlimited quantity of pad-elephants waiting at the foot of rich hill-preserves. Mount slowly and with dignity, and go in swinging procession, by the marble-faced border of one of the most lovely lakes on earth. Strike off on a semi-road, semi-hill-torrent path through unthrifty, thorny jungle, and so climb up and up and up, till you see, spread like a map below the lake and the Palace and the City, hemmed in by the sea of hills that lies between Udaipur and Mount Abu a hundred miles away. Then take your seat in a comfortable chair, in a pukka, two-storied Grand Stand, with an awning spread atop to keep off the sun, while the

Rawat of Amet and the Prime Minister's heir—no less—invite you to take your choice of the many rifles spread on a ledge at the front of the building. This, gentlemen who screw your pet ponies at early dawn after the sounder that vanishes into cover soon as sighted, or painfully follow the tiger through the burning heats of Mewar in May, this is shooting after the fashion of Ouida—in musk and ambergris and patchouli.

It is demoralizing. One of the best and hardest riders of the Lahore Tent Club in the old days, as the boars of Bouli Lena Singh knew well, said openly: "This is a first-class *bundobust*," and fell to testing his triggers as though he had been a pot-hunter from his birth. Derision and threats of exposure moved him not. "Give me an arm-chair!" said he. "This is the proper way to deal with pig!" And he put up his feet on the ledge and stretched himself.

There were many weapons to have choice among—from the double-barrelled '500 Express, whose bullet is a tearing, rending shell, to the Rawat of Amet's regulation military Martini-Henri. A profane public at the Residency had suggested clubs and saws as amply sufficient for the work in hand. Herein they were moved by envy, which passion was ten-fold increased when—but this comes later on. The beat was along a deep gorge in the hills, flanked on either crest by stone walls, manned with beaters. Immediately opposite the shooting-box, the wall on the upper or higher hill made a sharp turn downhill, contracting the space through which the pig would have to pass to a gut which was variously said to be from one hundred and fifty to four hundred yards across. Most of the shooting was up or downhill.

A philanthropic desire to murder more Bhils than were absolutely necessary to maintain a healthy current of human life in the Hilly Tracts, coupled with a well-founded dread of the hinder, or horse, end of a double-barrelled '500 Express which would be sure to go off both barrels together, led the Englishman to take a gunless seat in the background; while a silence fell upon the party, and very far away up the gorge the heated afternoon air was cut by the shrill tremolo squeal of the Bhil beaters. Now a man may be in no sort or fashion a *shikari*—may hold Buddhistic objections to the slaughter of living things—but there is something in the extraordinary noise of an agitated Bhil, which makes even the most peaceful mortals get up and yearn, like Tartarin of Tarescon for "lions," always at a safe distance be it understood. As the beat drew nearer, under the squealing—the "*ul-al-lu-lu-lu*"—was heard a long-drawn bittern-like boom of "*So-oor!*" "*So-oor!*" and the crashing of boulders. The guns rose in their places, forgetting that each and all had merely come "to see the fun," and began to fumble among the little mounds of cartridges under the chairs. Presently, tripping delicately among the rocks, a pig stepped out of a cactus-bush, and the fusillade began. The dust flew and the branches chipped, but the pig went on—a blue-grey shadow almost undistinguishable against the rocks, and took no harm. "Sighting shots," said the guns sulkily; and the company mourned that the brute had got away. The beat came nearer, and then the listener discovered what the bubbling scream was like ; for he forgot straightway about the beat and went back to the dusk of an Easter Monday in the Gardens of the Crystal Palace before the bombardment of Kars, "set piece ten thousand feet square," had been illuminated, and about five hundred 'Arries were tickling a thousand 'Arriets. Their giggling and nothing else was the noise of the Bhil. So curiously does Sydenham and Western Rajputana meet. Then came another pig, who was smitten to the death and rolled down among the bushes, drawing his last breath in a human and horrible manner.

But full on the crest of the hill, blown along—there is no other word to describe it—like a ball of thistle-down, passed a brown shadow, and men cried : "*Bagheera*," or "Panther !" according to their nationalities, and blazed. The shadow leaped the wall that had turned the pig downhill, and vânished among the cactus. "Never mind," said the Prime Minister's son consolingly, "we'll beat the other side of the hill afterwards and get him yet." "Oh, he's a mile off by this time," said the guns ; but the Rawat of Amet, a magnificent young man, smiled a sweet smile and said nothing. More pig passed and were slain, and many more broke back through the beaters who presently came through the cover in scores. They were in russet green and red uniform, each man bearing a long spear, and the hill-side was turned on the instant to a camp of Robin Hood's foresters. Then they brought up the dead from behind bushes and under rocks—among others a twenty-seven-inch brute who bore on his flank (all pigs shot in a beat are *ex-officio* boars) a hideous, half-healed scar, big as a man's hand, of a bullet wound. Express bullets are ghastly things in their effects, for, as the *shikari* is never tired of demonstrating, they kock the inside of animals into pulp.

The second beat, of the reverse side of the hill, had barely begun when the panther returned—uneasily, as if something were keeping her back—much lower down the hill. Then the face of the Rawat of Amet changed, as he brought his gun up to his shoulder. Looking at him as he fired, one forgot all about the Mayo College at which he had been educated, and remembered only some trivial and out-of-date affairs, in which his forefathers had been concerned, when a bridegroom, with his bride at his side, charged down the slope of the Chitor road and died among Akbar's men. There are stories connected with the house of Amet, which are told in Mewar to-day. The young man's face, for as short a time as it takes to pull trigger and see where the bullet falls, was a light upon all these tales.

Then the mask shut down, as he clicked out the cartridge and, very sweetly, gave it as his opinion that some other gun, and not his own, had bagged the panther who lay shot through the spine, feebly trying to drag herself down-hill into cover. It is an awful thing to see a big beast die, when the soul is wrenched out of the struggling body in ten seconds. Wild horses shall not make the Englishman disclose the exact number of shots that were fired. It is enough to say that four Englishmen, now scattered to the four winds of heaven, are each morally certain that he and he alone shot that panther. In time when distance and the mirage of the sands of Uodhpur shall have softened the harsh outlines of truth, the Englishman who did *not* fire a shot will come to believe that he was the real slayer, and will carefully elaborate that lie.

A few minutes after the murder, a two-year old cub came trotting along the hill-side, and was bowled over by a very pretty shot behind the left ear and through the palate. Then the beaters' lances showed through the bushes, and the guns began to realize that they had allowed to escape, or had driven back by their fire, a multitude of pigs.

This ended the beat, and the procession returned to the Residency to heap dead panthers upon those who had called them "pork butchers," and to stir up the lake of envy with the torpedo of brilliant description. The Englishman's attempt to compare the fusillade which greeted the panther to the continuous drumming of a ten-barrelled Nordenfeldt was, however, coldly received. So harshly is truth treated all the world over.

And then, after a little time, came the end, and a return to the road in search of new countries. But shortly before the departure, the Padre-Sahib, who knows every one in Udaipur, read a sermon in a sentence. The Maharana's investiture, which has already been described in the Indian papers, had taken place, and the carriages, duly escorted by the Erinpura Horse, were returning to the Residency. In a niche of waste land, under the shadow of the main gate, a place strewn with rubbish and shards of pottery, a dilapidated old man was trying to control his horse and a *hookah* on the saddle-bow. The blundering garron had been made restive by the rush past, and the *hookah* all but fell from the hampered hands. "See that man," said the Padre tersely. "That's —— Singh. He intrigued for the throne not so very long ago." It was a pitiful little picture, and needed no further comment.

For the benefit of the loafer it should be noted that Udaipur will never be pleasant or accessible until the present Mail Contractors have been hanged. They are extortionate and untruthful, and their one set of harness and one tonga are as rotten as pears. However, the weariness of the flesh must be great indeed, to make the wanderer blind to the beauties of a journey by clear starlight and in biting cold to Chitor. About six miles from Udaipur, the granite hills close in upon the road, and the air grows warmer until, with a rush and a rattle, the tonga swings through the great Dobarra, the gate in the double circle of hills round Udaipur on to the pastures of Mewar. More than once the Girwa has been a death-trap to those who rashly entered it; and an army has been cut up on the borders of the Pichola lake. Even now the genius of the place is strong upon the hills, and as he felt the cold air from the open ground without the barrier, the Englishman found himself repeating the words of one of the Hat-marked tribe whose destiny kept him within the Dobarra. "You must have a *shouk* of some kind in these parts or you'll die." Very lovely is Udaipur, and thrice pleasant are a few days spent within her gates, but . . . read what Tod said who stayed two years behind the Dobarra, and accepted the deserts of Marwar as a delightful change.

It is good to be free, a wanderer upon the highways, knowing not what to-morrow will bring forth—whether the walled-in niceties of an English household, rich in all that makes life fair and desirable, or a sleepless night in the society of a goods-*cum*-booking-office-*cum*-parcels-clerk, on fifteen rupees a month, who tells in stilted English the story of his official life, while the telegraph gibbers like a maniac once in an hour and then is dumb, and the pariah dogs fight and howl over the cotton-bales on the platform.

Verily, there is no life like life on the road—when the skies are cool and all men are kind.

CHAPTER X.

THE ENGLISHMAN COMES UPON THE BLACK BULK OF CHITOR, AND LEARNS OF THE MAL-PRACTICES OF A SHE-ELEPHANT.

There is a certain want of taste, an almost actual indecency, in seeing the sun rise on the earth. Until the heat-haze begins and the distances thicken, Nature is so very naked that the Actæon who has surprised her dressing, blushes. Sunrise on the plains of Mewar is an especially brutal affair.

The moon was burnt out and the air was bitterly cold, when the Englishman headed due east in his tonga, and the patient sowar behind nodded and yawned in the saddle. There was no warning of the day's advent. The horses were unharnessed, at one halting-stage, in the thick, soft shadows of night, and ere their successors had limped under the bar, a raw and cruel light was upon all things, so that the Englishman could see every rent seam in the rocks around—see "even to the uttermost farthing." A little further, and he came upon the black bulk of Chitor between him and the morning sun. It has already been said that the Fort resembles a man-of-war. Every distant view heightens this impression, for the swell of the sides follows the form of a ship, and the bastions on the south wall make the sponsions in which the machine-guns are mounted. From bow to stern, the thing more than three miles long, is between three and five hundred feet high, and from one-half to one-quarter of a mile broad. Have patience, now, to listen to a rough history of Chitor.

In the beginning, no one knows clearly who scarped the hill-sides of the hill rising out of the bare plain, and made of it a place of strength. It is written that, eleven and a half centuries ago, Bappa Rawul, the demi-god whose stature was twenty cubits, whose loin-cloth was five hundred feet long, and whose spear was beyond the power of mortal man to lift, took Chitor from "Man Singh, the Mori Prince," and wrote the first chapter of the history of Mewar, which he received ready-made from Man Singh who, if the chronicles speak sooth, was his uncle. Many and very marvellous legends cluster round the name of Bappa Rawul; and he is said to have ended his days far away from India, in Khorasan, where he married an unlimited number of the Daughters of Heth, and was the father of all the Nowshera Pathans. Some who have wandered, by the sign-posts of inscription, into the fogs of old time, aver that, two centuries before Bappa Rawul took Chitor the Mori division of the Pramar Rajputs, who are the ruling family of Mewar, had found a hold in Bhilwar, and for four centuries before that time had ruled in Kathiawar; and had royally sacked and slain, and been sacked and slain in turn. But these things are for the curious and the scholar, and not for the reader who reads lightly. Nine princes succeeded Bappa, between 728 and 1068 A. D., and among these was one Alluji, who built a Jain tower upon the brow of the hill, for in those days, though the sun was worshipped, men were Jains.

And here they lived and sallied into the plains, and fought and increased the borders of their kingdom, or were suddenly and stealthily murdered, or stood shoulder to shoulder against the incursions of the "Devil men" from the north. In 1150 A. D. was born Samar Singh, and he married into the family of Prithi Raj, the last Hindu Emperor of Delhi, who was at feud, in regard to a succession question, with the Prince of Kanauj. In the war that followed, Kanauj, being hard pressed by Prithi Raj, and Samar

Singh, called Shahabuddin Ghori to his aid. At first, Samar Singh and Prithi Raj broke the army of the Northern somewhere in the lower Punjab, but two years later Shahabuddin came again, and, after three days' fighting on the banks of the Kaggar, slew Samar Singh, captured and murdered Prithi Raj, and sacked Delhi and Amber, while Samar Singh's favorite queen became *sati* at Chitor. But another wife, a princess of Patun, kept her life, and when Shahabuddin sent down Kutbuddin to waste her lands, led the Rajput army, in person, from Chitor, and defeated Kutbuddin.

Then followed confusion, through eleven turbulent reigns that the annalist has failed to unravel. Once in the years between 1193 and the opening of the fourteenth century, Chitor must have been taken by the Mussalman, for it is written that one prince "recovered Chitor and made the name of Rana to be recognized by all." Six princes were slain in battles against the Mussulman, in vain attempts to clear far away Gya from the presence of the infidel.

Then Ala-ud-din Khilji, the Pathan Emperor, swept the country to the Dekkan. In those days, and these things are confusedly set down as having happened at the end of the thirteenth century, a relative of Rana Lakhsman Singh, the then Rana of Chitor, had married a Rajput princess of Ceylon—Pudmini, "And she was fairest of all flesh on earth." Her fame was sung through the land by the poets, and she became, in some sort, the Helen of Chitor. Ala-ud-din heard of her beauty and promptly besieged the Fort. When he found his enterprise too difficult, he prayed that he might be permitted to see Pudmini's face in a mirror, and this wish, so says the tale, was granted. Knowing that the Rajput was a gentleman he entered Chitor almost unarmed, saw the face in the mirror, and was well treated; the husband of the fair Pudmini accompanying him, in return, to the camp at the foot of the hill. Like Raja Runjeet in the ballad the Rajput—

> " . . . trusted a Mussalman's word
> Wah! Wah! Trust a liar to lie.
> Out of his eyrie they tempted my bird,
> Fettered his wings that he could not fly."

Pudmini's husband was caught, and Ala-ud-din demanded Pudmini as the price of his return. The Rajputs here showed that they too could scheme, and sent, in great state, Pudmini's litter to the besiegers' entrenchments. But there was no Pudmini in the litter, and the following of handmaidens was a band of seven hundred armed men. Thus, in the confusion of a camp-fight, Pudmini's husband was rescued, and Ala-ud-din's soldiery followed hard on his heels to the gates of Chitor, where the best and bravest on the rock were killed before Ala-ud-din withdrew, only to return soon after and, with a doubled army, besiege in earnest. His first attack men called the half-sack of Chitor, for, though he failed to win within the walls, he killed the flower of the Rajputs. The second attack ended in the first sack and the awful *sati* of the women on the rock.

When everything was hopeless and the very terrible Goddes, who lives in the bowels of Chitor, had spoken and claimed for death eleven out of the twelve of the Rana's sons, all who were young or fair women betook themselves to a great underground chamber, and the fires were lit and the entrance was walled up and they died. The Rajputs opened the gates and fought till they could fight no more, and Ala-ud-din the victorious entered a wasted and desolated city. He wrecked everything except only the palace of Pudmini and the old Jain tower before mentioned. That was all he could do, for there were few men alive of the defenders of Chitor when the day was won, and the women were ashes in the underground palace.

Ajai Singh, the one surviving son of Lakshman Singh, had at his father's insistence, escaped from Chitor to "carry on the line" when better days should come. He brought up Hamir, son of one of his elder brothers, to be a thorn in the side of the invader, and Hamir overthrew Maldeo, chief of Jhalore and vassal of Ala-ud-din, into whose hands Ala-ud-din had, not too generously, given what was left of Chitor. So the Sesodias came to their own again, and the successors of Hamir extended their kingdoms and rebuilt Chitor, as kings know how to rebuild cities in a land where human labor and life are cheaper than bread and water. For two centuries, saith Tod, Mewar flourished exceedingly and was the paramount kingdom of all Rajasthan. Greatest of all the successors of Hamir, was Kumbha Rana who, when the Ghilzai dynasty was rotting away and Viceroys declared themselves kings, met, defeated, took captive and released without ransom, Mahmoud of Malwa. Kumbha Rana built a Tower of Victory, nine stories high, to commemorate this and the other successes of his reign, and the tower stands to-day a mark for miles across the plains. Of this, more hereafter.

But the well-established kingdom weakened, and the rulers took favorites and disgusted their best supporters—after the immemorial custom of too prosperous rulers. Also they murdered one another. In 1535 A. D. Bahadur Shah, King of Gujarat, seeing the decay, and remembering how one of his predecessors, together with Mahmoud of Malwa, had been humbled by Mewar in years gone by, set out to take his revenge of Time and Mewar then ruled by Rana Bikrmajit, who had made a new capital at Deola. Bikrmajit did not stay to give battle in that place. His chiefs were out of hand, and Chitor was the heart and brain of Mewar; so he marched thither, and the gods were against him. Bahadur Shah mined one of the Chitor bastions and wiped out in the explosion the Hara Prince of Boondee with five hundred followers. Jowahir Bae, Bikrmajit's mother, headed a sally from the walls and was slain. There were Frank gunners among Bahadur Shah's forces, and they hastened the end. The Rajputs made a second *johur* greater than the *johur* of Pudmini; and thirteen thousand were blown up in the magazines, or stabbed or poisoned, before the gates were opened and the defenders rushed down.

Out of the carnage was saved Udai Singh, a babe of the Blood Royal, who grew up to be a coward and a shame to his line. The story of his preservation is written large in Tod, and Edwin Arnold sings it. Read it, who are interested. But, when Udai Singh came to the throne of Chitor, through blood and mis-rule, after Bahadur Shah had withdrawn from the wreck of the Fort, Akbar sat on the throne of Delhi, and it was written that few people should withstand the "Guardian of Mankind." Moreover, Udai Singh was the slave of a woman. It was Akbar's destiny to subdue the Rajputs and to win many of them to his own service; sending a Rajput Prince of Amber to get him Arraken. Akbar marched against Chitor once and was repulsed; the woman who ruled Udai Singh heading a charge against the besiegers because of the love she bore to her lover. Something of this sort had happened in Ala-ud-din's time, and, like Ala-ud-din, Akbar returned and sat down, in a huge camp, before Chitor in 1568, A. D. Udai Singh fled what was coming; and because the Goddess of Chitor demands always that a crowned head must fall if the defence of her home is to be successful, Chitor fell as it had fallen before—in a *johur* of thousands, a last rush of the men, and the entry of the conqueror into a reeking, ruined slaughter-pen. Akbar's sack was the most terrible of the three, for he killed everything that had life upon the rock, and wrecked and overturned and spoiled. The wonder, the lasting wonder, is that he did not destroy Kumbha Rana's Tower of Victory and memorial of the defeat of a Mahomedan prince. With the third sack the glory of Chitor departed, and Udai Singh founded himself a new capital, the city of Udaipur. Though Chitor was recovered in Jehangir's time by Udai Singh's grandson, it was never again made the capital of Mewar. It stood and rotted where it stood, till enlightened and loyal feudatories in the present years of grace, made attempts, with the help of Executive Engineers, to sweep it up and keep it in repair. The above is roughly, very roughly indeed, the tale of the sacks of Chitor.

Follows an interlude, for the study even of inaccurate history is indigestible to many. There was an elephant at Chitor, to take birds of passage up the hill, and she—she was fifty-one years old and her name was Gerowlia—came to the dak-bungalow for the Englishman. Let not the word dak-bungalow deceive any man into believing that there is even moderate comfort at Chitor. Gerowlia waited in the sunshine, and chuckled to herself like a female pauper when she receives snuff. The *mahout* said that he would go away for a drink of water. So he walked, and walked, and walked, till he disappeared on the stone-strewn plains, and the Englishman was left alone with Gerowlia aged fifty-one. She had been tied by the chain on her near hind-leg to a pillar of the verandah ; but the string was *moonj* string only, and more an emblem of authority than a means of restraint. When she had thoroughly exhausted all the resources of the country within range of her trunk, she ate up the string and began to investigate the verandah. There was more *moonj* string, and she ate it all, while the *mistri* who was repairing the dak-bungalow cursed her and her ancestry from afar. About this time the Englishman was roused to a knowledge of the business, for Gerowlia, having exhausted the string, tried to come into the verandah. She had, most unwisely, been pampered with biscuits an hour before. The *mistri* stood on an outcrop of rock and said angrily :—" See what damage your *hathi* has done, Sahib." "Tisn't my *hathi*," said the Sahib plaintively. "You ordered it," quoth the *mistri*, " and it has been here ever so long, eating up everything." Herewith he threw pieces of stone at Gerowlia and went away. It is a terrible thing to be left alone with an unshackled elephant, even though she be a venerable spinster. Gerowlia moved round the dak-bungalow, blowing her nose in a nervous and undecided manner and, presently, found some more string, which she ate. This was too much. The Englishman went out and spoke to her. She opened her mouth and salaamed ; meaning thereby " biscuits." So long as she remained in this position she could do no harm.

Imagine a boundless rock-strewn plain, broken here and there by low hills, dominated by the rock of Chitor and bisected by a single, metre-gauge railway track running into the Infinite, and unrelieved by even a way-inspector's trolly. In the foreground put a brand-new dak-bunglow furnished with a French bedstead and nothing else ; and, in the verandah, place an embarrassed Englishman, smiling into the open mouth of an idiotic female elephant. But Gerowlia could not live on smiles alone. Finding that no food was forthcoming, she shut her mouth and renewed her attempts to get into the verandah and ate more *moonj* string. To say " H !" to an elephant is a misdirected courtesy. It quickens the pace, and if you flick her on the trunk with a wet towel, she curls the trunk out of harm's way. Special education is necessary. A little breechless boy passed, carrying a lump of stone. "Hit on the feet, Sahib," said he; "Hit on the feet." Gerowlia had by this time nearly scraped off her pad and there were no signs of the *mahout*. The Englishman went out and found a tent-peg, and returning, in the extremity of his wrath, smote her bitterly on the nails of the near forefoot.

Then, as Rider Haggard used to say—though the expression was patented by at least one writer before he made it his own—a curious thing happened. Gerowlia held up her foot to be beaten, and made the most absurd noises—squawked in fact, exactly like an old lady who has narrowly escaped being run over. She backed out of the verandah, still squawking, on three feet and in the open held up near and off forefoot alternately to be beaten. It was very pitiful, for one swing of her trunk could have knocked the Englishman flat. He ceased whacking her, but she squawked for some minutes and then fell placidly asleep in the sunshine. When the *mahout* returned, he beat her for breaking her tether exactly as the Englishman had done, but much more severely, and the ridiculous old thing hopped on three legs for fully five minutes. "Come along, Sahib," said the *mahout*. I will show this mother of bastards who is the *mahout*. Fat daughter of the Devil sit down. You would eat string, would you? How does the iron taste?" And he gave Gerowlia a headache, which affected her temper all through the afternoon. She set off, across the railway line which runs below the rock of Chitor, into broken ground cut up with *mullahs* and covered with low scrub, over which it would have been difficult to have taken a sure-footed horse, so fragmentary and disconnected was its nature.

CHAPTER XI.

SHOWS THE DISCOVERY OF THE TOWER VISITED BY CHILDE ROLANDE, AND THE "BOGEY" WHO FRIGHTENS CHILDREN.

The Gamberi river—clear as a trout-stream—runs through the waste round Chitor, and is spanned by an old bridge, very solid and massive, said to have been built before the sack of Ala-ud-din. The bridge is in the middle of the stream—the floods have raced round either ends of it—and is reached by a steeply sloping stone causeway. From the bridge to the new town of Chitor, which lies at the foot of the hill, runs a straight and well-kept road, flanked on either side by the scattered remnants of old houses, and, here and there, fallen temples. The road, like the bridge, is no new thing, and is wide enough for twenty horsemen to ride abreast.

New Chitor is a very dirty, and apparently thriving, little town, full of grain-merchants and sellers of arms. The ways are barely wide enough for the elephant of dignity and the little brown babies of impudence. The Englishman went through, always on a slope painfully accentuated by Gerowlia who, with all possible respect to her years, must have been a baggage-animal and no true *Sahib's* mount. Let the local Baedeker speak for a moment: "The ascent to Chitor, which begins from within the south-east angle of the town, is nearly a mile to the upper gate, with a slope of about 1 in 15. There are two zig-zag bends, and on the three portions thus formed, are seven gates, of which one, however, has only the basement left." This is the language of fact which, very properly, leaves out of all account the Genius of the Place who sits at the gate nearest the new city and is with the sightseer throughout. The first impression of repulsion and awe is given by a fragment of tumbled sculpture close to a red daubed *lingam*, near the Padal Pol or lowest gate. It is a piece of frieze, and the figures of the men are worn nearly smooth by time. What is visible is finely and frankly obscene to an English mind.

The road is protected on the *Khud* side by a thick stone wall, loopholed for musketry, one aperture to every two feet, between fifteen and twenty feet high. This wall is being repaired throughout its length by the Maharana of Udaipur. On the hill-side, among the boulders, loose stones and *dhao*-scrub, lies stone wreckage that must have come down from the brown bastions above.

As Gerowlia labored up the stone-shod slope, the Englishman wondered how much life had flowed down this sluice of battles, and been lost at the Padal Pol—the last and lowest gate—where, in the old days, the besieging armies put their best and bravest battalions. Once at the head of the lower slope, there is a clear run-down of a thousand yards with no chance of turning aside either to the right or left. Even as he wondered, he was brought abreast of two stone chhatris, each carrying a red daubed stone. They were the graves of two very brave men, Jeemal of Bedmore, and Kalla, who fell in Akbar's sack fighting like Rajputs. Read the story of their deaths, and learn what manner of warriors they were. Their graves were all that spoke openly of the hundreds of struggles on the lower slope where the fight was always fiercest.

At last, after half an hour's climb, the main gate, the Ram Pol, was gained, and the Englishman passed into the City of Chitor and—then and there formed a resolution, since broken, not to write one word about it for fear that he should be set down as a babbling and a gushing enthusiast. Objects of archæological interest are duly described in an admirable little book of Chitor which, after one look, the Englishman abandoned. One cannot "do" Chitor with a guide-book. The Padre of the English Mission to Jehangir said the best that was to be said, when he described the place three hundred years ago, writing quaintly: "Chitor, an ancient great kingdom, the chief city so called which standeth on a mighty high hill, flat on the top, walled about at the least ten English miles. There appear to this day above a hundred churches ruined and divers fair palaces which are lodged in like manner among their ruins, as many Englishmen by the observation have guessed. Its chief inhabitants to-day are Zum and Ohim, birds and wild beasts, but the stately ruins thereof give a shadow of its beauty while it flourished in its pride." Gerowlia struck into a narrow pathway, forcing herself through garden-trees and disturbing the peacocks. An evil guide-man on the ground waved his hand, and began to speak ; but was silenced. The death of Amber was as nothing to the death of Chitor—a body whence the life had been driven by riot and sword. Men had parcelled the gardens of her palaces and the courtyards of her temples into fields ; and cattle grazed among the remnants of the shattered tombs. But over all—over rent and bastion, split temple-wall, pierced roof and prone pillar—lay the "shadow of its beauty while it flourished in its pride." The Englishman walked into a stately palace of many rooms, where the sunlight streamed in through wall and roof, and up crazy stone stairways, held together, it seemed, by the marauding trees. In one bastion, a wind-sown peepul had wrenched a thick slab clear of the wall, but held it tight pressed in a crook of a branch, as a man holds down a fallen enemy under his elbow, shoulder and forearm. In another place, a strange, uncanny wind, sprung from nowhere, was singing all alone among the pillars of what may have been a Hall of Audience. The Englishman wandered so far in one palace that he came to an almost black-dark room, high up in a wall, and said proudly to himself: "I must be the first man who has been here ;" meaning thereby no harm or insult to any one. But he tripped and fell, and as he put out his hands, he felt that the stairs had been worn hollow and smooth by the tread of innumerable naked feet. Than he was afraid, and came away very quickly, stepping delicately over fallen friezes and bits of sculptured men, so as not to offend the dead ; and was mightily relieved when he recovered his elephant and allowed the guide to take him to Kumbha Rana's Tower of Victory.

This stands, like all things in Chitor, among ruins, but time and the other enemies have been good to it. It is a Jain edifice, nine storeys high, crowned atop—was this designed insult or undesigned repair ?—with a purely Mahomedan dome, wherein the pigeons and the bats live. Excepting this blemish, the Tower of Victory is nearly as fair as when it left the hands of the builder whose name has not been handed down to us. It is to be observed here that the first, or more ruined, Tower of Victory, built in Alluji's days, when Chitor was comparatively young, was raised by some pious Jain as proof of conquest over things spiritual. The second tower is more worldly in intent.

Those who care to look, may find elsewhere a definition of its architecture and its more striking peculiarities. It was in kind, but not in degree, like the Jugdesh Temple at Udaipur, and, as it exceeded it in magnificence, so its effect upon the mind was more intense. The confusing intricacy of the figures with which it was wreathed from top to bottom, the recurrence of the one calm face, the God enthroned, holding the Wheel of the Law, and the appalling lavishness of decoration, all worked towards the instilment of fear and aversion.

Surely this must have been one of the objects of the architect. The tower, in the arrangement of its stairways, is like the interior of a Chinese carved ivory puzzle-ball. The idea given is that, even while you are ascending, you are wrapping yourself deeper and deeper in the tangle of a mighty maze. Add to this the half-light, the thronging armies of sculptured figures, the mad profusion of design splashed as impartially upon the undersides of the stone window-slabs as upon the door-beam of the threshold—add, most abhorrent of all, the slippery sliminess of the walls worn smooth by naked men, and you will understand that the tower is not a soothing place to visit. The Englishman fancied presumptuously that he had, in a way, grasped the builder's idea ; and when he came to the top storey and sat among the pigeons his theory was this : To attain power, wrote the builder of old, in sentences of fine stone, it is necessary to pass through all sorts of close-packed horrors, treacheries, battles and insults, in darkness and without knowledge whether the road leads upward or into a hopeless *cul-de-sac.* Kumbha Rana must many times have climbed to the top storey, and looked out towards the uplands of Malaw on the one side and his own great Mewar on the other, in the days when all the rock hummed with life and the clatter of hooves upon the stony ways, and Mahmoud of Malwa was safe in hold.

How he must have swelled with pride—fine insolent pride of life and rule and power—power not only to break things but to compel such builders as those who piled the tower to his royal will! There was no decoration in the top storey to bewilder or amaze —nothing but well-grooved stone-slabs, and a boundless view fit for kings who traced their ancestry—

> "From times when forth from the sunlight, the first of
> our kings came down,
> And had the earth for his footstool, and wore the stars
> for his crown."

The builder had left no mark behind him—not even a mark on the threshold of the door, or a sign in the head of the topmost step. The Englishman looked in both places, believing that those were the places generally chosen for mark-cutting. So he sat and meditated on the beauties of kingship and the unholiness of Hindu art, and what power a shadow-land of lewd monstrosities had upon those who believed in it, and what Lord Dufferin, who is the nearest approach to a king in this India, must have thought when A.—D.—C.'s clanked after him up the narrow steps. But the day was wearing, and he came down—in both senses—and, in his descent, the carven things on every side of the tower, and above and below once more took hold of and perverted his fancy, so that he arrived at the bottom in a frame of mind eminently fitted for a descent into the Gau-Mukh, which is nothing more terrible than a little spring, falling into a reservoir, in the side of the hill.

He stumbled across more ruins and passed between tombs of dead Ranis, till he came to a flight of steps, built out and cut out from rock, going down as far as he could see into a growth of trees on a terrace below him. The stone of the steps had been worn and polished by naked feet till it showed its markings clearly as agate; and where the steps ended in a rock-slope, there was a visible glair, a great snail-track, upon the rocks. It was hard to keep safe footing on the sliminess. The air was thick with the sick smell of stale incense, and grains of rice were scattered upon the steps. But there was no one to be seen. Now this in itself was not specially alarming; but the Genius of the Place must be responsible for making it so. The Englishman slipped and bumped on the rocks, and arrived, more suddenly than he desired, upon the edge of a dull blue tank, sunk between walls of timeless masonary. In a slabbed-in recess, water was pouring through a shapeless stone gargoyle, into a trough; which trough again dripped into the tank. Almost under the little trickle of water, was the loathesome Emblem of Creation, and there were flowers and rice around it. Water was trickling from a score of places in the cut face of the hill oozing between the edges of the steps and welling up between the stone slabs of the terrace. Trees sprouted in the sides of the tank and hid its surroundings. It seemed as though the descent had led the Englishman, *firstly*, two thousand years away from his own century, and *secondly*, into a trap, and that he would fall off the polished stones into the stinking tank, or that the Gau-Mukh would continue to pour water placidly until the tank rose up and swamped him, or that some of the stone slabs would fall forward and crush him flat.

Then he was conscious of remembering, with peculiar and unnecessary distinctness, that, from the Gau-Mukh, a passage led to the subterranean chambers in which fair Pudmini and her handmaids had slain themselves. Also, that Tod had written and the Station-master at Chitor had said, that some sort of devil, or ghoul, or something, stood at the entrance of that approach. All of which was a nightmare bred in full day and folly to boot; but it was the fault of the Genius of the Place, who made the Englishman feel that he had done a great wrong in trespassing into the very heart and soul of all Chitor. And, behind him, the Gau-Mukh guggled and choked like a man in his death-throe. The Englishman endured as long as he could—about two minutes. Then it came upon him that he must go quickly out of this place of years and blood—must get back to the afternoon sunshine, and Gerowlia, and the dak-bungalow with the French bedstead. He desired no archæological information, he wished to take no notes, and, above all, he did not care to look behind him, where stood the reminder that he was no better than the beasts that perish. But he had to cross the smooth, worn rocks, and he felt their sliminess through his bootsoles. It was as though he were treading on the soft, oiled skin of a Hindu. As soon as the steps gave refuge, he floundered up them, and so came out of the Gau-Mukh, bedewed with that perspiration which follows alike on honest toil or—childish fear.

"This," said he to himself, "is absurd!" and sat down on the fallen top of a temple to review the situation. But the Gau-Mukh had disappeared. He could see the dip in the ground and the beginning of the steps, but nothing more.

Perhaps it was absurd. It undoubtedly appeared so, later. Yet there was something uncanny about it all. It was not exactly a feeling of danger or pain, but an odd sort of apprehension of evil.

Looking at the dip in the ground, he thought what a strange thing is the mind of man. It preserves its wonted state of uniform activity or comparative rest until it is compelled by some irresistible force to change that state. There was some such force in the awful solitude of that "heart of Chitor," and the unearthly death-gurgle of the Gau-Mukh.

Then came the reaction, and the Englishman did not know whether or not to be ashamed of his remarkable experience.

In defence, it may be urged that there is moral, just as much as there is mine, choke-damp. If you get into a place laden with the latter you die, and if into the home of the former you . . . behave unwisely, as constitution and temperament prompt. If any man doubt this, let him sit for two hours in a hot sun on an elephant, stay half-an-hour in the Tower of Victory, and then go down into the Gau-Mukh, which, it must never be forgotten, is merely a set of springs "three or four in number, issuing from the cliff face at cow-mouth carvings, now mutilated. The water, evidently percolating from the Hathi Kund above, falls first in an old pillared hall and thence into the masonry reservoir below, eventually, when abundant enough, supplying a little water-fall lower down." That, Gentlemen and Ladies, on the honor of one who has been frightened of the dark in broad daylight, is the Gau-Mukh, as though photographed.

The Englishman regained Gerowlia and demanded to be taken away, but Gerowlia's driver went forward instead and showed him a new Mahal just built by the present Maharana. If a fourth sack of Chitor could be managed for a Viceroy's edification, the blowing up of the new Mahal would supply a pleasant evening's entertainment. Near the Mahal lie the remains of the great tanks of Chitor, for the hill has through a great part of its length, a depression in the centre, by means of bunds, stored, in the old time, a full supply of water. A general keeping in order is visible throughout many of the ruins; and, in places, a carriage-drive is being constructed. Carriage-drives, however, do not consort well with Chitor and the "shadow of her ancient beauty." The return journey, past temple after temple and palace upon palace, began in the failing light, and Gerowlia was still blundering up and down narrow bye-paths—for she possessed all an old woman's delusion as to the slimness of her waist when the twilight fell, and the smoke from the town below began to creep up the brown flanks of Chitor, and the jackals howled. Then the sense of desolation, which had been strong enough in all conscience in the sunshine, began to grow and grow :—

> "The sun's eye had a sickly glare,
> The earth with age was wan,
> The skeletons of ages stood
> Around that lonely man."

Near the Ram Pol there was some semblance of a town with living people in it, and a priest sat in the middle of the road and howled aloud upon his gods, until a little boy came and laughed in his face heretically, and he went away grumbling. This touch was deeply refreshing ; in the contemplation of it, the Englishman clean forgot that he had overlooked the gathering in of materials for an elaborate statistical, historical, geographical account of Chitor. All that remained to him was a shuddering reminiscence of the Gau-Mukh and two lines of the "Holy Grail."

> "And up into the sounding halls he passed,
> But nothing in the sounding halls he saw."

Post Scriptum.—There was something very uncanny about the Genius of the Place. He dragged an ease-loving egotist out of the French bedstead with the gilt knobs at head and foot, into a more than usually big folly—nothing less than a seeing of Chitor by moonlight. There was no possibility of getting Gerowlia out of *her* bed, and a mistrust of the Maharana's soldiery who in the day time guarded the gates, prompted the Englishman to avoid the public way, and scramble straight up the hillside, along an attempt at a path which he had noted from Gerowlia's back. There was no one to interfere, and nothing but an infinity of pestilent nullahs and loose stones to check. Owls came out and hooted at him, and animals ran about in the dark and made uncouth noises. It was an idiotic journey, and it ended—Oh, horror! in that unspeakable Gau-Mukh—this time entered from the opposite or brushwooded side, as far as could be made out in the dusk and from the chuckle of the water which, by night, was peculiarly malevolent.

Escaping from this place, crab-fashion, the Englishman crawled into Chitor and sat upon a flat tomb till the moon, a very inferior and second-hand one, rose, and turned the city of the dead into a city of scurrying ghouls—in sobriety, jackals. Also, the ruins took strange shapes and shifted in the half light and cast objectionable shadows.

It was easy enough to fill the rock with the people of old times, and a very beautiful account of Chitor restored, made out by the help of Tod, and bristling with the names of the illustrious dead, would undoubtedly have been written, had not a woman, a living breathing woman, stolen out of a temple—what was she doing in that gallery?—and screamed in piercing and public-spirited fashion. The Englishman got off the tomb and departed rather more noisily than a jackal; feeling for the moment that he was not much better. Somebody opened a door with a crash, and a man cried out: "Who is there?"

But the cause of the disturbance was, for his sins, being most horribly scratched by some thorny scrub over the edge of the hill—there are no bastions worth speaking of near the Gau-Mukh—and the rest was partly rolling, partly scrambling, and mainly bad language.

When you are too lucky sacrifice something, a beloved pipe for choice, to Ganesh. The Englishman has seen Chitor by moonlight—not the best moonlight truly, but the watery glare of a nearly spent moon—and his sacrifice to Luck is this. He will never try to describe what he has seen—but will keep it as a love-letter, a thing for one pair of eyes only—a memory that few men to-day can be sharers in. And does he, through this fiction, evade insulting, by the dauberie of pen and ink, a scene as lovely, wild, and unmatchable as any that mortal eyes have been privileged to rest upon?

An intelligent and discriminating public are perfectly at liberty to form their own opinions.

CHAPTER XII.

AN ESCAPE NORTHWARD TO JHARWASA—SOME LITTLE INCIDENTS CONNECTED WITH THE BHUMIA—THE ENGLISHMAN LANDS IN JODHPUR, AND WISHES TO GIVE THE BRITISH GOVERNMENT ADVICE ON CERTAIN MATTERS.

Come away from the monstrous gloom of Chitor and escape northwards. The place is unclean and terrifying. Let us catch To-day by both hands and return to the Station-master who is also booking-parcels and telegraph-clerk, and who never seems to go to bed—and to the comfortably wadded bunks of the Rajputana-Malwa line.

While the train is running, be pleased to listen to the perfectly true story of the *bhumia* of Jharwasa, which is a story the sequel whereof has yet to be written. Once upon a time, a Rajput landholder, a *bhumia*, and a Mahomedan *jaghirdar*, were next-door neighbors in Ajmir territory. They hated each other thoroughly for many reasons, all connected with land; and the *jaghirdar* was the bigger man of the two. In those days, it was the law that the victims of robbery or dacoity should be reimbursed by the owner of the lands on which the affair had taken place. The ordinance is now swept away as impracticable. There was a highway robbery on the *bhumia's* holding; and he vowed that it had been "put up" by the Mahomedan who, he said, was an Ahab. The reive-gelt payable nearly ruined the Rajput, and he, laboring under a galling grievance or a groundless suspicion, fired the *jaghird's* crops, was detected and brought up before the English Judge who gave him four years' imprisonment. To the sentence was appended a recommendation that, on release, the Rajput should be put on heavy securities for good behavior. "Otherwise," wrote the Judge, who seems to have known the people he was dealing with, "he will certainly kill the *jaghirdar*." Four years passed, and the *jaghirdar* obtained wealth and consideration, and was made, let us say, a Khan Bahadur, and an Honorary Magistrate; but the *bhumia* remained in gaol and thought over the highway robbery. When the day of release came, a new Judge hunted up his predecessor's finding and recommendation, and would have put the *bhumia* on security. "Sahib," said the *bhumia*, "I have no people. I have been in gaol. What am I now? And who will find security for me? If you will send me back to gaol again I can do nothing, and I have no friends." So they released him, and he went away into an outlying village and borrowed a sword from one house, and had it sharpened in another, for love. Two days later fell the birthday of the Kahn Bahadur and the Honorary Magistrate, and his friends and servants and dependants made a little durbar and did him honor after the native custom. The *bhumia* also attended the levee, but no one knew him, and he was stopped at the door of the courtyard by the servant. "Say that the *bhumia* of Jharwasa has come to pay his salaams," said he. They let him in, and in the heart of Ajmir City, in broad daylight, and before all the *jaghirdar's* household, he smote off his enemy's head so that it rolled upon the ground. Then he fled, and though they raised the countryside against him he was never caught, and went into Bikanir.

Five years later, word came to Ajmir that Chimbo Singh, the *bhumia* of Jharwasa, had taken service under the Thakur Sahib of Palitana. The case was an old one, and the chances of identification misty, but the suspected was caught and brought in, and one of the leading native barristers of the Bombay Bar was retained to defend him. He said nothing and continued to say nothing, and the case fell through. He is believed to be "wanted" now for a fresh murder committed within the last few months, out Bikanir way.

And now that the train has reached Ajmir, the Crewe of Rajputana, whither shall a tramp turn his feet? The Englishman set his stick on end, and it fell with its point North-West as nearly as might be. This being translated, meant Jodhpur, which is the city of the Hounhnhyms, and, that all may be in keeping, the occasional resting-place of fugitive Yahoos. If you would enjoy Jodhpur thoroughly, quit at Ajmir the decent conventionalities of "station" life, and make it your business to move among gentlemen—gentlemen in the Ordnance of the Commissariat, or, better still, gentlemen on the Railway. At Ajmir, gentlemen will tell you what manner of place Jodhpur is, and their accounts, though flavored with crisp and curdling oaths, are amusing. In their eyes the desert that rings the city has no charms, and they discuss affairs of the State, as they understand them, in a manner that would curl the hair on a Political's august head. Jodhpur has been, but things are rather better now, a much-favored camping ground for the light-cavalry of the road—the loafers with a certain amount of brain and great assurance. The explanation is simple. There are more than four hundred horses in His Highness's city stables alone; and where the Houyhnhnm is, there also will be the Yahoo. This is sad but true.

Besides the Uhlans who come and go on Heaven knows what mysterious errands, there are bag-men travelling for the big English firms. Jodhpur is a good customer, and purchases all sorts of things, more or less useful, for the State or its friends. These are the gentlemen to know, if you would understand something of matters which are not written in reports.

The Englishman took a train from Ajmir to Marwar Junction, which is on the road to Mount Abu, westward from Ajmir, and at five in the morning, under pale moonlight, was uncarted at the beginning of the Jodhpur State Railway—one of the quaintest little lines that ever ran a locomotive. It is the Maharaja's very own, and pays about ten per cent.; but its quaintness does not lie in these things. It is worked with rude economy, and started life by singularly and completely falsifying the Government estimates for its construction. An intelligent Bureau asserted that it could not be laid down for less than

—but the error shall be glossed over. It was laid down for a little more than seventeen thousand rupees a mile, with the help of second-hand rails and sleepers; and it is currently asserted that the Station-masters are flagmen, pointsmen, ticket-collectors and everything else, except platforms, and lamp-rooms. As only two trains are run in the twenty-four hours, this economy of staff does not matter in the least. The State line, with the comparatively new branch to the Pachbadra salt-pits, pays handsomely and is exactly suited to the needs of its users. True, there is a certain haziness as to the hour of starting, but this allows laggards more time, and fills the packed carriages to overflowing.

From Marwar Junction to Jodhpur, the train leaves the Aravalis and goes northwards into "the region of death" that lies beyond the Luni River. Sand, *ak* bushes, and sand-hills varied with occasional patches of unthrifty cultivation, make up the scenery. Rain has been very scarce in Marwar this year, and the country, consequently, shows at its worst, for almost every square mile of a kingdom nearly as large as Scotland is dependent on the sky for its crops. In a good season, a large village can pay from seven to nine thousand rupees revenue without blenching. In a bad one, "all the king's horses and all the king's men" may think themselves lucky if they raise "rupees fifteen only" from the same place. The fluctuation is startling.

From a country-side, which to the uninitiated seems about as valuable as a stretch of West African beach, the State gets a revenue of nearly forty lakhs;

and men who know the country vow that it has not been one tithe exploited, and that there is more to be made from salt and the marble—curious thing in this wilderness—good forest conservancy, than an open-handed Durbar dreams of. An amiable weakness for unthinkingly giving away villages where ready cash failed, has somewhat hampered the revenue in past years ; but now—and for this the Maharaja deserves great credit—Jodhpur has a large and genuine surplus and a very compact little scheme of railway extension. Before turning to a consideration of the City of Jodhpur, hear a true story in connection with the Hyderabad-Pachbadra project which those interested in the scheme may lay to heart.

His State line, his "ownest own," as has been said, very much delighted the Maharaja who, in one or two points, is not unlike Sir Theodore Hope of sainted memory. Pleased with the toy, he said effusively, in words which may or may not have reached the ears of the Hyderabad-Pachbadra people : "This is a good business. If the Government will give me independent jurisdiction, I'll make and open the line straight away from Pachbadra to the end of my dominions, *i. e.*, all but to Hyderabad."

Then "up and spake an elder knight, sat at the King's right knee," who knew something about the railway map of India and the Controlling Power of strategical lines : "Maharaja Sahib—here is the Indus Valley State and here is the Bombay-Baroda. Where would you be ?" "By Jove," quoth the Maharaja, though he swore by quite another god : "I see !" and thus he abandoned the idea of a Hyderabad line, and turned his attention to an extension to Nagore, with a branch to the Makrana marble-quarries which are close to the Sambhar salt lake near Jeypore. And, in the fullness of time, that extension will be made and perhaps extended to Bahawalpur.

The Englishman came to Jodhpur at mid-day, in a hot, fierce sunshine that struck back from the sands and the ledges of red-rock, as though it were May instead of December. The line scorned such a thing as a regular ordained terminus. The single track gradually melted away into the sands. Close to the station was a grim stone dak-bungalow, and in the verandah stood a brisk, bag-and-flask-begirdled individual, cracking his joints with excess of irritation. He was also snorting like an impatient horse.

Nota Bene.—When one is on the road it is above all things necessary to "pass the time o' day" to fellow-wanderers. Failure to comply with this law implies that the offender is "too good for his company;" and this, on the road, is the unpardonable sin. The Englishman "passed the time o' day" in due and ample form. "Ha! Ha!" said the gentleman with the bag. "Isn't this a sweet place? There ain't no ticca-gharries, and there ain't nothing to eat, if you haven't brought your vittles, an' they charge you three-eight for a bottle of whiskey. An' Encore at that! Oh! it's a sweet place." Here he skipped about the verandah and puffed. Then turning upon the Englishman, he said fiercely: "What have you come here for?" Now this was rude, because the ordinary form of salutation on the road is usually: "And what are you for?" meaning "what house do you represent?" The Englishman answered dolefully that he was travelling for pleasure, which simple explanation offended the little man with the courier-bag. He snapped his joints more excruciatingly than ever: "For pleasure! My God! For pleasure! Come here an' wait five weeks for your money, an' mark what I'm tellin' you now, you don't get it then! But per'aps your ideas of pleasure is different from most people's. For pleasure! Yah!" He skipped across the sands towards the station, for he was going back with the down train, and vanished in a whirlwind of luggage and the fluttering of female-skirts: in Jodhpur women are baggage-coolies. A level, drawling voice spoke from an inner room: "'E's a bit upset. That's what 'e is! I remember when I was at Gworlior"—the rest of the story was lost, and the Englishman set to work to discover the nakedness of the dak-bungalow. For reasons which do not concern the public, it is made as bitterly uncomfortable as possible. The food is infamous, and the charges seem to be willfully pitched about eighty per cent. above the tariff, so that some portion of the bill, at least, may be paid without bloodshed, or the unseemly defilement of walls with the contents of drinking-glasses. This is short-sighted policy, and it would, perhaps, be better to lower the prices and hide the tariff, and put a guard about the house to prevent jackal-molested donkeys from stampeding into the verandahs. But these be details. Jodhpur dak-bungalow is a merry, merry place, and any writer in search of new ground to locate a madly improbable story in, could not do better than study it diligently. In front lies sand, riddled with innumerable ant-holes, and, beyond the sand, the red sandstone wall of the city, and the Mahomedan burying-ground that fringes it. Fragments of sandstone set on end mark the resting places of the faithful, who are of no great account here. Above everything, a mark for miles around, towers the dun-red pile of the Fort which is also a Palace. This is set upon sandstone rock whose sharper features have been worn smooth by the wash of the windblown sand. It is as monstrous as anything in Dore's illustrations of the *Contes Drolatiques* and, wherever it wanders, the eye comes back at last to its fantastic bulk. There is no greenery on the rock, nothing but fierce sunlight or black shadow. A line of red hills forms the background of the city, and this is as bare as the picked bones of camels that lie bleaching on the sand below.

Wherever the eye falls, it sees a camel or a string of camels—lean, racer-built *sowarri* camels, or heavy, black, shag-haired trading ships bent on their way to the Railway Station. Through the night the air is alive with the bubbling and howling of the brutes, who assuredly must suffer from nightmare. In the morning the chorus round the station is deafening. A camel has as wide a range of speech as an elephant. The Englishman found a little one, crooning happily to itself, all alone on the sands. Its nose-string was smashed. Hence its joy. But a big man left the station and beat it on the neck with a seven-foot stick, and it rose up and sobbed.

Knowing what these camels meant, but trusting

nevertheless that the road would not be *very* bad, the Englishman went into the city, left a well-kunkered road, turned through a sand-worn, red sandstone gate, and sank ankle-deep in fine reddish white sand. This was the main thoroughfare of the city. Two tame lynxes shared it with a donkey; and the rest of the population seemed to have gone to bed. In the hot weather, between ten in the morning and four in the afternoon all Jodhpur stays at home for fear of death by sun-stroke, and it is possible that the habit extends far into what is officially called the "cold weather;" or, perhaps, being brought up among sands, men do not care to tramp them for pleasure. The city internally is a walled and secret place; each courtyard being hidden from view by a red sandstone wall except in a few streets where the shops are poor and mean.

In an old house now used for the storing of tents, Akbar's mother lay two months, before the "Guardian of Mankind" was born, drawing breath for her flight to Umarkot across the desert. Seeing this place, the Englishman thought of many things not worth the putting down on paper, and went on till the sand grew deeper and deeper, and a great camel, heavily laden with stone, came round a corner and nearly stepped on him. As the evening drew on, the city woke up, and the goats and the camels and the kine came in by hundreds, and men said that wild pig, which are strictly preserved by the Princes for their own sport, were in the habit of wandering about the roads. Now if they do this in the capital, what damage must they not do to the crops in the district? Men said that they did a very great deal of damage, and it was hard to keep their noses out of anything they took a fancy to. On the evening of the Englishman's visit, the Maharaja went out, as is his laudable custom, alone and unattended, to a road actually *in* the city along which one specially big pig was in the habit of passing. His Highness got his game with a single shot behind the shoulder, and in a few days it will be pickled and sent off to the Maharana of Udaipur, as a love-gift, on account of the latter's investiture. There is great friendship between Jodhpur and Udaipur, and the idea of one King going abroad to shoot game for another has something very pretty and quaint in it.

Night fell and the Englishman became aware that the conservancy of Jodhpur might be vastly improved. Strong stenches, say the doctors, are of no importance; but there came upon every breath of heated air—and in Jodhpur City the air is warm in mid-winter—the faint, sweet, sickly reek that one has always been taught to consider specially deadly. A few months ago there was an impressive outbreak of cholera in Jodhpur, and the Residency Doctor, who really hoped that the people would be brought to see sense, did his best to bring forward a general cleansing-scheme. But the city fathers would have none of it. Their fathers had been trying to poison themselves in well-defined ways for an indefinite number of years; and they were not going to have any of the Sahib's "sweeper-nonsense."

To clinch everything, one travelled member of the community rose in his place and said: "Why, I've been to Simla. Yes, to Simla! And even I don't want it!" This compliment should be engrossed in the archives of the Simla Municipality. Sanitation on English lines is not yet acceptable to Jodhpur.

When the black dusk had shut down, the Englishman climbed up a little hill and saw the stars come out and shine over the desert. Very far away, some camel-drivers had lighted a fire and were singing as they sat by the side of their beasts. Sound travels as far over sand as over water, and their voices came into the city wall and beat against it in multiplied echoes.

Then he returned to the House of Strange Stories—the Dak-Bungalow—and passed the time o' day to the genial, light-hearted bagman—a Cockney, in whose heart there was no thought of India, though he had travelled for years throughout the length and breadth of the Empire and over New Burma as well. There was a fort in Jodhpur, but you see that was not in his line of business exactly, and there were stables, but "you may take my word for it, them who has much to do with horses is a bad lot. You get hold of the Maharaja's coachman and he'll drive you all round the shop. I'm only waiting here collecting money." Jodhpur dak-bungalow seems to be full of men "waiting here." They lie in long chairs in the verandah and tell each other interminable stories, or stare citywards and express their opinion of some dilatory debtor in language punctuated by free spitting. They are all waiting for something; and they vary the monotony of a life they make willfully dull beyond words, by waging war with the dak-bungalow khansama. Then they return to their long chairs or their couches, and sleep. Some of them, in old days, used to wait as long as six weeks—six weeks in May, when the sixty miles from Marwar Junction to Jodhpur was covered in three days by slow-pacing bullock carts! Some of them are bagmen, able to describe the demerits of every dak-bungalow from the Peshin to Pagan, and southward to Hyderabad—men of substance who have "The Trades," at their back. It is a terrible thing to be in "The Trades," that great Doomsday Book of Calcutta, in whose pages are written the names of doubtful debtors. Let light-hearted purchasers take note.

And the others, who wait and swear and spit and exchange anecdotes—what are they? Bummers, land-sharks, skirmishers for their bread. It would be cruel in a fellow-tramp to call them loafers. Their lien upon the State may have its origin in horses, or anything else; for the State buys anything vendible, from Abdul Raymon's most promising importations to—a patent, self-acting corkscrew. They are a mixed crew, but amusing and full of strange stories of adventure by land and sea. And their ends are as curiously brutal as their lives. A wanderer was once swept into the great, still backwater that divides the loaferdom of Upper India—that is to say, Calcutta and Bombay—from the north-going current of Madras, where Nym and Pistol are highly finished articles with certificates. This backwater is a dangerous place to break down in, as the men on the road know well. "You can run Rajputana in a pair o' sack breeches an' an old hat, but go to Central Injia with pice," says the wisdom of the road. So the waif died in the bazaar, and the Barrack-master Sahib gave orders for his burial. It might have been the bazaar sergeant, or it might have been an hireling who was charged with the disposal of the body. At any rate, it was an Irishman who said to the Barrack-master Sahib: "Fwhat about that loafer?" "Well, what's the matter?" "I'm considtherin whether I'm to mash in his thick head, or to break his long legs. He won't fit the store-coffin anyways."

Here the story ends. It may be an old one; but it struck the Englishman as being rather unsympathetic in its nature; and he has preserved it for this reason. Were the Englishman a mere Secretary of State instead of an enviable and unshackled vagabond, he would remodel that Philanthropic Institution for Teaching Young Subalterns how to Spell—variously called the Intelligence and the Political Department—and giving each *omedwar* the pair of sack breeches and old hat, above prescribed, would send him out for a twelvemonth on the road. Not that he might learn to swear Australian oaths (which are superior to any ones in the market) or to drink bazaar-drinks (which are very bad indeed), but in order that he might gain an insight into the tertiary politics of States—things less imposing than succession-cases and less wearisome than boundary disputes, but—here speaks Ferdinand Count Fathom, in an Intermediate compartment, very drunk and very happy—"Worth knowing a little—Oh no! Not at all."

A small volume might be written of the ways and the tales of Indian loafers of the more brilliant order—such Chevaliers of the Order of Industry as would throw their glasses in your face did you call them loafers. They are a genial, blasphemous, blustering crew, and pre-eminent even in a land of liars.

CHAPTER XIII.

SHOWING WHAT SORT OF A COUNTRY A KING WILL MAKE—THE HAT-MARKED CASTE RECEIVES ATTENTION.

The hospitality that spreads tables in the wilderness, and shifts the stranger from the back of the hired camel into the two-horse victoria, must be experienced to be appreciated.

To those unacquainted with the peculiarities of the native-trained horse, this advice may be worth something. Sit as far back as ever you can, and, if Oriental courtesy have put an English bit and bridoon in a mouth by education intended for a spiked curb, leave the whole contraption alone. Once acquainted with the comparative smoothness of English ironmongery, your mount will grow frivolous. In which event a four-pound steeplechase saddle, accepted through sheer shame, offers the very smallest amount of purchase to untrained legs.

The Englishman rode up to the Fort, and by the way learnt all these things and many more. He was provided with a racking, female horse who swept the gullies of the city by dancing sideways.

The road to the Fort which stands on the Hill of Strife, wound in and out of sixty-foot hills, with a skillful avoidance of all shade ; and this was at high noon, when puffs of heated air blew from the rocks on all sides. "What must the heat be in May ?" The Englishman's companion was a cheery Brahmin, who wore the lightest of turbans and sat the smallest of neat little country-breds. "Awful !" said the Brahmin. "But not so bad as in the district. Look there !" and he pointed from the brow of a bad eminence, across the quivering heat-haze, to where the white sand faded into bleach blue sky and the horizon was shaken and tremulous. "It's very bad in summer. Would knock you—Oh yes—all to smash, but we are accustomed to it." A rock-strewn hill, about half a mile, as the crow flies, from the Fort was pointed out as the place whence, at the beginning of this century, the Pretender Sowae besieged Raja Maun for five months, but could make no headway against his foe. One gun of the enemy's batteries specially galled the Fort, and the Jodhpur King offered a village to any of his gunners who should dismount it. "It was smashed," said the Brahmin. "Oh yes, all to pieces." Practically, the city which lies below the Fort is indefensible, and during the many wars of Marwar has generally been taken up by the assailants without resistance.

Entering the Fort by the Jeypore Gate, and studiously refraining from opening his umbrella, the Englishman found shadow and coolth, took off his hat to the tun-bellied, trunk-nosed God of Good-Luck who had been very kind to him in his wanderings, and sat down near half-a-dozen of the Maharaja's guns bearing the mark, "A Broome, Cossipore, 1857," or "G. Hutchinson, Cossipore, 1838." Now rock and masonry are so curiously blended in this great pile that he who walks through it loses sense of being among buildings. It is as though he walked through mountain-gorges. The stone-paved, inclined planes, and the tunnel-like passages driven under a hundred feet height of buildings, increase this impression. In many places the wall and rock runs up unbroken by any window for forty feet.

It would be a week's work to pick out even roughly the names of the dead who have added to the buildings, or to describe the bewildering multiplicity of courts and ranges of rooms; and, in the end, the result would be as satisfactory as an attempt to describe a night-mare. It is said that the rock on which the Fort stands is four miles in circuit, but no man yet has dared to estimate the size of the city that they call the Palace, or the mileage of its ways. Ever since Ras Joda, four hundred years ago, listened to the voice of a *Jogi*, and leaving Mundore built his eyrie on the "Bird's nest" as the Hill of Strife was called, the Palaces have grown and thickened. Even to-day the builders are still at work. Takht Singh, the present ruler's predecessor, built royally. An incomplete bastion and a Hall of Flowers are among the works of his pleasure. Hidden away behind a mighty wing of carved red sandstone, lie rooms set apart for Viceroys, Durbar Halls and dinner-rooms without end. A gentle gloom covers the evidences of the catholic taste of the State in articles of "bigotry and virtue;" but there is enough light to show the *raison d'etre* of the men who wait in the dak-bungalow. And, after all, what is the use of Royalty in these days if a man may not take delight in the pride of the eye? Kumbha Rana, the great man of Chitor, fought like a Rajput, but he had an instinct which made him build the Tower of Victory at, who knows what cost of money and life. The fighting-instinct thrown back upon itself, must have some sort of outlet; and a merciful Providence wisely ordains that the Kings of the East in the nineteenth century shall take pleasure in "shopping" on an imperial scale. Dresden China snuff-boxes, mechanical engines, electro-plated fish-slicers, musical boxes, and gilt blown-glass Christmas-tree balls do not go well with the splendors of a Palace that might have been built by Titans and colored by the morning sun. But there are excuses to be made for Kings who have no work to do—at least such work as their fathers understood best.

In one of the higher bastions stands a curious specimen of one of the earliest *mitrailleuses*—a cumbrous machine carrying twenty gun-barrels in two rows, which small-arm fire is flanked by two tiny cannon. As a muzzle-loading implement its value after the first discharge would be insignificant; but the soldiers lounging by assured the Englishman that it had done good service in its time; it was eaten with rust.

A man may spend a long hour in the upper tiers of the Palaces, but still far from the roof-tops, in looking out across the desert. There are Englishmen in these wastes, who say gravely that there is nothing so fascinating as the sand of Bikanir and Marwar. "You see," explained an enthusiast of the Hat-marked Caste, "you are not shut in by roads, and you can go just as you please. And, somehow, it grows upon you as you get used to it, and you end, y'know, by falling in love with the place." Look steadily from the Palace westward where the city with its tanks and serais is spread at your feet, and you will, in a lame way, begin to understand the fascination of the desert which, by those who have felt it, is said to be even stronger than the fascination of the road. The city is of red-sandstone and dull and sombre to look at. Beyond it, where the white sand lies, the country is dotted with camels limping into the Eiwigkeit or coming from the same place. Trees appear to be strictly confined to the suburbs of the city. Very good. If you look long enough across the sands, while a voice in your ear is telling you of half-buried cities, old as old Time and wholly unvisited by Sahibs, of districts where the white man is unknown, and of the wonders of far-away Jeysulmir ruled by a half distraught king, sand-locked and now smitten by a terrible food and water famine, you will, if it happen that you are of a sedentary and civilized nature, experience a new emotion—will be conscious of a great desire to take one of the lobbing camels and get away into the desert, away from the last touch of To-day, to meet the Past face to face. Some day a novelist will exploit the unknown land from the Rann, where the wild ass breeds, northward and eastward, till he comes to the Indus. That will be when Rider Haggard has used up Africa and a new " She " is needed.

But the officials of Marwar do not call their country a desert. On the contrary, they administer it very scientifically and raise, as has been said, about thirty-eight lakhs from it. To come back from the influence and the possible use of the desert to more prosaic facts. Read quickly a rough record of things in modern Marwar. The old is drawn in Tod, who speaks the truth. The Maharaja's right hand in the work of the State is Maharaj Sir Pertab Singh, Prime Minister A.—D.—C. to the Prince of Wales, capable of managing the Marwari who intrigues like a—Marwari, equally capable, as has been seen, of moving in London Society, and Colonel of a newly-raised "crack" cavalry corps. The Englishman would have liked to have seen him, but he was away in the desert somewhere, either marking a boundary or looking after a succession case. Not very long ago, as the Setts of Ajmir knew well, there was a State debt of fifty lakhs. This has now been changed into a surplus of three lakhs, and the revenue is growing. Also, the simple Dacoit who used to enjoy himself very pleasantly, has been put into a department, and the Thug with him.

Consequently, for the department takes a genuine interest in this form of *shikar*, and the gaol leg-irons are not too light, dacoities have been reduced to such an extent that men say "you may send a woman, with her ornaments upon her, from Sojat to Phalodi, and she will not lose a nose-ring. Also, and this in a Rajput State is an important matter, the boundaries of nearly every village in Marwar have been demarcated, and boundary *rixes*, in which both sides preferred small-arm fire to the regulation lathi, are unknown. The open-handed system of giving away villages had raised a large and unmannerly crop of *jaghirdars*. These have been taken and brought in hand by Sir Pertab Singh, to the better order of the State.

A Punjabi Sirdar, Har Dyal Singh, has reformed, or made rather, Courts on the Civil and Criminal Side; and his hand is said to be found in a good many sweepings out of old corners. It must always be borne in mind that everything that has been done, was carried through over and under unlimited intrigue, for Jodhpur is a Native State. Intrigue must be met with intrigue by all except Gordons or demigods; and it is curious to hear how a reduction in tariff, or a smoothing out of some tangled Court, had to be worked by shift and by-way. The tales are comic, but not for publication. Howbeit! Har Dayal Singh got his training in part under the Punjab Government, and in part in a little Native State far away in the Himalayas, where the *gumnameh* was not altogether an unknown animal. To the credit of the "Pauper Province" be it said, it is not easy to circumvent a Punjabi. The details of his work would be dry reading. The result of it is good, and there is justice in Marwar, and order and firmness in its administration.

Naturally, the land-revenue is the most interesting thing in Marwar from an administrative point of view. The basis of it is a tank about the size of a swimming-bath, with a catchment of several hundred square yards, draining through leeped channels. When God sends the rain, the people of the village drink from the tank. When the rains fail, as they failed this year, they take to their wells, which are brackish and breed guinea-worm. For these reasons the revenue, like the Republic of San Domingo, is never alike for two years runnning. There are no canal questions to harry the authorities; but the fluctuations are enormous. Under the Aravalis the soil is good: further north they grow millet and pasture cattle, though, said a Revenue Officer cheerfully, "God knows what the brutes find to eat." *Apropos* of irrigation, the one canal deserves special mention, as showing how George Stephenson came to Jodhpur and astonished the inhabitants. Six miles from the city proper lies the Balsamans Sagar, a great tank. In the hot weather, when the city tanks ran out or stank, it was the pleasant duty of the women to tramp twelve miles at the end of the day's work to fill their lotahs. In the hot weather Jodhpur is—let a simile suffice, Sukkur in June would be Simla to Jodhpur.

The State Engineer, who is also the Jodhpur State Line, for he has no European subordinates, conceived the idea of bringing the water from the Balsamans into the city. Was the city grateful? Not in the least. It is said that the Sahib wanted the water to run uphill and was throwing money into the tank. Being true Marwaris, men betted on the subject. The canal—a built out one, for water must not touch earth in these parts—was made at a cost of something over a lakh, and the water came down because the tank was a trifle higher than the city. Now, in the hot weather, the women need not go for long walks, but the Marwari cannot understand how it was that the "waters came down to Jodhpur." From the Marwari to money matters is an easy step. Formerly, that is to say up to within a very short time, the Treasury of Jodhpur was conducted in a shiftless, happy-go-lucky sort of fashion not uncommon in Native States, whereby the Mahajuns "held the bag" and made unholy profits on discount and other things, to the confusion of the Durbar Funds and their own enrichment. There is now a Treasury modelled on English lines, and English in the important particular that money is not to be got from it for the asking, and the items of expenditure are strictly looked after.

In the middle of all this bustle of reform planned, achieved, frustrated and re-planned, and the never-ending underground warfare that surges in a Native State, move the English officers—the irreducible minimum of exiles. As a caste, the working Englishmen in Native States are curiously interesting; and the traveller whose tact by this time has been Wilfred-blunted by tramping, sits in judgment upon them as he has seen them. In the first place, they are, they must be, the fittest who have survived; for though, here and there, you shall find one chafing bitterly against the burden of his life in the wilderness, one to be pitied more than any chained beast, the bulk of the caste are honestly and unaffectedly fond of their work, fond of the country around them, and fond of the people they deal with. In each State their answer to a question is the same. The men with whom they are in contact are "all right" when you know them, but you've got to "know them first," as the music-hall song says. Their hands are full of work; so full that, when the incult wanderer said: "What do you find to do?" they look upon him with contempt and amazement, exactly as the wanderer himself had once looked upon a Globe-Trotter, who had put to him the same impertinent query. And—but here the Englishman may be wrong—it seemed to him that in one respect their lives were a good deal more restful and concentrated than those of their brethren under the British Government. There was no talk of shiftings and transfers and promotions, stretching across a Province and a half, and no man said anything about Simla. To one who has hitherto believed that Simla is the hub of the Empire, it is disconcerting to hear: "Oh, Simla! That's where you Bengalis go. We haven't anything to do with Simla down here." And no more they have. Their talk and their interests run in the boundaries of the States they serve, and, most striking of all, the gossipy element seems to be cut altogether. It is a backwater of the river of Anglo-Indian life—or is it the main current, the broad stream that supplies the motive power, and is the other life only the noisy ripple on the surface? You who have lived, not merely looked at, both lives, decide. Much can be learnt from the talk of the caste, many curious, many amusing, and some startling things. One hears stories of men who take a poor, impoverished State as a man takes a wife, "for better or worse," and, moved by some incomprehensible ideal of virtue, consecrate—that is not too big a word—consecrate their lives to that State in all single-heartedness and purity. Such men are few, but they exist to-day, and their names are great in lands where no Englishman travels. Again the listener hears tales of grizzled diplomats of Rajputana—Machiavellis who have hoisted a powerful intriguer with his own intrigue, and bested priestly cunning, and the guile of the Oswal, simply that the way might be clear for some scheme which should put money into a tottering Treasury, or lighten the taxation of a few hundred thousand men—or both; for this can be done. One tithe of that force spent on their own advancement would have carried such men very far.

Those who know anything of the internals of government, know that such men must exist, for their works are written between the lines of the Administration Reports; but to hear about them and to have them pointed out, is quite a different thing. It breeds respect and a sense of shame and frivolity in the mind of the mere looker-on, which may be good for the soul. Truly the Hat-marked Caste are a strange people. They are so few and so lonely and so strong. They can sit down in one place for years, and see the works of their hands and the promptings of their brain grow to actual and beneficent life, bringing good to thousands. Less fettered than the direct servant of the Indian Government, and working over a much vaster charge, they seem a bigger and a more large-minded breed. And that is saying a good deal.

But let the others, the little people bound down and supervised, and strictly limited and income-taxed, always remember that the Hat-marked are very badly off for shops. If they want a neck-tie they must get it up from Bombay, and in the rains they can hardly move about; and they have no amusements and must go a day's railway journey for a rubber, and their drinking-water is doubtful; and there is rather less than one lady *per* ten thousand square miles.

After all, comparative civilization has its advantages.

CHAPTER XIV.

AMONG THE HOUYHNHNMS.

Jodhpur differs from the other States of Rajputana in that its Royalty are peculiarly accessible to an inquiring public. There are wanderers, the desire of whose life it is "to see Nabobs," which is the Globe-Trotter's title for any one in unusually clean clothes, or an Oudh Taluqdar in gala dress. Men asked in Jodhpur whether the Englishman would like to see

His Highness. The Englishman had a great desire to do so, if His Highness would be in no way inconvenienced. Then they scoffed : "Oh, he won't *durbar* you, you needn't flatter yourself. If he's in the humor he'll receive you like an English country-gentleman." How in the world could the owner of such a place as Jodhpur Palace be in any way like an English country-gentleman? The Englishman had not long to wait in doubt. His Highness intimated his readiness to see the Englishman between eight and nine in the morning at the Raika-Bagh. The Raika-Bagh is not a Palace, for the lower storey and all the detached buildings round it are filled with horses. Nor can it in any way be called a stable, because the upper storey contains sumptuous apartments full of all manner of valuables both of the East and the West. Nor is it in any sense a pleasure-garden, for it stands on soft white sand, close to a multitude of litter and sand training tracks, and is devoid of trees for the most part. Therefore the Raika-Bagh is simply the Raika-Bagh and nothing else. It is now the chosen residence of the Maharaja who loves to live among his four hundred or more horses. All Jodhpur is horse-mad by the way, and it behoves any one who wishes to be any one to keep his own race-course. The Englishman went to the Raika-Bagh, which stands half a mile or so from the city, and passing through a long room filled with saddles by the dozen, bridles by the score, and bits by the hundred, was aware of a very small and lively little cherub on the roof of a garden-house. He was carefully muffled, for the morning was chill. "Good-morning," he cried cheerfully in English, waving a mittened hand. "Are you going to see my fav(r and the horses?" It was the Maharaja Kanwar, the Crown Prince, the apple of the Maharaja's eye, and one of the quaintest little bodies that ever set an Englishman disrespectfully laughing. He studies English daily with one of the English officials of the State, and stands a very good chance of being thoroughly spoiled, for he is a general pet. Also, as befits his dignity, he has his own carriage or carriages, his own twelve-hand stable, his own house and retinue, and everything handsome about him.

A few steps further on, in a little enclosure in front of a small two-storied white bungalow, sat His Highness the Maharaja, deep in discussion with the State Engineer. He wore an English ultser, and within ten paces of him was the first of a long range of stalls. There was an informality of procedure about Jodhpur which, after the strained etiquette of other States, was very refreshing. The State Engineer, who has a growing line to attend to, cantered away and His Highness after a few introductory words, knowing what the Englishman would be after, said : "Come along, and look at the horses." Other formality there was absolutely none. Even the indispensable knot of hangers-on stood at a distance, and behind a paling, in this most rustic country residence. A well-bred fox-terrier took command of the proceedings, after the manner of dogs the world over, and the Maharaja led to the horse-boxes. But a man turned up, bending under the weight of much bacon. "Oh ! here's the pig I shot for Udaipur last night. You see that is the best piece. It's pickled, and that's what makes it yellow to look at." He patted the great side that was held up. "There will be a camel sowar to meet it half way to Udiapur; and I hope Udaipur will be pleased with it. It was a very big pig." "And where did you shoot it, Maharaja Sahib?" "Here," said His Highness, smiting himself high up under the armpit. "Where else would you have it?" Certainly this descendant of Raja Maun was more like an English country-gentleman than the Englishman in his ignorance had deemed possible. He led on from horse-box to horse-box, the terrier at his heels, pointing out each horse of note; and Jodhpur has many. "There's *Raja*, twice winner of the Civil Service Cup." The Englishman looked reverently and *Raja* rewarded his curiosity with a vicious snap, for he was being dressed over, and his temper was out of joint. Close to him stood *Autocrat*, the grey with the nutmeg marks on the off-shoulder, a picture of a horse, also disturbed in his mind. Next to him was a chestnut Arab, a hopeless cripple, for one of his knees had been smashed and the leg was doubled up under him. It was *Turquoise*, who, six or eight years ago, rewarded good feeding by getting away from his *sais*, falling down and ruining himself, but who, none the less, has lived an honored pensioner on the Maharaja's bounty ever since. No horses are shot in the Jodhpur stables, and when one dies—they have lost not more than twenty-five in six years—his funeral is an event. He is wrapped in a white sheet which is strewn with flowers, and, amid the weeping of the *saises*, is borne away to the burial ground.

After doing the honors for nearly half an hour the Maharaja departed, and as the Englishman has not seen more than forty horses, he felt justified in demanding more. And he got them. *Eclipse* and *Young Revenge* were out down-country, but *Sherwood*, at the stud, *Shere Ali*, *Conqueror*, *Tynedale*, *Sherewood II*, a maiden of Adbul Rahman's, and many others of note, were in, and were brought out. Among the veterans, a wrathful, rampant, red horse still, came *Brian Boru*, whose name has been written large in the chronicles of the Indian turf, jerking his *sais* across the road. His near-fore is altogether gone, but as a pensioner he condescends to go in harness, and is then said to be a "handful." He certainly looks it.

At the two hundred and fifty-seventy horse, and perhaps the twentieth block of stables, the Englishman's brain began to reel, and he demanded rest and information on a certain point. He had gone into some fifty stalls, and looked into all the rest, and in the looking had searchingly sniffed. But, as truly as he was then standing far below *Brian Boru's* bony withers never the ghost of a stench had polluted the keen morning air. The City of the Houyhnhnms was specklessly clean—cleaner than any stable, racing or private, that he had been into. How was it done? The pure white sand accounted for a good deal, and the rest was explained by one of the Masters of Horse: "Each horse has one *sais* at least—old *Ringwood* four—and we make 'em work. If we didn't, we'd be mucked up to the horses' bellies in no time. Everything is cleaned off at once ; and whenever the sand's tainted its renewed. There's quite enough sand you see hereabouts. Of course we can't keep their coats so good as in other stables, by reason of the rolling ; but we can keep 'em pretty clean."

To the eye of one who knew less than nothing about horse-flesh, this immaculate purity was very striking, and quite as impressive was the condition of the horses, which was English—quite English. Naturally, none of them were in any sort of training beyond daily exercise, but they were fit and in such thoroughly good fettle. Many of them were out on the various tracks, and many were coming in. Roughly, two hundred go out of a morning, and it is to be feared, learn from the heavy going of the Jodhpur courses, how to hang in their stride. This is a matter for those who know, but it struck the Englishman that a good deal of the unsatisfactory performances of the Jodhpur stables might be accounted for by their having lost the clean stride on the sand, and having to pick it up gradually on the less holding down-country courses—unfortunately when they were *not* doing training gallops, but the real thing. This small theory is given for instant contradiction by those who understand.

It was pleasant to sit down and watch the rush of the horses through the great opening—gates are not affected—going on to the country-side where they take the air. Here a boisterous, unschooled Arab shot out across the road and cried, "Ha! Ha!" in the scriptural manner, before trying to rid himself of the grinning black imp on his back. Behind him a Cabuli—surely all Cabulis must have been born with Pelhams in their mouths—bored sulkily across the road, or threw himself across the path of a tall, mild-eyed Kurnal-bred youngster, whose cocked ears and swinging head showed that, though he was so sedate, he was thoroughly taking in his surroundings, and would very much like to know if there were anybody better than himself on the course that morning. Impetuous as a schoolboy and irresponsible as a monkey, one of the Prince's polo ponies, not above racing in his own set, would answer the query by rioting past the pupil of Parrott, the monogram on his body-cloth flapping free in the wind, and his head and hogged tail in the elements as Uncle Remus hath it. The youngster would swing himself round, and polka-mazurka for a few paces, till his attention would be caught by some dainty Child of the Desert, fresh from the Bombay stables, sweating at every sound, backing and filling like a rudderless ship. Then, thanking his stars that he was wiser than some people, number 177 would lob on to the track and settle down to his spin like the gentleman he was. Elsewhere, the eye fell upon a cloud of nameless ones, purchases from Abdul Rahman, whose worth will be proved next hot weather, when they are seriously taken in hand—skirmishing over the face of the land and enjoying themselves immensely. High above everything else, like a collier among barges, screaming shrilly, a black, flamboyant Marwari stallion with a crest like the crest of a barb, barrel-bellied, goose-rumped and river-maned, pranced through the press, while the slow-pacing waler carriage-horses eyed him with deep disfavor, and the Maharaj Kanwar's tiny mount capered under his pink, Roman nose, kicking up as much dust as the *Foxhall* colt who had got on to a lovely patch of sand and was dancing a saraband in it. In and out of the tangle, going down to or coming back from the courses, ran, shuffled, rocketed, plunged, sulked or stampeded countless horses of all kinds, shapes and descriptions—so that the eye at last failed to see what they were, and only retained a general impression of a whirl of bays, greys, iron greys and chestnuts with white stockings, some as good as could be desired, others average, but not one distinctly bad.

"We have no downright bad 'uns in this stable. What's the use?" said the Master of Horse calmly. "They are all good beasts and, one with another, must cost more than a thousand each. This year's new ones bought from Bombay and the pick of our own studs, are a hundred strong about. May be more. Yes, they look all right enongh; but you can never know what they are going to turn out. Live-stock is very uncertain." "And how are the stables managed? how do you make room for the fresh stock?" Something this way.' Here are all the new ones and Parrott's lot, and the English colts that Maharaja Pertab Singh brought out with him from Home. *Winterlake* out o' *Queen's Consort*, that chestnut with the two white stockings you're looking at now. Well, next hot weather we shall see what they're made of and which is who. There's so many that the trainer hardly knows 'em one from another till they begin to be a good deal forward. Those that haven't got the pace, or that the Maharaja don't fancy, they're taken out and sold for what they'll bring. The man who takes the horses out has a good job of it. He comes back and says: "I sold such and such for so much, and here's the money." That's all. Well, our rejections are worth having. They have taken prizes at the Poona Horse Show. See for yourself. Is there one of those that you wouldn't be glad to take for a hack, and look well after too? Only they're no use to us, and so out they go by the score. We've got sixty riding-boys, perhaps more, and they've got their work cut out to keep them all going. What you've seen are only the stables. We've got one stud at Bellara, eighty miles out, and they come in sometimes in droves of three and four hundred from the stud. They raise Marwaris there too, but that's entirely under native management. We've got nothing to do with that. The natives reckon a Marwari the best country-bred you can lay hands on; and some of them are beauties! Crests on 'em like the top of a wave. Well, there's that stud and another stud and, reckoning one with another, I should say the Maharaja has nearer twelve hundred than a thousand horses of his own. For this place here, two wagon-loads of grass come in every day from Marwar Junction. Lord knows how many saddles and bridles we've got. I never counted. I suppose we've about forty carriages, not counting the ones that get shabby and are stacked in places in the city, as I suppose you've seen. We take 'em out in the morning, a regular string all together, brakes and all; but the prettiest turn-out we ever turned out was Lady Dufferin's pony four-in-hand. Walers—thirteen-two the wheelers I think, and thirteen-one the leaders. They took prizes in Poona. That *was* a pretty turn-out. The prettiest in India. Lady Dufferin, she drove it when the Viceroy was down here last year. There are bicycles and tricycles in the carriage department too. I don't know how many, but when the Viceroy's camp was held, there was about one apiece for the gentlemen, with remounts. They're somewhere about the place now, if you want to see them. How do we manage to keep the horses so quiet? You'll find some o' the youngsters play the goat a good deal when they come out o' stable, but, as you say, there's no vice generally. It's this way. We don't allow any curry-combs. If we did, the *saises* would be wearing out their brushes on the combs. Its all elbow grease here. They've got to go over the horses with their hands. They must handle 'em, and a native he's afraid of a horse. Now an English groom, when a horse is doing the fool, clips him over the head with a curry-comb, or punches him in the belly; and that hurts the horse's feelings. A native, he just stands back till the trouble is over. He *must* handle the horse or he'd get into trouble for not dressing him, so it comes to all handling and no licking, and that's why you won't get hold of a really vicious brute in these stables. Old *Ringwood* he had four *saises*, and he wanted 'em every one, but the other horses have no more than one *sais* a-piece. The Maharaja he keeps fourteen or fifteen horses for his own riding. Not that he cares to ride now, but he likes to have his horses ; and no one else can touch 'em. Then there's the horses that he mounts his visitors on, when they come for pig-sticking and such like, and then there's a lot of horses that go to Maharaja Pertab Singh's new cavalry regiment. So you see a horse can go through all three degrees sometimes before he gets sold, and be a good horse at the end of it. And I think that's about all !"

A cloud of youngsters, sweating freely and ready for any mischief, shot past on their way to breakfast, and the conversation ended in a cloud of sand and the drumming of hurrying hooves.

In the Raika-Bagh are more racing cups than this memory holds the names of. Chiefest of all was the Delhi Assemblage Cup—the Imperial Vase, of solid gold, won by *Crown Prince.* The other pieces of plate were not so imposing. But of all the Crown Jewels, the most valuable appeared at the end of the inspection. It was the small Maharaja Kanwar lolling in state in a huge barouche—his toes were at least two feet off the floor—that was taking him from his morning drive. Have you seen *my* horses ?" said the Maharaja Kanwar. The four twelve-hand ponies had been duly looked over, and the future ruler of Jodhpur departed satisfied.

CHAPTER XV.

THE REAL REASON OF THE DECADENCE OF THE EMPIRE FOUND IN A "TWENTY-FIVE PER CENT. REDUCTION ALL ROUN'," THEREBY LIMITING THE PLEASURES OF LOAFERDOM—THE TREACHERY OF GANESH OF SITUR.

"A twenty-five per cent. reduction all roun' an' no certain leave when you wants it. *Of* course the best men goes somewhere else. That's only natural, and 'eres this sanguinary down mail a stickin' in the eye of the Khundwa down! I tell you, Sir, India's a bad place—a very bad place. 'Tisn 't what it was when I came out one and thirty year ago, an' the drivers was getting their seven and eight 'undred rupees a month an' was treated as *men.*"

The Englishman was on his way to Nasirabad, and a gentleman in the Railway was explaining to him the real reason of the decadence of the Empire. It was because the Rajputana-Malwa Railway had cut all its employes twenty-five per cent. And in truth, there is a good deal of fine free language where gentlemen in the carriage department, foremen-fitters, station and assistant station masters do foregather. It is ungenerous to judge a caste by a few samples; but the Englishman had on the road and elsewhere seen a good deal of gentlemen on the Railway, and is prepared to write down here that they spend their pay in a manner that would do credit to an income of a thousand a month. Now they are saying that the twenty-five per cent. reduction is depriving them of the pleasures of life. So much the better if it makes them moderately economical in their expenditure. Revolving these things in his mind, together with one or two stories of extravagance not quite fit for publication, the Englishman came to Nasirabad, before sunrise, and there to a tonga. Imagine an icy pause of several minutes followed by language. Quoth Ram Baksh, proprietor, driver, *sais* and everything else, calmly: "At this time of the year and having regard to the heat of the sun who wants a top to a tonga? I have no top. I have a top, but it would take till twelve o'clock to put it on. And behold Sahib, Padre Martum Sahib went in this tonga to Deoli. All the officer Sahibs of Deoli and Nasirabad go in this tonga for *shikar*. This is a 'shut-in-tonga!'" "When Church and Army are brought against one, argument is in vain." But to take a soft, office-bred unfortunate into the wilderness, upon a skeleton, a diagram of a conveyance, is brutality. Ram Baksh did not see it, and headed his two thirteen-hand rats straight towards the morning sun, along a beautiful military road. "We shall get to Deoli in six hours," said Ram Baksh the boastful, and, even as he spoke, the spring of the tonga bar snapt "mit a harp-like melodious twang." "What does it matter?" said Ram Baksh. "Has the Sahib never seen a tonga-iron break before? Padre Martum Sahib and all the officer Sahibs in Deoli"—"Ram Baksh," said the Englishman sternly, "I am not a Padre Sahib nor an officer Sahib, and if you say anything more about Padre Martum Sahib or the officer in Deoli I shall grow very angry, and beat you with a stick, Ram Baksh."

"Humph," said Ram Baksh, "I knew you were not a Padre Sahib. The little mishap was patched up with string, and the tonga went on merrily. It is Stevenson who says that the "invitation to the road," nature's great morning song, has not yet been properly understood or put to music. The first note of it is the sound of the dawn-wind through long grass, and the last, in this country, the creaking of the bullock wains getting under way in some unseen *serai*. It is good, good beyond expression, to see the sun rise upon a strange land and to know that you have only to go forward and possess that land—that it will dower you before the day is ended with a hundred new impressions and, perhaps, one idea. It is good to snuff the wind when it comes in over grassy uplands or down from the tops of the blue Aravalis—dry and keen as a new-ground sword. Best of all is to light the First Pipe—is there any tobacco so good as that we burn in honor of the breaking day?—and, while the ponies wake the long white road with their hooves and the birds go abroad in companions together, to thank your stars that you are neither the Subaltern who has Orderly Room, the 'Stunt who has *kacherri*, or the Judge who has the Court to attend; but are only a loafer in a flannel shirt bound, if God pleases, to "Little Boondi," somewhere beyond the faint hills across the plain.

But there was alloy in this delight. Men had told the Englishman darkly that Boondi State had no love for Englishmen, that there was nowhere to stop, and that no one would do anything for money. Love was out of the question. Further, it was an acknowledged fact that there were no Englishmen of any kind in Boondi. But the Englishman trusted that Ganesh would be good to him, and that he would, somehow or other, fall upon his feet as he had fallen before. The road from Nasirabad to Deoli, being military in its nature, is nearly as straight as a ruler and about as smooth. It runs for the most part through "Arthurian" country, just such a land as the Knights of the Round Table went a-looting in—is gently sloping pasture ground where a man could see his enemy a long way off and "ride a wallop" at him, as the Morte D'Arthur puts it, of a clear half mile. Here and there little rocky hills, the last off-shoots of the Aravalis to the west, break the ground; but the bulk of it is fair and without pimples. The Deoli Force are apparently so utterly Irregular that they can do without a telegraph, have their mails carried by runners, and dispense with bridges over all the fifty-six miles that separate them from Nasirabad. However, a man who goes shikarring for any length of time in one of Ram Baksh's tongas would soon learn to dispense with anything and everything. "All the Sahibs use my tonga; I've got eight of them and twenty pairs of horses," said Ram Baksh. "They go as far as Gangra, where the tigers are, for they are 'shutin-tongas'." Now the Englishman knew Gangra slightly, having seen it on the way to Udaipur; and it was as perverse and rocky a place as any man would desire to see. He politely expressed doubt. "I tell you my tongas go anywhere," said Ram Baksh testily. A hay-waggon—they cut and stack their hay in these parts—blocked the road. Ram Baksh ran the tonga to one side, into a rut, fetched up on a tree-stump, rebounded on to a rock, and struck the kunkur. "Observe," said Ram Baksh; "but that is nothing. You wait till we get on the Boondi Road, and I'll make you shake, shake like a *botal*." "Is it *very* bad?" "I've never been to Boondi myself, but I hear it is all rocks—great rocks as big as the tonga." But though he boasted himself and his horses nearly all the way, he could not reach Deoli in anything like the time he had set forth. "If I am not at Boondi by four," he had said, at six in the morning, "let me go without my fare." But by midday he was still far from Deoli, and Boondi lay twenty-eight miles beyond that station. "What can I do?" said he. "I've laid out lots of horses—any amount. But the fact is I've never been to Boondi. I shan't go there in the night." Ram Baksh's "lots of horses" were three pair between Nasirabad and Deoli—three pair of undersized ponies who did wonders. One place, after he had quitted a cotton wagon, a drove of *Bunjaras* and a man on horseback, with his carbine across his saddle-bow, the Englishman came to a stretch of road so utterly desolate that he said: "Now I am clear of everybody who ever knew me. This is the beginning of the waste into which the scape-goat was sent.'

From a bush by the road side sprang up a fat man who cried aloud in English: "How does Your Honor do? I met your Honor in Simla this year. Are you quite well? Ya-as, I am here. Your Honor remembers me? I am travelling. Ya-as. Ha! Ha!" and he went on, leaving His Honor bemazed. It was a Babu—a Simla Babu, of that there could be no doubt; but who he was or what he was doing, thirty miles from anywhere, His Honor could not make out. The native moves about more than most folk, except railway people, imagine. The big banking firms of Upper India naturally keep in close touch with their great change-houses in Ajmir, despatching and receiving messengers regularly. So it comes to pass that the necessitous circumstances of Lieutenant McRannamack, of the Tyneside Tail-twisters, quartered on the Frontier, are thoroughly known and discussed, a thousand miles south of the cantonment where the light-hearted Lieutenant goes to the "beastly *shroff*."

This is by the way. Let us return to the banks of the Banas river, where "poor Carey," as Tod calls him, came when he was sickening for his last illness. The Banas is one of those streams which runs "over golden sands with feet of silver," but, from the scarp of its banks, Deoli in the rains must be isolated. Ram Baksh, questioned hereon, vowed that all the Officer Sahibs never dreamed of halting, but went over in boats or on elephants. According to Ram Baksh the men of Deoli must be wonderful creatures. They do nothing but use his tongas. A break in some low hills give on to the dead flat plain in which Deoli stands. "You must stop here for the night," said Ram Baksh. "I will not take my horses forward in the dark ; God knows where the dak-bungalow is. I've forgotten, but anyone of the Officer Sahibs in Deoli will tell you." Those in search of a new emotion would do well to run about an apparently empty cantonment, in a disgraceful shooting-tonga, in search of a place to sleep in. Chaprassis come out of back verandahs, and are rude, and regimental Babus hop of godowns and are flippant, while in the distance a Sahib looks out of his room, where he has evidently been sleeping, and eyes the dusty forlorn-hope with silent contempt. It should be mentioned that the dust on the Deoli road not only powders but masks the face and raiment of the passenger.

Next morning Ram Baksh was awake with the dawn, and clamorous to go on to Boondi. "I've sent a pair of horses, big horses, out there and the *sais* is a fool. Perhaps they will be lost, I want to find them." He dragged his unhappy passenger on the road once more and demanded of all who passed the dak-bungalow which was the way to Boondi. "Observe," said he, "there can be only one road, and if I hit it we are all right, and I'll show you what the tonga can do." "Amen," said the Englishman devoutly, as the tonga jumped into and out of a larger hole. "Without doubt this is the Boondi road," said Ram Baksh ; "it is too bad."

Beyond Deoli the cultivated land gave place to more hills peppered with stones, stretches of *ak*-scrub and clumps of thorn varied with a little jhil here and there for the benefit of the officers of the Deoli Irregular Force.

It has been before said that the Boondi State has no great love for Sahibs. The state of the road proves it. "This," said Ram Baksh, tapping the wheel to see whether the last plunge had smashed a spoke, "is a very good road. You wait till you see what is ahead." And the funeral staggered on—over irrigation cuts, through buffalo wallows, and dried pools stamped with the hundred feet of kine (this by the way is the most cruel road of all), up rough banks where the rock ledges peered out of the dust, down steep-cut dips ornamented with large stones, and along two-feet deep ruts of the rains, where the tonga went slantwise even to the verge of upsetting. It was a royal road—a native road—a Raj road of the roughest, and, through all its jolts and bangs and bumps and dips and heaves, the eye of Ram Baksh rolled in its blood-shot socket, seeking for the "big horses" he had so rashly sent into the wilderness. The ponies that had done the last twenty miles into Deoli were nearly used up, and did their best to lie down in the dry beds of nullahs. (*Nota bene.*—There was an unabridged nullah every five minutes, for the set of the country was towards the Mej river. In the rains it must be utterly impassable).

A man came by on horseback, his servant walking before with platter and meal bag. "Have you seen any horses hereabouts?" cried Ram Baksh. "Horses. Horses. What the Devil have I to do with your horses? D'you think I've stolen them?" Now this was decidedly a strange answer, and showed the rudeness of the land. An old woman under a tree cried out in a strange tongue and ran away. It was a dream-like experience, this hunting for horses on a "blasted heath" with neither house nor hut nor shed in sight. "If we keep to the road long enough we must find them. Look at the road. This Raj ought to be smitten with bullets." Ram Baksh had been pitched forward nearly on the off-pony's rump, and was in a very bad temper indeed. The funeral found a house—a house walled with thorns—and near by were the two big horses, thirteen-two if an inch, and harnessed quite regardless of expense.

Everything was re-packed and re-bound with triple ropes, and the Sahib was provided with an extra cushion ; but he had reached a sort of dream-some Nirvana ; having several times bitten his tongue through, cut his boot against the wheel-edge and twisted his legs into a true-lover's-knot. There was no further sense of suffering in him. He was even beginning to enjoy himself faintly and by gasps. The road struck boldly into hills with all their teeth on edge, that is to say, their strata breaking across the road in a series of little ripples. The effect of this was amazing. The tonga skipped merrily as a young fawn, from ridge to ridge, and never seemed to have both wheels on the ground at the same time. It shivered, it palpitated, it shook, it slid, it hopped, it waltzed, it ricochetted, it bounded like a kangaroo, it blundered like a sledge, it swayed like a top-heavy coach on a down-grade, it "kicked" like a badly coupled railway carriage, it squelched like a country-cart, it squeaked in its torment, and, lastly, it essayed to plough up the ground with its nose. After three hours of this performance, it struck a tiny little ford, set between steeply-sloping banks of white dust, where the water was clear brown and full of fish. And here a blissful halt was called under the shadow of the high bank of a tobacco field.

Would you taste one of the real pleasures of Life? Go through severe acrobatic exercises in and about a tonga for four hours; then, having eaten and drank till you can no more, sprawl in the cool of a nullah bed with your head among the green tobacco, and your mind adrift within the one little cloud in a royally blue sky. Earth has nothing more to offer her children than this deep delight of animal well-being. There were butterflies in the tobacco—six different kinds, and a little rat came out and drank at the ford. To him succeeded the flight into Egypt. The white bank of the ford framed the picture perfectly—the Mother in blue, on a great white donkey, holding the Child in her arms, and Joseph walking beside, his hand upon the donkey's withers. By all the laws of the East, Joseph should have been riding and the Mother walking. This was an exception decreed for the Englishman's special benefit. It was very warm and very pleasant, and, somehow, the passers by the ford grew indistinct, and the nullah became a big English garden, with a cuckoo singing far down in the orchard, among the apple-blossoms. The cuckoo started the dream. He was the only real thing in it, for the garden slipped back into the water, but the cuckoo remained and called and called for all the world as though he had been a veritable English cuckoo. "Cuckoo—cuckoo—cuck;" then a pause and renewal of the cry from another quarter of the horizon. After that the ford became distasteful, so the procession was driven forward and in time plunged into what must have been a big city once, but the only inhabitants were oil-men. There were abundance of tombs here, and one carried a life-like carving in high relief of a man on horseback spearing a foot-soldier. Hard by this place the road or rut turned by great gardens, very cool and pleasant, full of tombs and black-faced monkeys who quarreled among the tombs, and shut in from the sun by gigantic banians and mango trees. Under the trees and behind the walls, priests sat sighing; and the Englishman would have inquired into what strange place he had fallen, but the men did not understand him.

Ganesh is a mean little god of circumscribed powers. He was dreaming, with a red and flushed face, under a banian tree; and the Englishman gave him four annas to arrange matters comfortably at Boondi. His priest took the four annas, but Ganesh did nothing whatever, as shall be shown later. His only excuse is that his trunk was a good deal worn, and he would have been better for some more silver leaf, but that was no fault of the Englishman.

Beyond the dead city was a jhil, full of snipe and duck, winding in and out of the hills; and beyond the jhil, hidden altogether among the hills, was Boondi. The nearer to the city the viler grew the road and the more overwhelming the curiosity of the inhabitants. But what befel at Boondi must be reserved for another chapter.

CHAPTER XVI.

A NEW TREATY IS NEEDED WITH MAHA RAO RAJA RAM SINGH, BAHADUR, RAJA OF BOONDI—BOYS AND OTHER THINGS BY THE WAY—SHIELDS.

It is high time that a new treaty were made with Maha Rao Raja Ram Singh, Bahadur, Raja of Boondi. He keeps the third article of the old one too faithfully, which says that he "shall not enter into negotiations with anyone without the consent of the British Government." He does not negotiate at all. Arrived at Boondi Gate, the Englishman asked where he might lay his head for the night, and the Quarter Guard with one accord said: "The Sukh Mahal, which is beyond the city," and the tonga went thither through the length of the town, of which more presently, till it arrived at a pavilion on a lake—a place of two turrets connected by an open colonnade. The "house" was open to the winds of heaven and the pigeons of the Raj; but the latter had polluted more than the first could purify. A snowy-bearded chowkidar crawled out of a place of tombs, which he seemed to share with some monkeys, and threw himself into Anglo-Saxon attitudes. He was a great deal worse than Ram Baksh, for he said that all the Officer Sahibs of Deoli came to the Sukh Mahal for *shikar* and—never went away again, so pleased were they. The Sahib had brought the honor of his Presence, and he was a very old man, and without a *purwana* could do nothing. Then he fell deeply asleep without warning ; and there was a pause, of one hour only, which the Englishman spent in seeing the lake. It, like the jhils on the road, wound in and out among the hills, and, on the bund side, was bounded by a hill of black rock crowned with a *chhatri* of grey stone. Below the bund was a garden as fair as eye could wish, and the shores of the lake were dotted with little temples. Given a habitable house—a mere dak-bungalow—it would be a delightful spot to rest in. Warned by some bitter experiences in the past, the Englishman knew that he was in for the demi-semi-royal or embarrassing reception, when a man, being the unwelcome guest of a paternal State, is neither allowed to pay his way and make himself comfortable, nor is he willingly entertained. When he saw a one-eyed *munshi*, he felt certain that Ganesh had turned upon him at last. The munshi demanded and received the purwana. Then he sat down and questioned the traveller exhaustively as to his character and profession. Having thoroughly satisfied himself that the visitor was in no way connected with the Government or the "Agenty Sahib Bahadur," he took no further thought of the matter ; and the day began to draw in upon a grassy bund, an open work pavilion, and a disconsolate tonga.

At last the faithful servitor, who had helped to fight the Battle of the Mail Bags at Udaipur, broke his silence, and vowing that all these devil-people—not more than twelve—had only come to see the tamasha, suggested the breaking of the munshi's head. And, indeed, that seemed the only way of breaking the ice; for the munshi had, in the politest possible language, put forward the suggestion that there was nothing particular to show that the Sahib who held the *purwana* had really any right to hold it. The chowkidar woke up and chaunted a weird chaunt, accompanied by the Anglo-Saxon attitudes, a new set. He was an old man, and all the Sahib-log said so, and within the pavilion were tables and chairs and lamps and bath-tubs, and everything that the heart of man could desire. Even now an enormous staff of *khalassis* were arranging all these things for the comfort of the Sahib Bahadur and Protector of the Poor, who had brought the honor and glory of his Presence all the way from Deoli. What did tables and chairs and eggs and fowls and very bright lamps matter to the Raj? He was an old man and . . . "Who put the present Raja on the guddee?" "Lake Sahib," promptly answered the chowkidar. "I was there. That is the news of many old years." Now Tod says it was he himself who installed "Lalji the beloved" in the year 1821. The Englishman began to lose faith in the chowkidar. The munshi said nothing but followed the Englishman with his one workable eye. A merry little breeze crisped the waters of the lake, and the fish began to frolic before going to bed.

"Is nobody going to do or bring anything?" said the Englishman faintly, wondering whether the local jail would give him a bed if he killed the munshi. "I am an old man," said the chowkidar, "and because of their great respect and reverence for the Sahib in whose Presence I am only a bearer of orders and a servant awaiting them, men, many men, are bringing now *kanats* which I with my own hands will wrap, here and there, there and here, in and about the pillars of the place; and thus you, O Sahib, who have brought the honor of your Presence to the Boondi Raj over the road to Deoli, which is a *kutcha* road, will be provided with a very fine and large apartment over which I will watch while you go to kill the tigers in these hills.

By this time two youths had twisted *kanats* round some of the pillars of the colonnade, making a sort of loose-box with a two-foot air-way all round the top. There was no door, but there were unlimited windows. Into this enclosure the chowkidar heaped furniture on which many generations of pigeons had evidently been carried off by cholera, until he was entreated to desist. "What," said he scornfully, "are tables and chairs to this Raj?" If six be not enough, let the Presence give an order, and twelve shall be forthcoming. Everything shall be forthcoming." Here he filled a *chirag* with kerosene oil and set it in a box upon a stick. Luckily, the oil which he poured so lavishly from a quart bottle was bad, or he would have been altogether consumed.

Night had fallen long before this magnificence was ended. The superfluous furniture—chairs for the most part—was shovelled out into the darkness and by the light of a flamboyant chirag—a merry wind forbade candles—the Englishman went to bed, and was lulled to sleep by the rush of the water escaping from the overflow trap and the splash of the water-turtle as he missed the evasive fish. It was a curious sight. Cats and dogs rioted about the enclosure, and a wind from the lake bellied the kanats. The brushwood of the hills around snapped and cracked as beasts went through it, and creatures—not jackals—made dolorous noises. On the lake it seemed that hundreds of water-birds were keeping a hotel, and that there were arrivals and departures throughout the night. The Raj insisted upon providing a guard of two sepoys, very pleasant men on four rupees a month. These said tigers sometimes wandered about on the hills above the lake, but were most generally to be found five miles away. And the Englishman promptly dreamed that a one-eyed tiger came into his tent without a *purwana*. But it was only a wild cat after all ; and it fled before the shoes of civilization.

The Sukh Mahal was completely separated from the city, and might have been a country-house. It should be mentioned that Boondi is jammed into a V-shaped gorge—the valley at the main entrance being something less than five hundred yards across. As it splays out, the thickly-packed houses follow its lines, and, seen from above, seem like cattle being herded together preparatory to a stampede through the gate. Owing to the set of the hills, very little of the city is visible except from the Palace. It was in search of this latter that the Englishman went abroad and became so interested in the streets that he forgot all about it for a time. Jeypore is a show-city and is decently drained ; Udaipur is blessed with a State Engineer and a printed form of Government; for Jodhpur the dry sand, the burning sun, and an energetic doctor have done a good deal, but Boondi has none of these things. The crampedness of the locality aggravates the evil, and it can only be in the rains which channel and furrow the rocky hill-sides that Boondi is at all swept out. The Nal Sagar, a lovely little stretch of water, takes up the head of the valley called the Banda Gorge, and must, in the nature of things, receive a good deal of unholy drainage. But setting aside this weakness, it is a fascinating place—this jumbled city of straight streets and cool gardens, where gigantic mangoes and peepuls intertwine over gurgling water-courses, and the cuckoo comes at mid-day. It boasts no foolish Municipality to decree when a house is dangerous and uninhabitable. The newer shops are built into, on to, over and under, time-blackened ruins of an older day, and the little children skip about tottering arcades and grass-gown walls, while their parents chatter below in the crowded bazaar. In the black slums, the same stones seem to be used over and over again for house-building, perhaps, because there is no space to bring up laden buffaloes. Wheeled conveyances are scarce in Boondi city—there is scant room for carts, and the streets are paved with knobsome stones, unpleasant to walk over. From time to time an inroad of *Bunjaras'* pack-bullocks sweeps the main streets clear of life, or one of the Raja's elephants—he has twelve of them—blocks the way. But, for the most part, the foot passengers have all the city for their own.

They do not hurry themselves. They sit in the sun and think, or put on all the arms in the family, and, hung with ironmongery, parade before their admiring friends. Other men, lean, dark men, with bound jaws and only a tulwar for weapon, dive in and out of the dark allies, on errands of State. It is a blissfully lazy city, doing everything in the real, true, original native way, and it is kept in very good order by the Durbar. There either is or is not an order for everything. There is no order to sell fishing-hooks, or to supply an Englishman with milk, or to change for him Currency Notes. He must only deal with the Durbar for whatever he requires ; and wherever he goes he must be accompanied by at least two men. They will tell him nothing, for they know or affect to know nothing of the city. They will do nothing except shout at the little innocents who joyfully run after the stranger and demand *pice*, but there they are, and there they will stay till he leaves the city, accompanying him to the gate, and waiting there a little to see that he is fairly off and away. Englishmen are not encouraged in Boondi. The intending traveller would do well to take a full suit of Political uniform with the sunflowers, and the little black sword to sit down upon. The local god is the "Agenty Sahib," and he is an incarnation without a name—at least among the lower classes. The educated, when speaking of him, always use the courtly "Bahadur" affix ; and yet it is a mean thing to gird at a State which, after all, is not bound to do anything for intrusive Englishmen without any visible means of livelihood. The King of this fair city should declare the blockade absolute, and refuse to be troubled with anyone except "Colon-nel Baltah Agenty Sahib Bahadur" and the Politicals. If ever a railway is run through Kotah, as men on the Bombay side declare it must be, the cloistered glory of Boondi will depart, for Kotah is only twenty miles easterly of the city and the road is moderately good. In that day the Globe-Trotter will pry about the place, and the Charitable Dispensary—a gem among dispensaries—will be public property.

The Englishman was hunting for the statue of a horse, a great horse hight Hunja, who was a steed of Irak, and a King's gift to Rao Omeda, one time monarch of Boondi. He found it in the city square as Tod had said ; and it was an unlovely statue, carven after the dropsical fashion of later Hindu art. No one seemed to know anything about it. A little further on, one cried from a byeway in rusty English : "Come and see my Dispensary." There are only two men in Boondi who speak English. One is the head, and the other the assistant, teacher of the English side of Boondi Free School. The third was, some twenty years ago, a pupil of the Lahore Medical College when that institution was young ; and he only remembered a word here and there. He was head of the Charitable Dispensary ; and insisted upon, then and there, organizing a small durbar, and pulling out all his books for inspection. Escape was hopeless : nothing less than a formal inspection and introduction to all the native Baids would serve. There were sixteen beds in and about the courtyard, and between twenty and thirty out-patients stood in attendance. Making allowances for untouched Orientalism, the Dispensary is a good one, and must relieve a certain amount of human misery. There is no other in all Boondi. The operation-book, kept in English, showed the principal complaints of the country. They were: "Asthama," "Numonia," "Skindiseas," "Dabalaty" and "Loin-bite." This last item occurred again and again—three and four cases per week—and it was not until the Doctor said: "*Sher se mara*" that the Englishman read it aright. It was "lion-bite," or tiger, if you insist upon zoological accuracy. There was one incorrigible idiot, a handsome young man, naked as the day, who sat in the sunshine, shivering and pressing his hands to his head. "I have given him blisters and setons—have tried native and English treatment for two years, but it is no use. He is always as you see him, and now he stays here by the favor of the Durbar, which is a very good and pitiful Durbar," said the Doctor. There were many such pensioners of the Durbar—men afflicted with chronic "asthama" who stayed "by favor," and were kindly treated. They were resting in the sunshine their hands on their knees, sure that their daily dole of grain and tobacco and opium would be forthcoming. "All folk, even little children, eat opium here," said the Doctor, and the diet-book proved it. After laborious investigation of everything, down to the last indent to Bombay for Europe medicines, the Englishman was suffered to depart. "Sir, I thank . . .," began the Native Doctor, but the rest of the sentence stuck. Sixteen years in Boondi does not increase knowledge of English; and he went back to his patients, gravely conning over the name of the Principal of the Lahore Medical School—a College now—who had taught him all he knew, and to whom he intended to write. There was something pathetic in the man's catching at news from the outside world of men he had known as Assistant and House Surgeons who are now Rai Bahadurs, and his parade of the few shreds of English that still clung to him. May he treat "loin-bites" and "catrack" successfully for many years. In the happy, indolent fashion that must have merits which we cannot understand, he is doing a good work, and the Durbar allows his Dispensary as much as it wants.

What a narrow life it must be for these doctors, aside, of course, from the exercising of their professional skill. They seem far happier, however, than many favored residents of a busy thriving metropolis. A stranger falls to considering what might be the amusements of a Surgeon in Boondi, and he concludes that the simple fact of a perpetual existence in the place precludes the possibility of the residents caring especially for entertainment aside from the scenes and labors in the precincts of the school and hospital.

Close to the Dispensary stood the Free School, and thither an importunate munshi steered the Englishman who, by this time, was beginning to persuade himself that he really was an accredited agent of Government sent to report on the progress of Boondi. From a peepul-shaded courtyard came a clamor of young voices. Thirty or forty little ones, from five to eight years old, were sitting in an open verandah learning *hissab* and Hindustani, said the teacher. No need to ask from what castes they came, for it was written on their faces that they were Mahajans, Oswals, Aggerwals, and in one or two cases it seemed, Sharawaks of Guzerat. They were learning the business of their lives and, in time, would take their father's places, and show in how many ways money may be manipulated. Here the profession-type came out with startling distinctness. Through the chubbiness of almost babyhood, or the delicate suppleness of maturer years, in mouth and eyes and hands, it betrayed itself. The Rahtor, who comes of a fighting-stock, is a fine animal and well-bred ; the Hara, who seems to be more compactly-built, is also a fine animal ; but for a race that show blood in every line of their frame, from the arch of the instep to the modelling of the head, the financial—trading is too coarse a word—the financial class of Rajputana appears to be the most remarkable. Later in life may become clouded with fat jowl and paunch ; but in his youth, his quick-eyed nimble youth, the young Marwar, to give him his business-title, is really a thing of beauty. Also his manners are courtly. The bare ground and a few slates sufficed for the children who were merely learning the ropes that drag States ; but the English class, of boys from ten to twelve, was supplied with benches and forms and a table with a cloth top. The assistant teacher, for the head was on leave, was a self-taught man of Boondi, young and delicate looking, who preferred reading to speaking English. His youngsters were supplied with "The Third English Reading Book," and were painfully thumbing their way through a doggerel poem about an "old man with hoary hair." One boy, bolder than the rest, slung an English sentence at the visitor and collapsed. It was his little stock-in-trade, and the rest regarded him enviously. The Durbar supports the school, which is entirely free and open; a just distinction being maintained between the various castes. The old race prejudice against payment for knowledge came out in reply to a question. "You must not sell teaching," said the teacher, and the class murmured applausively: "You must not sell teaching."

The population of Boondi seems more obviously mixed than that of the other States. There are four or five thousand Mahomedans within its walls and a sprinkling of aborigines of various varieties, besides the human raffle that the Bunjaras bring in their train, with Pathans and sleek Delhi men. The new heraldry of the Sate is curious—something after this sort. *Or*, a demi-man, *sable*, issuant of flames, holding in right hand a sword and in the left a bow—*all proper*. In chief, a dagger of the *second*, sheathed *vest*, fessewise over seven arrows in sheaf of the *second*. This latter blazon Boondi holds in commemoration of the defeat of an Imperial Prince who rebelled against the Delhi Throne in the days of Jehangir, when Boondi, for value received, took service under the Mahomedan. It might be, but here there is no certainty, the memorial of Rao Rutton's victory over Prince Khoorm, when the latter strove to raise all Rajputana against Jehangir his father; or of a second victory over a riotous lordling who harried Mewar a little later. For this exploit, the annals say, Jehangir gave Rao Rutton honorary flags and kettle-drums which may have been melted down by the science of the Heralds College into the blazon aforesaid. All the heraldry of Rajputana is curious and, for such as hold that there is any worth in the "Royal Science," interesting. Udaipur's shield is naturally *gules*, a sun in splendor, as befits the "children of the sun and fire," and one of the most ancient houses in India. Her crest is the straight Rajput sword, the *Khanda*, for an account of the worship of which very powerful divinity read Tod. The supporters are a Bhil and a Rajput, attired for the forlorn-hope; commemorating not only the defences of Chitor, but also the connection of the great Bappa Rawul with the Bhils who even now play the principal part in the Crown-Marking of a Rana of Udaipur. Here, again, Tod explains the matter at length. Banswara claims alliance with Udaipur and carries a sun, with a label of difference of some kind. Jeypore has the five-colored flag of Amber with a sun, because the House claim descent from Rama, and her crest is a kuchnar tree, which is the bearing of Dasaratha, father of Rama. The white horse, which faces the tiger as supporter, may or may not be memorial of the great *aswamedha yuga* or horse sacrifice that Jey Singh, who built Jeypore, did *not* carry out.

Jodhpur has the five-colored flag, with a falcon, in which shape Durga, the patron Goddess of the State, has been sometimes good enough to appear. She has perched in the form of a wagtail on the howdah of the Chief of Jeysulmir, whose shield is blazoned with "forts in a desert island," and a naked left arm holding a broken spear, because, the legend goes, Jeysulmir was once galled by a horse with a magic spear. They tell the story to-day, but it is a long one. The supporters of the shield—this is canting heraldry with a vengeance!—are antelopes of the desert spangled with gold coin, because the State was long the refuge of the wealthy bankers of India.

Bikanir, a younger House of Jodhpur, carries three white hawks on the five-colored flag. The patron Goddess of Bikanir once turned the thorny jungle round the city to fruit-trees, and the crest therefore is a green tree—strange emblem for a desert principality. The motto, however, is a good one. When the greater part of the Rajput States were vassals of Akbar, and he sent them abroad to do his will, certain Princes objected to crossing the Indus, and asked Bikanir to head the mutiny because his State was the least accessible. He consented, on condition that they would all for one day greet him thus: "*Jey Jangal dar Badshah!*" History shows what became of the objector, and Bikanir's motto: "Hail to the King of the Waste!" proves that the tale *must* be true. But from Boondi to Bikanir is a long digression, bred by blissful idleness on the bund of the Burra. It would have been sinful not to let down a line into those crowded waters, and the Guards, who were Mahomedans, said that if the Sahib did not eat fish, they did. And the Sahib fished luxuriously, catching two and three-pounders, of a perch-like build, whenever he chose to cast. He was wearied of schools and dispensaries, and the futility of heraldry accorded well with laziness—that is to say Boondi.

It should be noted, none the less, that in this part of the world the soberest mind will believe anything—believe in the ghosts by the Gow Mukh, and the dead Thakurs who get out of their tombs and ride round the Burra Talao at Boondi—will credit every legend and lie that rises as naturally as the red flush of sunset, to gild the dead glories of Rajasthan.

CHAPTER XVII.

POETRY MAY BE FOUND IN A BANK, AND THERE ARE OTHER WONDERS THAN POETRY IN THE PALACE OF BOONDI.

"This is a devil's place you have come to, Sahib. No grass for the horses, and the people don't understand anything, and their dirty pice are no good in Nasirabad. Look here." And Ram Baksh wrathfully exhibited a handful of lumps of copper. The nuisance of taking a native out of his own beat is that he forthwith regards you not only as the author of his being, but of all his misfortunes as well. He is as hampering as a frightened child and as irritating as a man. "*Padre Martum Sahib* never came here," said Ram Baksh, with an air of one who had been led against his will into bad company.

A story about a rat that found a piece of turmeric and set up a bunnia's shop had sent the one-eyed munshi away, but a company of lesser munshis, runners and the like, were in attendance, and they said that money might be changed at the Treasury, which was in the Palace. It was quite impossible to change it anywhere else—there was no *hookum*. From the Sukh Mahal to the Palace the road ran through the heart of the city, and by reason of the continual shouting of the munshis, not more than ten thousand of the fifty thousand people of Boondi knew for what purpose the Sahib was journeying through their midst. Cataract was the most prevalent affliction, cataract in its worst forms, and it was, therefore, necessary that men should come very close to look at the stranger. They were in no sense rude, but they stared devoutly. "He has not come for *shikar*, and he will not take petitions. He has come to see the place, and God knows what he is." The description was quite correct, as far as it went; but, somehow or another, when shouted out at four cross-ways in the midst of a very pleasant little gathering it did not seem to add to dignity or command respect.

It has been written "the *coup d'œil* of the castellated Palace of Boondi, from whichever side you approach it, is perhaps the most striking in India. Whoever has seen the Palace of Boondi can easily picture to himself the hanging gardens of Semiramis." This is true—and more too. To give on paper any adequate idea of the Boondi-ki-Mahal is impossible. Jeypore Palace may be called the Versailles of India ; Udaipur's House of State is dwarfed by the hills round it and the spread of the Pichola Lake ; Jodhpur's House of Strife grey towers on red rock, is the work of giants, but the Palace of Boondi, even in broad daylight, is such a Palace as men build for themselves in uneasy dreams—the work of goblins more than the work of men. It is built into and out of the hill side, in gigantic terrace on terrace, and dominates the whole of the city. But a detailed description of it were useless. Owing to the dip of the valley in which the city stands, it can only be well seen from one place, the main road of the city ; and from that point seems like an avalanche of masonry ready to rush down and whelm the gorge. Like all the other Palaces of Rajputana, it is the work of many hands, and the present Raja has thrown out a bastion of no small size on one of the lower levels, which has been four or five years in the building. Only by scaling this annex, and, from the other side of the valley, seeing how insignificant is its great bulk in the entire scheme, is it possible to get some idea of the stupendous size of the Palace. No one knows where the hill begins and where the Palace ends. Men say that there are subterranean chambers leading into the heart of the hills, and passages communicating with the extreme limits of Taragarh, the giant fortress that crowns the hill and flanks the whole of the valley on the Palace side. They say that there is as much room under as above ground, and that none know the whole extent of the Palace. Looking at it from below, the Englishman could readily believe that nothing was impossible for those who had built it. The dominant impression was of height—height that heaved itself out of the hillside and weighed upon the eyelids of the beholder. The steep slope of the land had helped the builders in securing this effect. From the main road of the city a steep stone-paved ascent led to the first gate—name not communicated by the zealous following. Two gaudily painted fishes faced each other over the arch, and there was little except glaring color ornamentation visible. This gate gave into what they called the *chowk* of the Palace, and one had need to look twice ere realizing that this open space, crammed with human life, was a spur of the hill on which the Palace stood, paved and built over. There had been little attempt at levelling the ground. The foot-worn stones followed the contour of the ground, and ran up to the walls of the Palace smooth as glass. Immediately facing the Gate of the Fish was the Quarter-Guard barracks, a dark and dirty room, and here, in a chamber hollowed out in a wall, were stored the big drums of State, the *nakarras*. The appearance of the Englishman seemed to be the signal for smiting the biggest of all the drums, and the dull thunder rolled up the Palace *chowk*, and came back from the unpierced Palace walls in hollow groaning. It was an eerie welcome—this single, sullen boom. In this enclosure, four hundred years ago, if the legend be true, a son of the great Rao Bando, who dreamed a dream as Pharoah did and saved Boondi from famine, left a little band of Haras to wait his bidding while he went up into the Palace and slew his two uncles who had usurped the throne and abandoned the faith of their fathers. When he had pierced one and hacked the other, as they sat alone and unattended, he called out to his followers, who made a slaughter-house of the enclosure and cut up the usurpers' adherents. At the best of times men slip on these smooth stones; and when the place was swimming in blood, foothold must have been treacherous indeed.

An inquiry for the place of the murder of the uncles—it is marked by a staircase slab, or Tod, the accurate, is at fault—was met by the answer that the Treasury was close at hand. They speak a pagan tongue in Boondi, swallow half their words, and adulterate the remainder with local *patois*. What can be extracted from a people who call four miles variously *do kosh*, *do kush*, *dhi hkas*, *doo-a koth* and *diakast*, all one word? The country-folk are quite unintelligible; which simplifies matters. It is the catching of a shadow of a meaning here and there, the hunting for directions cloaked in dialect, that is annoying. Foregoing his archæological researches, the Englishman sought the Treasury. He took careful notes; he even made a very bad drawing, but the Treasury of Boondi defied pinning down before the public. There was a gash in the brown flank of the Palace—and this gash was filled with people. A broken bees' comb with the whole hive busily at work on repairs, will give a very fair idea of this extraordinary place—the Heart of Boondi. The sunlight was very vivid without and the shadows were heavy within, so that little could be seen except this clinging mass of humanity huggling like maggots in a carcass. A stone staircase ran up to a rough verandah built out of the wall, and in the wall was a cave-like room, the guardian of whose snow-carpeted depths was one of the refined financial classes, a man with very small hands and soft, low voice. He was girt with a sword, and held authority over the Durbar funds. He referred the Englishman courteously to another branch of the department, to find which necessitated a blundering progress up another narrow staircase crowded with loungers of all kinds. Here everything shone from constant contact of bare feet and hurrying bare shoulders. The staircase was the thing that, seen from without, had produced the bees' comb impression. At the top was a long verandah shaded from the sun, and here the Boondi Treasury worked, under the guidance of a grey-haired old man, whose sword lay by the side of his comfortably wadded cushion. He controlled twenty or thirty writers, each wrapped round a huge, country paper account-book, and each far too busy to raise his eyes.

The babble on the staircase might have been the noise of the sea so far as these men were concerned. It ebbed and flowed in regular beats, and spread out far into the courtyard below. Now and again the *click-click-click* of a scabbard tip being dragged against the wall, cut the dead sound of tramping naked feet, and a soilder would stumble up the narrow way into the sunlight. He was received, and sent back or forward by a knot of keen-eyed loungers, who seemed to act as a buffer between the peace of the Secretariat and the pandemonium of the Administrative. Saises and grass-cutters, mahouts of elephants, brokers, mahajuns, villagers from the district, and here and there a shock-headed aborigine, swelled the mob on and at the foot of the stairs. As they came up, they met the buffer-men who spoke in low voices and appeared to filter them according to their merits. Some were sent to the far end of the verandah, where everything melted away in a fresh crowd of dark faces. Others were sent back, and joined the detachment shuffling for shoes in the *chowk*. One servant of the Palace withdrew himself to the open, underneath the verandah, and there sat yapping from time to time like a hungry dog: "The grass. The grass. The grass." But the men with the account-books never stirred. And they bowed their heads gravely and made entry or erasure, turning back the rustling leaves. Not often does a reach of the River of Life so present itself that it can without alteration be transferred to canvas. But the Treasury of Boondi, the view up the long verandah, stood complete and ready for any artist who cared to make it his own. And by that lighter and less malicious irony of Fate, who is always giving nuts to those who have no teeth, the picture was clinched and brought together by a winking, brass hookah-bowl of quaint design, pitched carelessly upon a roll of dull red cloth in the foreground. The faces of the accountants were of pale gold, for they were an untanned breed, and the face of the old man their controller, was like frosted silver.

It was a strange Treasury, but no other could have

suited the Palace. The Englishman watched open-mouthed, blaming himself because he could not catch the meaning of the orders given to the flying chaprassies, nor make anything of the hum in the verandah and the tumult on the stairs. The old man took the common-place Currency Note and announced his willingness to give change in silver. "We have no small notes here," he said. "They are not wanted. In a little while, when you next bring the Honor of your Presence this way, you shall find the silver."

The Englishman was taken down the steps and fell into the arms of a bristled giant who had left his horse in the courtyard, and the giant spoke at length waving his arms in the air, but the Englishman could not understand him and dropped into the hubbub at the Palace foot. Except the main lines of the building there is nothing straight or angular about it. The rush of people seems to have rounded and softened every corner, as a river grinds down boulders. From the lowest tier, two zigzags, all of rounded stones sunk in mortar, took the Englishman to a gate where two carved elephants were thrusting at each other over the arch; and, because neither he nor any one round him could give the gate a name, he called it the "Gate of the Elephants." Here the noise from the Treasury was softened, and entry through the gate brought him into a well-known world, the drowsy peace of a King's Palace. There was a courtyard surrounded by stables, in which were kept chosen horses, and two or three *saises* were sleeping in the sun. There was no other life except the whirr and coo of the pigeons. In time—though there really is no such a thing as time off the line of railway—an official appeared begirt with the skewer-like keys that open the native bayonet-locks, each from six inches to a foot long. Where was the Raj Mahal in which, sixty-six years ago, Tod formally installed Ram Singh, "who is now in his eleventh year, fair and with a lively intelligent cast of face?" The warden made no answer, but led to a room, overlooking the courtyard, in which two armed men stood before an empty throne of white marble. They motioned silently that none must pass immediately before the *takht* of the King, but go round, keeping to the far side of the double row of pillars. Near the walls were stone slabs pierced to take the butts of long, venomous, black bamboo lances; rude coffers were disposed about the room, and ruder sketches of Ganesh adorned the walls. "The men," said the warden, "watch here day and night because this place is the Rutton Daulat." That, you will concede, is lucid enough. He who does not understand it, may go to for a thick-headed barbarian.

From the Rutton Daulat the warden unlocked doors that led into a hall of audience—the Chutter Mahal—built by Raja Chutter Lal, who was killed more than two hundred years ago in the latter days of Shah Jehan for whom he fought. Two rooms, each supported on double rows of pillars, flank the open space, in the centre of which is a marble reservoir. Here the Englishman looked anxiously for some of the atrocities of the West, and was pleased to find that, with the exception of a vase of artificial flowers and a clock, both hid in *mihrabs*, there was nothing that jarred with the exquisite pillars, and the raw blaze of color in the roofs of the rooms. In the middle of these impertinent observations, something sighed—sighed like a distressed ghost. Unaccountable voices are at all times unpleasant, especially when the hearer is some hundred feet or so above ground in an unknown Palace in an unknown land. A gust of wind had found its way through one of the latticed balconies, and had breathed upon a thin plate of metal, some astrological instrument, slung gongwise on a tripod. The tone was as soft as that of an Æolian harp, and, because of the surroundings, infinitely more plaintive.

There was an inlaid ivory door, set in lintel and posts crusted with looking-glass—all apparently old work. This opened into a darkened room where there were gilt and silver charpoys, and portraits, in the native fashion, of the illustrious dead of Boondi. Beyond the darkness was a balcony clinging to the sheer side of the Palace, and it was then that the Englishman realized to what a height he had climbed without knowing it. He looked down upon the bustle of the Treasury and the stream of life flowing into and out of the Gate of the Fishes where the big *nakarras* lie. Lifting his eyes, he saw how Boondi City had built itself, spreading from west to east as the confined valley became too narrow and the years more peaceable. The Boondi hills are the barrier that separates the stony, uneven ground near Deoli from the flats of Kotah, twenty miles away. From the Palace balcony the road to the eye is clear to the banks of the Chumbul river, which was the Debateable Ford in times gone by and was leaped, as all rivers with any pretensions to a pedigree have been, by more than one magic horse. Northward and easterly the hills run out to Indurgarh, and southward and westerly to territory marked "disputed" on the map in the present year of grace. From this balcony the Raja can see to the limit of his territory eastward, like the good King of Yves, his empire is all under his hand. He is, or the politicals err, that same Ram Singh who was installed by Tod in 1821, and for whose success in killing his first deer, Tod was, by the Queen-Mother of Boondi, bidden to rejoice. To-day the people of Boondi say: "This Durbar is very old, so old that few men remember its beginning, for they were in our fathers' time." It is related also of Boondi that, on the occasion of the Queen's Jubilee, they said proudly that their ruler had reigned for sixty years, and he was a man. They saw nothing astonishing in the fact of a woman having reigned for fifty. History does not say whether they jubilated; for there are no Englishmen in Boondi to write accounts of demonstrations and foundation-stone laying to the daily newspaper, and then Boondi is very, very small. In the early morning you may see a man being pantingly chased out of the city by another man with a naked sword. This is the dak and the dak-guard; and the effect is as though runner and swordsman lay under a doom —the one to fly with the fear of death always before him, as men fly in dreams, and the other to perpetually fail of his revenge. But this leaves us still in the swallow-nest balcony.

The warden unlocked more doors and led the Englishman still higher, but into a garden—a heavily timbered garden with a tank for gold fish in the midst. For once the impassive following smiled when they saw that the Englishman was impressed. "This," said they, "is the Rang Bilas." "But who made it?" "Who knows? It was made long ago." The Englishman looked over the garden-wall, a foot-high parapet, and shuddered. There was only the flat side of the Palace, and a drop on to the stones of the zig-zags scores of feet below. Above him was the riven hillside and the decaying wall of Taragarh, and behind him this fair garden, hung like Mahomet's coffin, full of the noise of birds and the talking of the wind in the branches. The warden entered into a lengthy explanation of the nature of the delusion, showing how—but he was stopped before he was finished. His listener did not want to know "how the trick was done." Here was the garden, and there were three or four storeys climbed to reach it. At one end of the garden was a small room, under treatment by native artists who were painting the panels with historical pictures, in distemper. Their's was florid polychromatic art, but skirting the floor was a series of frescoes in red, black and white, of combats with elephants, bold and temperate as good German work. They were worn and defaced in places; but the hand of some byegone limner, who did not know how to waste a line, showed under the bruises and scratches, and put the newer work to shame.

Here the tour of the Palace ended ; and it must be remembered that the Englishman had not gone the depth of three rooms into one flank. Acres of building lay to the right of him, and above the lines of the terraces he could see the tops of green trees. Who knew how many gardens, such as the Rang Bilas, were to be found in the Palace?" No one answered directly, but all said that there were many. The warden gathered up his keys, and locking each door behind him as he passed, led the way down to earth. But before he had crossed the garden the Englishman heard, deep down in the bowels of the Palace, a woman's voice singing, and the voice rang as do voices in caves. All Palaces in India excepting dead ones such as that of Amber, are full of eyes. In some, as has been said, the idea of being watched is stronger than in others. In Boondi Palace it was overpowering—being far worse than in the green shuttered corridors of Jodhpur. There were trap-doors on the tops of terraces, and windows veiled in foliage, and bull's-eyes set low in unexpected walls, and many other peep-holes and places of vantage. In the end, the Englishman looked devoutly at the floor, but when the voice of the woman came up from under his feet, he felt that there was nothing left for him but to go. Yet, excepting only this voice, there was deep silence everywhere, and nothing could be seen.

The warden returned to the Chutter Mahal to pick up a lost key. The brass table of the planets was sighing softly to itself as it swung to and fro in the wind. That was the last view of the interior of the Palace, the empty court, and the swinging, sighing *jantar*.

About two hours afterwards, when he had reached the other side of the valley and seen the full extent of the buildings, the Englishman began to realize first that he had not been taken through one-tenth of the Palace; and secondly, that he would do well to measure its extent by acres, in preference to meaner measures. But what made him blush hotly, all alone among the tombs on the hill side, was the idea that he with his ridiculous demands for eggs, firewood and sweet drinking water, should have clattered and chattered through any part of it at all.

He began to understand why Boondi does not encourage Englishmen.

CHAPTER XVIII.

FROM UNCIVILIZED SIGHT TO THINGS CIVILIZED—WALTER BESANT'S MR. MALIPHANT IS FOUND BY THE WAY—HOW A FRIEND MAY KEEP AN APPOINTMENT TOO WELL.

"Let us go hence my songs, she will not hear. Let us go hence together without fear." But Ram Baksh the irrepressible sang it in altogether a baser key. He came by night to the pavilion on the lake, while the sepoys were cooking their fish, and reiterated his whine about the devildom of the country into which the Englishman had dragged him. *Padre Martum Sahib* would never have thus treated the owner of sixteen horses, all fast and big ones, and eight superior "shutin tongas." "Let us get away," said Ram Baksh. "You are not here for *shikar*, and the water is very bad." It was indeed, except when taken from the lake, and then it only tasted fishy. "We will go, Ram Baksh," said the Englishman. "We will go in the very early morning, and in the meantime here is fish to stay your stomach with."

When a transparent *kanat*, which fails by three feet to reach ceiling or floor, is the only bar between the East and the West, he would be a churl indeed who stood upon "invidious race distinctions." The Englishman went out and fraternized with the Military—the four-rupee soldiers of Boondi who guarded him. They were armed, one with an old Tower musket crazy as to nipple and hammer, one with a native-made smooth-bore, and one with a composite contrivance—English sporting muzzle-loader stock with a compartment for a jointed cleaning-rod, and hammered octagonal native barrel, wire-fastened, with a tuft of cotton on the foresight. All three guns were loaded, and the owners were very proud of them. They were simple folk, these men-at-arms, with an inordinate appetite for broiled fish. They were not *always* soldiers they explained. They cultivated their crops until wanted for any duty that might turn up. They were paid now and again, at intervals, but they were paid in coin and not in kind.

The *munshis* and the vakils and the runners had departed after seeing that the Englishman was safe for the night, so the freedom of the little gathering on the bund was unrestrained. The *chowkidar* came out of his cave into the firelight. Warm wood ashes, by the way, like Epp's cocoa, are "grateful and comforting to" cold toes. He took a fish and incontinently choked, for he was a feeble old man. Set right again, he launched into a very long and quite unintelligible story while the sepoys said reverently: "He is an old man and remembers many things." As he babbled, the night shut in upon the lake and the valley of Boondi. The last cows were driven into the water for their evening drink, the waterfowl and the monkeys went to bed, and the stars came out and made a new firmament in the untroubled bosom of the lake. The light of the fire showed the ruled lines of the bund springing out of the soft darkness of the wooded hill on the left and disappearing into the solid darkness of a bare hill on the right. Below the bund a man cried aloud to keep wandering pigs from the gardens whose tree-tops rose to a level with the bund-edge. Beyond the trees all was swaddled in gloom. When the gentle buzz of the unseen city died out, it seemed as though the bund were the very Swordwide Bridge that runs, as every one knows, between this world and the next. The water lapped and muttered, and now and again a fish jumped, with the shatter of broken glass, blurring the peace of the reflected heavens.

> " And duller should I be than some fat weed
> That rolls itself at ease on Lethe's wharf."

The poet who wrote those lines knew nothing whatever of Lethe's wharf. The Englishman had found it, and it seemed to him, at that hour and in that place, that it would be good and desirable never to return to the Commissioners and the Deputy Commissioners any more, but to lie at ease on the warm sunlit bund by day, and, at night, near a shadow-breeding fire, to listen for the strangled voices and whispers of the darkness in the hills ; thus after as long a life as the *chowkidar's* dying easily and pleasantly, and being buried in a red tomb on the borders of the lake. Surely no one would come to reclaim him, across those weary, weary miles of rock-strewn road. . . . " And this," said the *chowkidar*, raising his voice to enforce attention, " is true talk. Everybody knows it, and now the Sahib knows it. I am an old man." He fell asleep at once, with his head on the *chillan* that was doing duty for a whole *hukka* among the company. He had been talking for nearly a quarter of an hour.

See how great a man is the true novelist. Six or seven thousand miles away, Walter Besant of the Golden Pen, had created Mr. Maliphant—the ancient of figureheads in the *All Sorts and Conditions of Men*, and here, in Boondi, the Englishman had found Mr. Maliphant in the withered flesh. So he drank Walter Besant's health in the water of the Burra Talao. One of the sepoys turned himself round, with a clatter of accoutrements, shifted his blanket under his elbow, and told a tale. It had something to do with his *khet*, and a *gunna* which certainly was not sugar-cane. It was elusive. At times it seemed that it was a woman, then changed to a right of way, and lastly appeared to be a tax; but the more he attempted to get at its meaning through the curious patois in which its doings or its merits were enveloped, the more dazed the Englishman became. None the less the story was a fine one, embellished with much dramatic gesture which told powerfully against the firelight. Then the second sepoy, who had been enjoying the *chillam* all the time, told a tale, the purport of which was that the dead in the tombs round the lake were won t to get up of nights and *shikar*. This was a fine and ghostly story; and its dismal effect was much heightened by some clamor of the night far up the lake beyond the floor of stars.

The third sepoy said nothing. He had eaten too

much fish and was fast asleep by the side of the *chowkidar*.

They were all Mahomedans, and consequently all easy to deal with. A Hindu is an excellent person, but . . . but . . . there is no knowing what is in his heart, and he is hedged about with so many strange observances.

The Hindu or Mahomedan bent, which each Englishman's mind must take before he has been three years in the country is, of course, influenced by Province or Presidency. In Rajputana generally, the Political swears by the Hindu, and holds that the Mahomedan is untrustworthy. But a man who will eat with you and take your tobacco, sinking the fiction that it has been doctored with *shrab*, cannot be very bad after all.

That night when the tales were all told and the guard, bless them, were snoring peaceably in the starlight, a man came stealthily into the enclosure of *kanats* and woke the Englishman by muttering *Sahib, Sahib*, in his ear. It was no robber but some poor devil with a petition—a grimy, welted paper. He was absolutely unintelligible, and additionally so in that he stammered almost to dumbness. He stood by the bed, alternately bowing to the earth and standing erect, his arms spread aloft, and his whole body working as he tried to force out some rebellious word in a key that should not wake the men without. What could the Englishman do? He was no Government servant, and had no concern with *urzis*. It was laughable to lie in a warm bed and watch this unfortunate heathen, clicking and choking and gasping in his desperate desire to make the *Sahib* understand. It was also unpleasantly pathetic, and the listener found himself as blindly striving to catch the meaning as the pleader to make himself comprehended. But it was no use ; and in the end the man departed as he had come—bowed, abject and unintelligible.

Let every word written against Ganesh be rescinded. It was by his ordering that the Englishman saw such a dawn on the Burra Talao as he had never before set eyes on. Every fair morning is a reprint, blurred perhaps, of the opening of the First Day ; but this splendor was a thing to be put aside from all other days and remembered. The stars had no fire in them and the fish had stopped jumping, when the black water of the lake paled and grew grey. While he watched it seemed to the Englishman that some voices on the hills were intoning the first verses of Genesis. The grey light moved on the face of the waters till, with no interval, a blood-red glare shot up from the horizon and, inky black against the intense red, a giant crane floated out towards the sun. In the still shadowed city the great Palace drum boomed and throbbed to show that the gates were open, while the dawn swept up the valley and made all things clear. The blind man who said : "The blast of a trumpet is red" spoke only the truth. The breaking of the red dawn is like the blast of a trumpet.

"What," said the *chowkidar*, picking the ashes of the overnight fire out of his beard, "what, I say, are five eggs or twelve eggs to such a Raj as ours ?"

What also are fowls—what are" . . . "There was no talk of fowls. Where is the fowl-man from whom you got the eggs?" "He is here. No, he is there. I do not know. I am an old man, and I and the Raj supply everything without price. The *murghiwalla* will be paid by the State—liberally paid. Let the *Sahib* be happy. *Wah. Wah.*

Experience of *beegar* in Himalayayan villages had made the Englishman very tender in raising supplies that were given gratis; but the *murghiwalla* could not be found, and the value of his wares was, later, paid to Ganesh—Ganesh of Situr, for that is the name of the village full of priests, through which the Englishman had passed in ignorance two days before. A double handful of sweet smelling flowers made the receipt.

Boondi was wide awake before half-past seven in the morning. Her hunters, on foot and on horse, were filing towards the Deoli Gate to go *shikarring*. They would hunt tiger and deer they said, even with matchlocks and muzzle-loaders as uncouth as those the *Sahib* saw. They were a merry company and chaffed the Quarter-Guard at the gate unmercifully when a bullock-cart, laden with the cases of the "Batoum Naptha and Oil Company" blocked the road. One of them had been a soldier of the Queen, and, excited by the appearance of a *Sahib*, did so rebuke and badger the Quarter-Guard for their slovenliness that they threatened to come out of the barracks and destroy him.

So, after one last look at the Palace high up the hill side, the Englishman was borne away along the

Deoli road. The peculiarity of Boondi is the peculiarity of the covered pitfall. One does not see it till one falls into it. A quarter of a mile from the gate, it and its Palace were invisible. The runners who had chivalrously volunteered to protect the wanderer against possible dacoits had been satisfactorily disposed of, and all was peace and unruffled loaferdom. But the Englishman was grieved at heart. He had fallen in love with Boondi the beauful, and believed that he would never again see anything half so fair. The utter untouchedness of the town was one-half the charm and its association the other. Read Tod, who is far too good to be chipped or sampled, read Tod luxuriously on the bund of the Burra Talao, and the spirit of the place will enter into you and you will be happy.

To enjoy life thoroughly, haste and bustle must be abandoned. Ram Baksh has said that Englishmen are always *dikking* to go forward, and for this reason, though beyond doubt they pay well and readily, are not wise men. He gave utterance to this philosophy after he had mistaken his road and pulled up in what must have been a disused quarry hard by a cane-field. There were patches and pockets of cultivation along the rocky road, where men grew cotton, *til*, chillies, tobacco and sugar-cane. "I will get you sugar-cane," said Ram Baksh. "Then we will go forward, and perhaps some of these jungly fools will tell us where the road is." A "jungly fool," a tender of goats, did in time appear, but there was no hurry; the sugar-cane was sweet and purple and the sun warm.

The Englishman lay out at high noon on the crest of a rolling upland crowned with rock, and heard, as a loafer had told him he would hear, the "set of the day," which is as easily discernible as the change of tone between the rising and the falling tide. At a certain hour the impetus of the morning dies out, and all things, living and inanimate, turn their thoughts to the prophecy of the coming night. The little wandering breezes drop for a time, and, when they blow afresh, bring the message. The "set of day" as the loafer said, has changed, the machinery is beginning to run down, the unseen tides of the air are falling. The moment of the change can only be felt in the open and in touch with the earth, and once discovered, seems to place the finder in deep accord and fellowship with all things on earth. Perhaps this is why the genuine loafer, though "frequently drunk," is "always polite to the stranger," and shows such a genial tolerance towards the weaknesses of mankind, black, white or brown.

In the evening when the jackals were scuttling across the roads and the cranes had gone to roost, came Deoli the desolate, and an unpleasant meeting. Six days away from his kind had bred in a Cockney heart a great desire to see an Englishman again. An elaborate loaf through the cantonment—fifteen minutes' walk from end to end—showed only one distant dog-cart and a small English child with an ayah. There was grass in the soldierly-straight roads, and some of the cross-cuts had never been used at all from the days when the cantonment had been first laid out. In the western corner lay the cemetery—the only carefully-tended and newly-white-washed thing in this God-forgotten place. Some years ago a man had said good-bye to the Englishman; adding cheerily: "We shall meet again. The world's a very little place y' know." His prophecy was a true one, for the two met indeed, but the prophet was lying in Deoli Cemetery near the well, which is decorated so ecclesiastically with funeral urns. Truly the world is a *very* little place that a man should so stumble upon dead acquaintances when he goes abroad.

CHAPTER XIX.

CERTAIN CONCLUDING INCIDENTS AND AN APOLOGY O THE READER.

In the morning the tonga rattled past Deoli Cemetery into the open, where the Deoli Irregulars were drilling. They marked the beginning of civilization and white shirts; for which reason they seemed altogether detestable. Yet another day's jolting, enlivened by the philosophy of Ram Baksh, and then came Nasirabad. The last pair of ponies suggested serious thought. They had covered eighteen miles at an average speed of eight miles an hour, and were well conditioned little rats. "A Colonel Sahib gave me this one for *bakshish*," said Ram Baksh, flicking the near one. "It was his *baba's* pony, The *baba* was five years old. When he went away, the Colonel Sahib said : " Ram Baksh, you are a good man. Never have I seen such a good man. This horse is yours." Ram Baksh was getting a horse's work out of a child's pony. Surely we in India work the land much as the Colonel Sahib worked his son's mount ; making it do child's work when so much more can be screwed out of it. A native and a native State deals otherwise with horse and holding. Perhaps our extreme scrupulousness in handling may be Statecraft, but, after even a short sojourn in places which are dealt with not so tenderly, it seems absurd. There are States where things are done, and done without protest, that would make the hair of the educated native stand on end with horror. These things are of course not expedient to write ; because their publication would give a great deal of unnecessary pain and heart-searching to estimable native administrators who have the hope of a Star before their eyes and would not better matters in the least.

Note this fact though. With the exception of such journals as, occupying a central position in British territory, levy blackmail from the neighboring States, there are no independent papers in Rajputana. A King may start a weekly, to encourage a taste for Sanskirt and high Hindi, or a Prince may create a Court Chronicle ; but that is all. A "free press" is not allowed, and this the native journalist knows. With good management he can, keeping under the shadow of our flag, raise two hundred rupees from a big man here, and five hundred from a rich man there, but he does not establish himself across the Border. To one who has reason to hold a stubborn disbelief in even the elementary morality of the native press, this bashfulness and lack of enterprise is amusing. But to return to the over-the-way administrations. There is nothing exactly wrong in the methods of government that are overlaid with English terms and forms. They are vigorous, in certain points, and where they are not vigorous, there is a cheery happy-go-luckiness about the arrangement that must be seen to be understood. The shift and play of a man's fortune across the Border is as sudden as anything in the days of Haroun-al-Raschid of blessed memory, and there are stories, to be got for the unearthing, as wild and as improbable as those in the *Thousand and One Nights.* Most impressive of all is the way in which the country is "used," and its elasticity under pressure. In the good old days the Durbar raised everything it could from the people, and the King spent as much as ever he could on his personal pleasures.

Now the institution of the Political has stopped the grabbing, for which, by the way, some of the monarchs are not in the least grateful—and smoothed the outward face of things. But there is still a difference, and such a difference, between our ways and the ways of the other places. A year spent among native States ought to send a man back to the Decencies and the Law Courts and the Rights of the Subject with a supreme contempt for those who rave about the oppressions of the brutal bureaucrat. One month nearly taught an average Englishman that it was the proper thing to smite anybody of mean aspect and obstructive tendencies on the mouth with a shoe. Hear what an intelligent loafer said. His words are at least as valuable as these babblings. He was, as usual, wonderfully drunk, and the gift of speech came down upon him. The conversation—he was a great politician this loafer—had turned on the poverty of India. "Poor?" said he. "Of course it's poor. Oh, yes, D—d poor. And I'm poor, an' you're poor, altogether. Do you expect people will give you money without you ask 'em? No, I tell you, Sir, there's enough money in India to pave *Hell* with if you could only get at it. I've kep' servants in my day. Did they ever leave me without a hundred or a hundred and fifty put by—and never touched? *You mark that.* Does any black man who has been in Guv'ment service go away without hundreds an' hundreds put by, and never touched? You mark that. Money. The place stinks o' money—just kept out o' sight. Do you ever know a native that didn't say *Garib admi*? They've been sayin' *Garib admi* so long that the Guv'ment learns to believe 'em, and now they're all bein' treated as though they was paupers. I'm a pauper, an' you're a pauper—we 'aven't got anything hid in the ground—an' so's every white man in this forsaken country. But the Injian he's a rich man. How do I know? Because I've tramped on foot, or warrant pretty well from one end of the place to the other, an' I know what I'm talkin' about, and this ere Guv'ment goes peckin' an' fiddlin' over its tuppenny-ha'penny little taxes as if it was afraid.

Which it is. You see how they do things in ——. It's six sowars here, and ten sowars there, and—Pay up you brutes or we'll pull your ears over your head. And when they've taken all they can get, the head-man, he says: "This is a dashed poor yield. I'll come again." *Of course* the people digs up something out of the ground, and they pay. I know the way it's done, and that's the way to do it. You can't go to an Injian an' say: "Look here. Can you pay me five rupees? He says: '*Garib admi*,' of course, an' would say it if he was as rich as banker. But if you send half a dozen swords at him and shift the thatch off of his roof, he'll pay. Guv'ment can't do that. I don't suppose it could. There is no reason why it shouldn't. But it might do something like it, to show that it wasn't going to have no nonsense. Why, I'd undertake to raise a hundred million—what am I talking of?—a hundred and fifty million pounds from this country *per annum*, and it wouldn't be strained *then*. One hundred and fifty millions you could raise as easy as paint, if you just made these 'ere Injians understand that they had to pay an' make no bones about it. It's enough to make a man sick to go in over yonder to —— and see what they do; and then come back an' see what we do. Perfectly sickenin' it is. Borrer money. Why the country could pay herself an' everything she wants, if she was only made to do it. It's this bloomin' *Garib admi* swindle that's been going on all these years, that has made fools o' the Guv'ment." Then he became egotistical, this ragged ruffian who conceived that he knew the road to illimitable wealth and told the story of his life, interspersed with anecdotes that would blister the paper they were written on. But through all his ravings, he stuck to his hundred-and-fifty-million-theory, and though the listener dissented from him and the brutal cruelty with which his views were stated, an unscientific impression remained and was not to be shaken off. Across the Border one feels that the country is being used, exploited, "made to sit up" so to speak. In our territories the feeling is equally strong of wealth "just round the corner," as the loafer said, and a people wrapped up in cotton wool and ungetable. Will any man, who really knows something of a little piece of India and has not the fear of running counter to custom before his eyes, explain how this impression is produced, and why it is an erroneous one? This digression has taken us far from the child's pony of Ram Baksh.

Nasirabad marked the end of the Englishman's holiday, and there was sorrow in his heart. "Come back again," said Ram Baksh cheerfully, "and bring a gun with you. Then I'll take you to Gungra, and I'll drive you myself. Drive you just as well as I've driven these four days past." An amicable open-minded soul was Ram Baksh. May his tongas never grow less.

"This 'ere Burma fever is a bad thing to have. It's pulled me down awful; an' now I am going to Peshawar. *Are* you the Station-Master?" It was Thomas—white-cheeked, sunken-eyed, drawn-mouthed Thomas—traveling from Nasirabad to Peshawar on pass; and with him was a Corporal new to his stripes and doing station duty. Every Thomas is interesting, except when he is too drunk to speak. This Thomas was an enthusiast. He had volunteered, from a Home-going regiment shattered by Burma fever, into a regiment at Peshawar, had broken down at Nasirabad on his way up with his draft, and was now journeying into the unknown to pick up another medal. "There's sure to be something on the Frontier," said this gaunt, haggard boy —he was little more, though he reckoned four years' service and considered himself somebody. "When there's anything going, Peshawar's the place to be in, they tell me ; but I hear we shall have to march down to Calcutta in no time. The Corporal was a little man and showed his friend off with great pride : "Ah, you should have come to us," said he ; "we're the regiment, we are." "Well, I went with the rest of our men," said Thomas. "There's three hundred of us volunteered to stay on, and we all went for the same regiment. Not but what I'm saying your's is a good regiment," he added with grave courtesy. This loosed the Corporal's tongue, and he discanted on the virtues of the regiment and the merits of the officers. It has been written that Thomas is devoid of *esprit de corps*, because of the jerkiness of the arrangements under which he now serves. If this be true, he managas to conceal his feelings very well ; for he speaks most fluently in praise of his own regiment ; and, for all his youth, has a keen appreciation of the merits of his officers. Go to him when his heart is opened, and hear him going through the roll of the subalterns, by a grading totally unknown in the *Army List*, and you will pick up something worth the hearing. Thomas, with the Burma fever on him, tried to cut in, from time to time, with stories of his officers and what they had done "when we was marchin' all up and down Burma," but the little Corporal went on gaily.

They made a curious contrast—these two types. The lathy, town-bred Thomas with hock-bottle shoulders, a little education, and a keen desire to get more medals and stripes; and the little, deep-chested, bull-necked Corporal brimming over with vitality and devoid of any ideas beyond the "regiment." And the end of both lives, in all likelihood, would be a nameless grave in some cantonment burying-ground with, if the case were specially interesting and the Regimental Doctor had a turn for the pen, an obituary notice in the *Indian Medical Journal.* It was an unpleasant thought.

From the Army to the Navy is a perfectly natural transition, but one hardly to be expected in the heart of India. Dawn showed the railway carriage full of riotous boys, for the Agra and Mount Abu schools had broken up for holidays. Surely it was natural enough to ask a child—not a boy, but a child—whether he was going home for the holidays; and surely it was a crushing, a petrifying thing, to hear in a clear treble tinged with icy *hauteur*: "No. I'm on leave. I'm a midshipman." Two "officers of Her Majesty's Navy"—mids of a man-o'-war in Bombay—were going Up-country on ten days' leave. They had not travelled much more than twice round the world; but they should have printed the fact on a label. They chattered like daws, and their talk was as a whiff of fresh air from the open sea, while the train ran eastward under the Aravalis. At that hour their lives were bound up in and made glorious by the hope of riding a horse when they reached their journey's end. Much had they seen "cities and men," and the artless way in which they interlarded their conversation with allusions to "one of those shore-going chaps you see" was delicious. They had no cares, no fears, no servants, and an unlimited stock of wonder and admiration for everything they saw, from the "cute little well-scoops" to a herd of deer grazing on the horizon. It was not until they had opened their young hearts with infantile abandon that the listener could guess from the incidental *argot* where these pocket-Ulysseses had travelled. South African, Norweigan, and Arabian words were used to help out the slang of Haslar, and a copious vocabulary of ship-board terms, complicated with modern Greek. As free from self-consciousness as children, as ignorant as beings from another planet of the Anglo-Indian life into which they were going to dip for a few days, shrewd and observant as befits men of the world who have authority, and neat-handed and resourceful as—blue-jackets, they were a delightful study, and accepted freely and frankly the elaborate apologies tendered to them for the unfortunate mistake about the "holidays." The roads divided and they went their way; and there was a shadow after they had gone, for the Globe-Trotter said to his wife: "What I like about Jeypore"—accent on the first syllable, if you please—"is its characteristic earnestness." And the Globe-Trotter's wife said, "Yes. It is purely Oriental."

It is curious what an attraction anything oriental has for a woman. It may only be that they like to utter the word, for there is in it a possible langorous and delicious enunciation from the lips of a pretty woman. Or again, it might be some really mysterious charm in the gorgeous colors and fantastic shapes of Eastern fabrics and carvings. Be this as it may, it is to be observed that the wife of a tourist, returned to her native soil, has always much more to say of the Orient than of any other country or object.

This was Jeypore with the gas-jets and the water-pipes as was shown at the beginning of these trivial letters; and the Globe-Trotter and his wife had not been to Amber. Joyful thought. They had not seen the soft splendors of Udaipur, the night-mare of Chitor, the grim power of Jodhpur and the virgin beauties of Boondi—fairest of all places that the Englishman had set eyes on. The Globe-Trotter was great in the matter of hotels and food, but he had not lain under the shadow of a tonga in soft warm sand, eating cold pork with a pocket-knife, and thanking Providence who put sweet-water streams where wayfarers wanted them. He had not drunk out the brilliant cold-weather night in the company of a King of loafers, a grimy scallawag with a six days' beard and an unholy knowledge of native States. He had attended service in cantonment churches; but he had not known what it was to witness the simple, solemn ceremonial in the dining-room of a far-away Residency, when all the English folk within a hundred-mile circuit bowed their heads before the God of the Christians. He had blundered about temples of strange deities with a guide at his elbow; but he had not known what it was to attempt conversation with a temple dancing-girl (*not* such an one as Edwin Arnold invented), and to be rewarded for a misturned compliment with a deftly heaved bunch of marigold buds on his respectable bosom. Yes he had undoubtedly lost much, and the measure of his loss was proven in his estimate of the Orientalism of Jeypore.

But what had he who sat in judgment upon him gained? One perfect month of loaferdom, to be remembered above all others and the night of the visit to Chitor, to be remembered even when the month is forgotten. Also the sad knowledge that of all the fair things seen, the inept pen gives but a feeble and blurred picture.

Let those who have read to the end, pardon a hundred blemishes.

END OF PART ONE.

PART SECOND.

CHAPTER I.

A REAL LIVE CITY.

We are all backwoodsmen and barbarians together —we others dwelling beyond the Ditch, in the outer darkness of the Mofussil. There are no such things as commissioners and heads of departments in the world, and there is only one city in India. Bombay is too green, too pretty and too stragglesome ; and Madras died ever so long ago. Let us take off our hats to Calcutta, the many-sided the smoky, the magnificent, as we drive in over the Hugli Bridge in the dawn of a still February morning. We have left India behind us at Howrah Station, and now we enter foreign parts. No, not wholly foreign. Say rather too familiar.

All men of certain age know the feeling of caged irritation—an illustration in the *Graphic*, a bar of music of the light words of a friend from home may set it ablaze—that comes from the knowledge of our lost heritage of London. At home they, the other men, our equals, have at their disposal all that town can supply—the roar of the streets, the lights, the music, the pleasant places, the millions of their own kind, and a wilderness full of pretty, fresh-colored Englishwomen, theatres and restaurants. It is their right. They accept it as such, and even affect to look upon it with contempt. And we, we have nothing except the few amusements that we painfully build up for ourselves—the dolorous dissipations of gymkhanas where everyone knows everybody else, or the chastened intoxication of dances where all engagements are booked, in ink, ten days ahead, and where everybody's antecedents are as patent as his or her method of waltzing. We have been deprived of our inheritance. The men at home are enjoying it all, not knowing how fair and rich it is, and we at the most can only fly westward for a few months and gorge what, properly speaking, should take seven or eight or ten luxurious years. That is the lost heritage of London; and the knowledge of the forfeiture, willful or forced, comes to most men at times and seasons, and they get cross.

Calcutta holds out false hopes of some return. The dense smoke hangs low, in the chill of the morning, over an ocean of roofs, and, as the city wakes, there goes up to the smoke a deep, full-throated boom of life and motion and humanity. For this reason does he who sees Calcutta for the first time hang joyously out of the *ticca-gharri* and sniff the smoke, and turn his face towards the tumult, saying: "This is, at last, some portion of my heritage returned to me. This is a city. There is life here, and there should be all manner of pleasant things for the having, across the river and under the smoke." When Leland, he who wrote the Hans Breitmann Ballads, once desired to know the name of an austere, plug-hatted redskin of repute, his answer, from the lips of a half-bred, was :

"He Injun. He big Injun. He heap big Injun. He dam big heap Injun. He dam mighty great big heap Injun. He Jones!" The litany is an expressive one, and exactly describes the first emotions of a wandering savage adrift in Calcutta. The eye has lost its sense of proportion, the focus has contracted through overmuch residence in up-country stations —twenty minutes' canter from hospital to parade-ground, you know—and the mind has shrunk with the eye. Both say together, as they take in the sweep of shipping above and below the Hugli Bridge : "Why, this is London! This is the docks. This is Imperial. This is worth coming across India to see!"

Then a distinctly wicked idea takes possession of the mind : "What a divine—what a heavenly place to *loot!*" This gives place to a much worse devil—that of Conservatism. It seems not only a wrong but a criminal thing to allow natives to have any voice in the control of such a city—adorned, docked, wharfed, fronted and reclaimed by Englishmen, existing only because England lives, and dependent for its life on England. All India knows of the Calcutta Municipality ; but has anyone thoroughly investigated the Big Calcutta Stink? There is only one. Benares is fouler in point of concentrated, pent-up muck, and there are local stenches in Peshawur which are stronger than the B. C. S.; but, for diffused, soul-sickening expansiveness, the reek of Calcutta beats both Benares and Peshawur. Bombay cloaks her stenches with a veneer of assafœtida and *huqa*-tobacco; Calcutta is above pretence. There is no tracing back the Calcutta plague to any one source. It is faint, it is sickly, and it is indescribable; but Americans at the Great Eastern Hotel say that it is something like the smell of the Chinese quarter in San Francisco. It is certainly not an Indian smell. It resembles the essence of corruption that has rotted for the second time—the clammy odor of blue slime. And there is no escape from it. It blows across the *maidan;* it comes in gusts into the corridors of the Great Eastern Hotel; what they are pleased to call the "Palaces of Chouringhi" carry it; it swirls round the Bengal Club; it pours out of bye-streets with sickening intensity, and the breeze of the morning is laden with it. It is first found, in spite of the fume of the engines, in Howrah Station. It seems to be worst in the little lanes at the back of Lal Bazar where the drinking-shops are, but it is nearly as bad opposite Government House and in the Public Offices. The thing is intermittent. Six moderately pure mouthfuls of air may be drawn without offence. Then comes the seventh wave and the queasiness of an uncultured stomach. If you live long enough in Calcutta you grow used to it. The regular residents admit the disgrace, but their answer is: "Wait till the wind blows off the Salt Lakes where all the sewage goes, and *then* you'll smell something." That is their defence! Small wonder that they consider Calcutta is a fit place for a permanent Viceroy. Englishmen who can calmly extenuate one shame by another are capable of asking for anything—and expecting to get it.

If an up-country station holding three thousand troops and twenty civilians owned such a possession as Calcutta does, the Deputy Commissioner or the Cantonment Magistrate would have all the natives off the board of management or decently shovelled into the background until the mess was abated. Then they might come on again and talk of "high-handed oppression" as much as they liked. That stink, to an unprejudiced nose, damns Calcutta as a City of Kings. And, in spite of that stink, they allow, they even encourage, natives to look after the place! The damp, drainage-soaked soil is sick with the teeming life of a hundred years, and the Municipal Board list is choked with the names of natives—men of the breed born in and raised off this surfeited muck-heap! They own property, these amiable Aryans on the Municipal and the Bengal Legislative Council. Launch a proposal to tax them on that property, and they naturally howl. They also howl up-country, but there the halls for mass-meetings are few, and the vernacular papers fewer, and with a *zubbardusti* Secretary and a President whose favor is worth the having and whose wrath is undesirable, men are kept clean despite themselves, and may not poison their neighbors. Why, asks a savage, let them vote at all? They can put up with this filthiness. They *cannot* have any feelings worth caring a rush for. Let them live quietly and hide away their money under our protection, while we tax them till they know through their purses the measure of their neglect in the past, and when a little of the smell has been abolished, bring them back again to talk and take the credit of enlightenment. The better classes own their broughams and barouches; the worse can shoulder an Englishman into the kennel and talk to him as though he were a *khidmatgar.* They can refer to an English lady as an *aurat;* they are permitted a freedom—not to put it too coarsely—of speech which, if used by an Englishman towards an Englishman, would end in serious trouble. They are fenced and protected and made inviolate. Surely they might be content with all those things without entering into matters which they cannot, by the nature of their birth, understand.

Now, whether all this genial diatribe be the outcome of an unbiased mind or the result first of sickness caused by that ferocious stench, and secondly of headache due to day-long smoking to drown the stench, is an open question. Anyway, Calcutta is a fearsome place for a man not educated up to it.

A word of advice to other barbarians. Do not bring a north-country servant into Calcutta. He is sure to get into trouble, because he does not understand the customs of the city. A Punjabi in this place for the first time esteems it his bounden duty to go to the *Ajaib-ghar*—the Museum. Such an one has gone and is even now returned very angry and troubled in the spirit. "I went to the Museum," says he, "and no one gave me any *gali.* I went to the market to buy my food, and then I sat upon a seat. There came a *chaprissi* who said: 'Go away, I want to sit here.' I said: 'I am here first.' He said: 'I am a *chaprissi! nikal jao!*' and he hit me, Now that sitting-place was open to all, so I hit him till he wept. He ran away for the Police, and I went away too, for the Police here are all *Sahibs.* Can I have leave from two o'clock to go and look for that *chaprissi* and hit him again?"

Behold the situation! An unknown city full of smell that makes one long for rest and retirement, and a champing *naukar*, not yet six hours in the stew, who has started a blood-feud with an unknown *chaprissi* and clamors to go forth to the fray. General orders that, whatever may be said or done to him, he must not say or do anything in return lead to an eloquent harangue on the quality of *izzat* and the nature of "face blackening." There is no *izzat* in Calcutta, and this Awful Smell blackens the face of any Englishman who sniffs it.

Alas! for the lost delusion of the heritage that was to be restored. Let us sleep, let us sleep, and pray that Calcutta may be better to-morrow.

At present it is remarkably like sleeping with a corpse.

CHAPTER II.

THE REFLECTIONS OF A SAVAGE.

Morning brings counsel. *Does* Calcutta smell so pestiferously after all? Heavy rain has fallen in the night. She is newly-washed, and the clear sunlight shows her at her best. Where, oh where, in all this wilderness of life shall a man go? Newman and Co. publish a three-rupee guide which produces first despair and then fear in the mind of the reader. Let us drop Newman and Co. out of the topmost window of the Great Eastern, trusting to luck and the flight of the hours to evolve wonders and mysteries and amusements.

The Great Eastern hums with life through all its hundred rooms. Doors slam merrily, and all the nations of the earth run up and down the staircases. This alone is refreshing, because the passers bump you and ask you to stand aside. Fancy finding any place outside a Levée-room where Englishmen are crowded together to this extent! Fancy sitting down seventy strong to *tâble d'hôte* and with a deafening clatter of knives and forks! Fancy finding a real bar whence drinks may be obtained! and, joy of joys, fancy stepping out of the hotel into the arms of a live, white, helmeted, buttoned, truncheoned Bobby! A beautiful, burly Bobby—just the sort of man who, seven thousand miles away, staves off the stuttering witticism of the three-o'clock-in-the-morning reveller by the strong badged arm of authority. What would happen if one spoke to this Bobby? Would he be offended? He is not offended. He is affable. He has to patrol the pavement in front of the Great Eastern and to see that the crowding *ticca-gharris* do not jam. Towards a presumably respectable white he behaves as a man and a brother. There is no arrogance about him. And this is disappointing. Closer inspection shows that he is not a *real* Bobby after all. He is a Municipal Police something and his uniform is not correct; at least if they have not changed the dress of the men at home. But no matter. Later on we will inquire into the Calcutta Bobby, because he is a white man, and has to deal with some of the "toughest" folk that ever set out of malice aforethought to paint Job Charnock's city vermillion. You must not, you cannot cross Old Court House Street without looking carefully to see that you stand no chance of being run over. This is beautiful. There is a steady roar of traffic, cut every two minutes by the deeper roll of the trams. The driving is eccentric, not to say bad, but there is the traffic—more than unsophisticated eyes have beheld for a certain number of years. It means business, it means money-making, it means crowded and hurrying life, and it gets into the blood and makes it move. Here be big shops with plate-glass fronts—all displaying the well-known names of firms that we savages only correspond with through the V. P. P. and Parcels Post. They are all here, as large as life, ready to supply anything you need if you only care to sign. Great is the fascination of being able to obtain a thing on the spot without having to write for a week and wait for a month, and then get something quite different. No wonder pretty ladies, who live anywhere within a reasonable distance, come down to do their shopping personally.

"Look here. If you want to be respectable you musn't smoke in the streets. Nobody does it." This is advice kindly tendered by a friend in a black coat. There is no Levée or Lieutenant-Governor in sight; but he wears the frock-coat because it is daylight, and he can be seen. He also refrains from smoking for the same reason. He admits that Providence built the open air to be smoked in, but he says that "it isn't the thing." This man has a brougham, a remarkably natty little pill-box with a curious wabble about the wheels. He steps into the brougham and puts on—a top hat, a shiny black "plug."

There was a man up-country once who owned a top-hat. He leased it to amateur theatrical companies for some seasons until the nap wore off. Then he threw it into a tree and wild bees hived in it. Men were wont to come and look at the hat, in its palmy days, for the sake of feeling homesick. It interested all the station, and died with two seers of *babul* flower honey in its bosom. But top-hats are not intended to be worn in India. They are as sacred as home letters and old rose-buds. The friend cannot see this. He allows that if he stepped out of his brougham and walked about in the sunshine for ten minutes he would get a bad headache. In half-an-hour he would probably catch sunstroke. He allows all this, but he keeps to his hat and cannot see why a barbarian is moved to inextinguishable laughter at the sight. Everyone who owns a brougham and many people who hire *ticca gharris* keep top-hats and black frock-coats. The effect is curious, and at first fills the beholder with surprise.

And now, "let us see the handsome houses where the wealthy nobles dwell." Northerly lies the great human jungle of the native city, stretching from Burra Bazar to Chitpore. That can keep. Southerly is the *maidan* and Chouringhi. "If you get out into the centre of the *maidan* you will understand why Calcutta is called the City of Palaces." The travelled American said so at the Great Eastern. There is a short tower, falsely called a "memorial," standing in a waste of soft, sour green. That is as good a place to get to as any other. Near here the newly-landed waler is taught the whole duty of the trap-horse and careers madly in a brake. Near here young Calcutta gets upon a horse and is incontinently run away with. Near here hundreds of kine feed, close to the innumerable trams and the whirl of traffic along the face of Chouringhi Road. The size of the *maidan* takes the heart out of anyone accustomed to the "gardens" of up-country, just as they say Newmarket Heath cows a horse accustomed to more shut-in course. The huge level is studded with brazen statues of eminent gentlemen riding fretful horses on diabolically severe curbs. The expanse dwarfs the statues, dwarfs everything except the frontage of the far-away Chouringhi Road. It is big—it is impressive. There is no escaping the fact.

They built houses in the old days when the rupee was two shillings and a penny. Those houses are three-storied, and ornamented with service-staircases like houses in the Hills. They are also very close together, and they own garden walls of *pukka*-masonry pierced with a single gate. In their shutupness they are British. In their spaciousness they are Oriental, but those service-staircases do not look healthy. We will form an amateur sanitary commission and call upon Chouringhi.

A first introduction to the Calcutta *durwan* is not nice. If he is chewing *pan*, he does not take the trouble to get rid of his quid. If he is sitting on his *charpoy* chewing sugarcane, he does not think it worth his while to rise. He has to be taught those things, and he cannot understand why he should be reproved. Clearly he is a survival of a played-out system. Providence never intended that any native should be made a *concierge* more insolent than any of the French variety. The people of Calcutta put an Uria in a little lodge close to the gate of their house, in order that loafers may be turned away, and the houses protected from theft. The natural result is that the *durwan* treats everybody whom he does not know as a loafer, has an intimate and vendible knowledge of all the outgoings and incomings in that house, and controls, to a large extent, the nomination of the *naukar-log*. They say that one of the estimable class is now suing a bank for about three lakhs of rupees. Up-country, a Lieutenant-Governor's *charprassi* has to work for thirty years before he can retire on seventy thousand rupees of savings.

The Calcutta *durwan* is a great institution. The head and front of his offence is that he will insist upon trying to talk English. How he protects the houses Calcutta only knows. He can be frightened out of his wits by severe speech, and is generally asleep in calling hours. If a rough round of visits be any guide, three times out of seven he is fragrant of drink. So much for the *durwan*. Now for the houses he guards.

Very pleasant is the sensation of being ushered into a pestiferously stablesome drawing-room. "Does this always happen?" "No, not unless you shut up the room for some time; but if you open the *jhilmills* there are other smells. You see the stables and the servants' quarters are close too." People pay five hundred a month for half-a-dozen rooms filled with *attr* of this kind. They make no complaint. When they think the honor of the city is at stake they say defiantly: "Yes, but you must remember we're a metropolis. We are crowded here. We have no room. We aren't like your little stations." Chouringhi is a stately place full of sumptuous houses, but it is best to look at it hastily. Stop to consider for a moment what the cramped compounds, the black soaked soil, the netted intricacies, of the service-staircases, the packed stables, the seethment of human life round the *durwans'* lodges and the curious arrangement of little open drains means, and you will call it a whited sepulchre.

Men living in expensive tenements suffer from chronic sore-throat, and will tell you cheerily that "we've got typhoid in Calcutta now." Is the pest ever out of it? Everything seems to be built with a view to its comfort. It can lodge comfortably on roofs, climb along from the gutter-pipe to piazza, or rise from sink to verandah and thence to the topmost story. But Calcutta says that all is sound and produces figures to prove it; at the same time admitting that healthy cut flesh will not readily heal. Further evidence may be dispensed with.

Here come pouring down Park Street on the *maidan* a rush of broughams, neat buggies, the lightest of gigs, trim office brownberrys, shining victorias, and a sprinkling of veritable hansom cabs. In the broughams sit men in top-hats. In the other carts, young men, all very much alike, and all immaculately turned out. A fresh stream from Chouringhi joins the Park Street detachment, and the two together stream away across the *maidan* towards the business quarter of the city. This is Calcutta going to office —the civilians to the Government Buildings and the young men to their firms and their blocks and their wharves. Here one sees that Calcutta has the best turn-out in the Empire. Horses and traps alike are enviably perfect, and—mark the touchstone of civilization—*the lamps are in the sockets.* This is distinctly refreshing. Once more we will take off our hats to Calcutta, the well-appointed, the luxurious. The country-bred is a rare beast here; his place is taken by the waler, and the waler, though a ruffian at heart, can be made to look like a gentleman. It would be indecorous as well as insane to applaud the winking harness, the perfectly lacquered panels, and the liveried *saises*. They show well in the outwardly fair roads shadowed by the Palaces.

How many sections of the complex society of the place do the carts carry? *Imprimis*, the Bengal Civilian who goes to Writers' Buildings and sits in a perfect office and speaks flippantly of "sending things into India," meaning thereby the Supreme Government. He is a great person, and his mouth is full of promotion-and-appointment "shop." Generally he is referred to as a "rising man." Calcutta seems full of "rising men." *Secondly*, the Government of India man, who wears a familiar Simla face, rents a flat when he is not up in the Hills, and is rational on the subject of the drawbacks of Calcutta. *Thirdly*, the man of the "firms," the pure non-official who fights under the banner of one of the great houses of the City, or for his own hand in a neat office, or dashes about Clive Street in a brougham doing "share work" or something of the kind. He fears not "Bengal," nor regards he "India." He swears impartially at both when their actions interfere with his operations. His "shop ' is quite unintelligible. He is like the English city man with the chill off, lives well and entertains hospitably. In the old days he was greater than he is now, but still he bulks large. He is rational in so far that he will help the abuse of the Municipality, but womanish in his insistence on the excellencies of Culcutta. Over and above these who are hurrying to work are the various brigades, squads and detachments of the other interests. But they are sets and not sections, and revolve round Belvedere, Government House, and

Fort William. Simla and Darjeeling claim them in the hot weather. Let them go. They wear top-hats and frock-coats.

It is time to escape from Chouringhi Road and get among the long-shore folk, who have no prejudices against tobacco, and who all use pretty nearly the same sort of hat.

CHAPTER III.

THE COUNCIL OF THE GODS.

He set up conclusions to the number of nine thousand seven hundred and sixty four . . . he went afterwards to the Sorbonne, where he maintained argument against the theologians for the space of six weeks, from four o'clock in the morning till six in the evening, except for an interval of two hours to refresh themselves and take their repasts, and at this were present the greatest part of the lords of the court the masters of request, presidents, counsellors, those of the accompts, secretaries, advocates, and others; as also the sheriffs of the said town.—*Pantagruel.*

"The Bengal Legislative Council is sitting now. You will find it in an octagonal wing of Writers' Buildings: straight across the *maidan.* It's worth seeing." "What are they sitting on?" "Municipal business. No end of a debate." So much for trying to keep low company. The long-shore loafers must stand over. Without doubt this Council is going to hang some one for the state of the City, and Sir Steuart Bayley will be chief executioner. One does not come across Councils every day.

Writers' Buildings are large. You can trouble the busy workers of half-a-dozen departments before you stumble upon the black-stained staircase that leads to an upper chamber looking out over a populous street. Wild *chuprassis* block the way. The Councillor Sahibs are sitting, but anyone can enter. "To the right of the Lât Sahib's chair, and go quietly." Ill-mannered minion! Does he expect the awe-stricken spectator to prance in with a jubilant war-whoop or turn Catherine-wheels round that sumptuous octagonal room with the blue-domed roof? There are gilt capitals to the half pillars and an Egyptian patterned lotus-stencil makes the walls decorously gay. A thick piled carpet covers all the floor, and must be delightful in the hot weather. On a black wooden throne, comfortably cushioned in green leather, sits Sir Steuart Bayley, Ruler of Bengal. The rest are all great men, or else they would not be there. Not to know them argues oneself unknown. There are a dozen of them, and sit six aside at two slightly curved lines of beautifully polished desks. Thus Sir Steuart Bayley occupies the frog of a badly made horse-shoe split at the toe. In front of him, at a table covered with books and pamphlets and papers, toils a secretary. There is a seat for the Reporters, and that is all. The place enjoys a chastened gloom, and its very atmosphere fills one with awe. This is the heart of Bengal, and uncommonly well upholstered. If the work matches the first-class furniture, the inkpots, the carpet, and the resplendent ceiling, there will be something worth seeing. But where is the criminal who is to be hanged for the stench that runs up and down Writers' Buildings staircases, for the rubbish heaps in the Chitpore Road, for the sickly savor of Chouringhi, for the dirty little tanks at the back of Belvedere, for the street full of small-pox, for the reeking gharri-stand outside the Great Eastern, for the state of the stone and dirt pavements, for the condition of the gullies of Shampooker, and for a hundred other things?

"This, I submit, is an artificial scheme in supersession of Nature's unit, the individual." The speaker is a slight, spare native in a flat hat-turban, and a black alpaca frock-coat. He looks like a *vakil* to the boot-heels, and, with his unvarying smile and regulated gesticulation, recalls memories of up-country courts. He never hesitates, is never at a loss for a word, and never in one sentence repeats himself. He talks and talks and talks in a level voice, rising occasionally half an octave when a point has to be driven home. Some of his periods sound very familiar. This, for instance, might be a sentence from the *Mirror:* "So much for the principle. Let us now examine how far it is supported by precedent." This sounds bad. When a fluent native is discoursing of "principles" and "precedents," the chances are that he will go on for some time. Moreover, where is the criminal, and what is all this talk about abstractions? They want shovels not sentiments, in this part of the world.

A friendly whisper brings enlightenment: "They are plowing through the Calcutta Municipal Bill—plurality of votes you know; here are the papers." And so it is! A mass of motions and amendments on matters relating to ward votes. Is *A* to be allowed to give two votes in one ward and one in another? Is section 10 to be omitted, and is one man to be allowed one vote and no more? How many votes does three hundred rupees' worth of landed property carry? Is it better to kiss a post or throw it in the fire? Not a word about carbolic acid and gangs of *domes*. The little man in the black *choga* revels in his subject. He is great on principles and precedents, and the necessity of "popularizing our system." He fears that under certain circumstances "the status of the candidates will decline." He riots in "self-adjusting majorities," and the healthy influence of the educated middle classes."

For a practical answer to this, there steals across the council chamber just one faint whiff. It is as though some one laughed low and bitterly. But no man heeds. The Englishmen look supremely bored, the native members stare stolidly in front of them. Sir Steuart Bayley's face is as set as the face of the Sphinx. For these things he draws his pay, and his is a low wage for heavy labor. But the speaker, now adrift, is not altogether to be blamed. He is a Bengali, who has got before him just such a subject as his soul loveth—an elaborate piece of academical reform leading no-whither. Here is a quiet room full of pens and papers, and there are men who must listen to him. Apparently there is no time limit to the speeches. Can you wonder that he talks? He says "I submit" once every ninety seconds, varying the form with "I do submit." The popular element in the electoral body should have prominence." Quite so. He quotes one John Stuart Mill to prove it. There steals over the listener a numbing sense of nightmare. He has heard all this before somewhere—yea; even down to J. S. Mill and the references to the "true interests of the ratepayers." He sees what is coming next. Yes, there is the old Sabha Anjuman journalistic formula—"Western education is an exotic plant of recent importation." How on earth did this man drag Western education into this discussion? Who knows? Perhaps Sir Steuart Bayley does. He seems to be listening. The others are looking at their watches. The spell of the level voice sinks the listener yet deeper into a trance. He is haunted by the ghosts of all the cant of all the political platforms of Great Britain. He hears all the old, old vestry phrases, and once more he smells the smell. *That* is no dream. Western education is an exotic plant. It is the upas tree, and it is all our fault. We brought it out from England exactly as we brought out the ink bottles and the patterns for the chairs. We planted it and it grew—monstrous as a banian. Now we are choked by the roots of it spreading so thickly in this fat soil of Bengal. The speaker continues. Bit by bit. We builded this dome, visible and invisible, the crown of Writers' Buildings, as we have built and peopled the buildings. Now we have gone too far to retreat, being "tied and bound with the chain of our own sins." The speech continues. We made that florid sentence. That torrent of verbiage is ours. We taught him what was constitutional and what was unconstitutional in the days when Calcutta smelt. Calcutta smells still, but we must listen to all that he has to say about the plurality of votes and the threshing of wind and the weaving of ropes of sand. It is our own fault absolutely.

The speech ends, and there rises a grey Englishman in a black frock-coat. He looks a strong man, and a worldly. Surely he will say: "Yes, Lala Sahib, all this may be true talk, but there's a *burra krab* smell in this place, and everything must be *saf karoed* in a week, or the Deputy Commissioner will not take any notice of you in *durbar*." He says nothing of the kind. This is a Legislative Council, where they call each other "Honorable So-and-So's." The Englishman in the frock-coat begs all to remember that "we are discussing principles, and no consideration of the details ought to influence the verdict on the principles." Is he then like the rest? How does this strange thing come about? Perhaps these so English office fittings are responsible for the warp. The Council Chamber might be a London Board-room. Perhaps after long years among the pens and papers its occupants grow to think that it really is, and in this belief give *résumés* of the history of Local Self-Government in England.

The black frock-coat, emphasizing his points with his spectacle-case, is telling his friends how the parish was first the unit of self-government. He then explains how burgesses were elected, and in tones of deep fervor announces: "Commissioners of Sewers are elected in the same way." Whereunto all this lecture? Is he trying to run a motion through under cover of a cloud of words, essaying the well-known "cuttle-fish trick" of the West?

He abandons England for a while, and *now* we get a glimpse of the cloven hoof in a casual reference to Hindus and Mahomedans. The Hindus will lose nothing by the complete establishment of plurality of votes. They will have the control of their own wards as they used to have. So there is race-feeling, to be explained away, even among these beautiful desks. Scratch the Council, and you come to the old, old trouble. The black frock-coat sits down, and a keen-eyed, black-bearded Englishman rises with one hand in his pocket to explain his views on an alteration of the vote qualification. The idea of an amendment seems to have just struck him. He hints that he will bring it forward later on. He is academical like the others, but not half so good a speaker. All this is dreary beyond words. Why do they talk and talk about owners and occupiers and burgesses in England and the growth of autonomous institutions when the city, the great city, is here crying out to be cleansed? What has England to do with Calcutta's evil, and why should Englishmen be forced to wander through mazes of unprofitable argument against men who cannot understand the iniquity of dirt?

A pause follows the black-bearded man's speech. Rises another native, a heavily-built Babu, in a black gown and a strange head-dress. A snowy white strip of cloth is thrown *jharun*-wise over his shoulders. His voice is high, and not always under control. He begins: "I will try to be as brief as possible." This is ominous. By the way, in Council there seems to be no necessity for a form of address. The orators plunge in *medias res*, and only when they are well launched throw an occasional "Sir" towards Sir Steuart Bayley, who sits with one leg doubled under him and a dry pen in his hand. This speaker is no good. He talks, but he says nothing, and he only knows where he is drifting to. He says: "We must remember that we are legislating for the Metropolis of India, and therefore we should borrow our institutions from large English towns, and not from parochial institutions." If you think for a minute, that shows a large and healthy knowledge of the history of Local Self-Government. It also reveals the attitude of Calcutta. If the city thought less about itself as a metropolis and more as a midden, its state would be better. The speaker talks patronizingly of "my friend," alluding to the black frock-coat. Then he flounders afresh, and his voice gallops up the gamut as he declares, "and therefore that makes all the difference." He hints vaguely at threats, something to do with the Hindus and the Mahomedans, but what he means it is difficult to discover. Here, however, is a sentence taken *verbatim*. It is not likely to appear in this form in the Calcutta papers. The black frock-coat had said that if a wealthy native "had eight votes to his credit, his vanity would prompt him to go to the polling-booth, because he would feel better than half-a-dozen *gharri-wans* or petty traders." (Fancy allowing a *gharri-wan* to vote! He has yet to learn how to drive!) Hereon the gentleman with the white cloth: "Then the complaint is that influential voters will not take the trouble to vote. In my humble opinion, if that be so, adopt voting papers. *That* is the way to meet them. In the same way—The Calcutta Trades' Association—you abolish all plurality of votes: and that is the way to meet *them.*" Lucid, is it not? Up flies the irresponsible voice, and delivers this statement: "In the election for the House of Commons plurality are allowed for persons having interest in different districts." Then hopeless, hopeless fog. It is a great pity that India ever heard of anybody higher than the heads of the Civil Service. The country appeals from the *Chota* to the *Burra Sahib* all too readily as it is. Once more a whiff. The gentleman gives a defiant jerk of his shoulder-cloth, and sits down.

Then Sir Steuart Bayley: "The question before the Council is," etc. There is a ripple of "Ayes" and "Noes," and the "Noes" have it, whatever it may be. The black-bearded gentleman springs his amendment about the voting qualifications. A large senator in a white waistcoat, and with a most genial smile, rises and proceeds to smash up the amendment. Can't see the use of it. Calls it in effect rubbish. The black frock-coat rises to explain his friend's amendment, and incidentally makes a funny little slip. He is a knight, and his friend has been newly knighted. He refers to him as "Mister." The black *choga*, he who spoke first of all, speaks again, and talks of the "*sojorner* who comes here for a little time, and then leaves the land." Well it is for the black *choga* that the sojourner does come, or there would be no comfy places wherein to talk about the power that can be measured by wealth and the intellect "which, sir, I submit, cannot be so measured." The amendment is lost, and trebly and quadruply lost is the listener. In the name of sanity and to preserve the tattered shirt tails of a torn illusion, let us escape. This is the Calcutta Municipal Bill. They have been at it for several Saturdays. Last Saturday Sir Steuart Bayley pointed out that at their present rate they would be about two years in getting it through. Now they will sit till dusk, unless Sir Steuart Bayley, who wants to see Lord Connemara off, puts up the black frock-coat to move an adjournment. It is not good to see a Government close to. This leads to the formation of blatantly self-satisfied judgments, which may be quite as wrong as the cramping system with which we have encompassed ourselves. And in the streets outside Englishmen summarize the situation brutally, thus: "The whole thing is a farce. Time is money to us. We can't stick out those everlasting speeches in the municipality. The natives choke us off, but we know that if things get too bad the Government will step in and interfere, and so we worry along somehow." Meantime Calcutta continues to cry out for the bucket and the broom.

CHAPTER IV.

ON THE BANKS OF THE HUGLI.

The clocks of the city have struck two. Where can a man get food? Calcutta is not rich in respect of dainty accommodation. You can stayyour stomach at Peliti's or Bonsard's, but their shops are not to be found in Hasting Street, or in the places where brokers fly to and fro in office-jauns, sweating and growing visibly *rich*. There must be some sort of entertainment where sailors congregate. "Honest Bombay Jack" supplies nothing but Burma cheroots and whisky in liqueur-glasses, but in Lal Bazar, not far from "The Sailors' Coffee-rooms," a board gives bold advertisement that "officers and seamen can find good quarters." In evidence a row of neat officers and seamen are sitting on a bench by the "hotel" door smoking. There is an almost military likeness in their clothes. Perhaps "Honest Bombay Jack" only keeps one kind of felt hat and one brand of suit. When Jack of the mercantile marine is sober, he is very sober. When he is drunk he is—but ask the river police what a lean, mad Yankee can do with his nails and teeth. These gentlemen smoking on the bench are impassive almost as Red Indians. Their attitudes are unrestrained, and they do not wear braces. Nor, it would appear from the bill of fare, are they particular as to what they eat when they attend *tâble d'hôte*. The fare is substantial and the regulation peg—every house has its own depth of peg if you will refrain from stopping Ganymede—something to wonder at. Three fingers and a trifle over seems to be the use of the officers and seamen who are talking so quietly in the doorway. One says—he has evidently finished a long story—"and so he shipped for four pound ten with a first mate's certificate and all, and that was in a German barque." Another spits with conviction and says genially, without raising his voice: "That was a hell of a ship; who knows her?" No answer from the *panchayet*, but a Dane or a German wants to know whether the *Myra* is "up" yet. A dry, red-haired man gives her exact position in the river—(How in the world can he know?)—and the probable hour of her arrival. The grave debate drifts into a discussion of a recent river accident, whereby a big steamer was damaged, and had to put back and discharge cargo. A burly gentleman who is taking a constitutional down Lal Bazar strolls up and says: "I tell you she fouled her own chain with her own forefoot. Hev you seen the plates?" "No." "Then how the —— can any —— like you —— say what it ——well was?" He passes on, having delivered his highly-flavored opinion without heat or passion. No one seems to resent the expletives.

Let us get down to the river and see this stamp of men more thoroughly. Clarke Russell has told us that their lives are hard enough in all conscience. What are their pleasures and diversions? The Port Office, where lives the gentlemen who make improvements in the Port of Calcutta, ought to supply information. It stands large and fair, and built in an orientalized manner after the Italians at the corner of Fairlie Place upon the great Strand Road, and a continual clamor of traffic by land and by sea goes up throughout the day and far into the night against its windows. This is a place to enter more reverently than the Bengal Legislative Council, for it houses the direction of the uncertain Hugli down to the Sandheads, owns enormous wealth, and spends huge sums on the frontaging of river banks, the expansion of jetties, and the manufacture of docks costing two hundred lakhs of rupees. Two million tons of sea-going shippage yearly find their way up and down the river by the guidance of the Port Office, and the men of the Port Office know more than it is good for men to hold in their heads. They can without reference to telegraphic bulletins give the position of all the big steamers, coming up or going down, from the Hugli to the sea, day by day with their tonnage, the names of their captains and the nature of their cargo. Looking out from the verandah of their officer over a lancer-regiment of masts, they can declare truthfully the name of every ship within eye-scope, with the day and hour when she will depart.

In a room at the bottom of the building lounge big men, carefully dressed. Now there is a type of face which belongs almost exclusively to Bengal Cavalry officers—majors for choice. Everybody knows the bronzed, black-moustached, clear-speaking Native Cavalry officer. He exists unnaturally in novels, and naturally on the frontier. These men in the big room have its caste of face so strongly marked that one marvels what officers are doing by the river. "Have they come to book passengers for home?" "Those men! They're pilots. Some of them draw between two and three thousand rupees a month. They are responsible for half-a-million pounds' worth of cargo sometimes." They certainly are men, and they carry themselves as such. They confer together by twos and threes, and appeal frequently to shipping lists.

"*Isn't* a pilot a man who always wears a pea-jacket and shouts through a speaking-trumpet?" "Well, you can ask those gentlemen if you like. You've got your notions from home pilots. Ours aren't that kind exactly. They are a picked service, as carefully weeded as the Indian Civil. Some of 'em have brothers in it, and some belong to the old Indian army families." But they are not all equally well paid. The Calcutta papers sometimes echo the groans of the junior pilots who are not allowed the handling of ships over a certain tonnage. As it is yearly growing cheaper to build one big steamer than two little ones, these juniors are crowded out, and, while the seniors get their thousands, some of the youngsters make at the end of one month exactly thirty rupees. This is a grievance with them; and it seems well-founded.

In the flats above the pilots' room are hushed and chapel-like offices, all sumptuously fitted, where Englishmen write and telephone and telegraph, and deft Babus for ever draw maps of the shifting Hugli,

Any hope of understanding the work of the Port Commissioners is thoroughly dashed by being taken through the Port maps of a quarter of a century past. Men have played with the Hugli as children play with a gutter-runnel, and, in return, the Hugli once rose and played with men and ships till the Strand Road was littered with the raffle and the carcasses of big ships. There are photos on the walls of the cyclone of '64, when the *Thunder* came inland and sat upon an American barque, obstructing all the traffic. Very curious are these photos, and almost impossible to believe. How can a big, strong steamer have her three masts razed to deck level? How can a heavy, country boat be pitched on to the poop of a high-walled liner? and how can the side be bodily torn out of a ship? The photos say that all these things are possible, and men aver that a cyclone may come again and scatter the craft like chaff. Outside the Port Office are the export and import sheds, buildings that can hold a ship's cargo a-piece, all standing on reclaimed ground. Here be several strong smells, a mass of railway lines, and a multitude of men. "Do you see where that trolly is standing, behind the big P. and O. berth? In that place as nearly as may be the *Govindpur* went down about twenty years ago, and began to shift out!" "But that is solid ground." "She sank there, and the next tide made a scour-hole on one side of her. The returning tide knocked her into it. Then the mud made up behind her. Next tide the business was repeated—always the scour-hole in the mud and the filling up behind her. So she rolled and was pushed out and out until she got in the way of the shipping right out yonder, and we had to blow her up. When a ship sinks in mud or quicksand she regularly digs her own grave and wriggles herself into it deeper and deeper till she reaches moderately solid stuff. Then she sticks." Horrible idea, is it not, to go down and down with each tide into the foul Hugli mud?

Close to the Port Offices is the Shipping Office, where the captains engage their crews. The men must produce their discharges from their last ships in the presence of the shipping master, or as they call him—"The Deputy Shipping." He passes them as correct after having satisfied himself that they are not deserters from other ships, and they then sign articles for the voyage. This is the ceremony, beginning with the "dearly beloved" of the crew-hunting captain down to the "amazement" of the identified deserter. There is a dingy building, next door to the Sailors' Home, at whose gate stand the cast-ups of all the seas in all manner of raiment. There are Seedee boys, Bombay *serangs* and Madras fishermen of the salt villages, Malays who insist upon marrying native women grow jealous and run *amok:* Malay-Hindus, Hindu-Malay-whites, Burmese, Burma-whites, Burma-native-whites, Italians with gold earrings and a thirst for gambling, Yankees of all the States, with Mulattoes and pure buck-niggers, red and rough Danes, Cingalese, Cornish boys who seem fresh taken from the plough-tail "corn-stalks from colonial ships where they got four pound ten a month as seamen, tun-bellied Germans, Cockney mates keeping a little aloof from the crowd and talking in knots together, unmistakable "Tommies" who have tumbled into seafaring life by some mistake, cockatoo-tufted Welshmen spitting and swearing like cats, broken-down loafers, grey-headed, penniless, and pitiful, swaggering boys, and very quiet men with gashes and cuts on their faces. It is an ethnological museum where all the specimens are playing comedies and tragedies. The head of it all is the "Deputy Shipping," and he sits, supported by an English policeman whose fists are knobby, in a great Chair of State. The "Deputy Shipping" knows all the iniquity of the river-side, all the ships, all the captains, and a fair amount of the men. He is fenced off from the crowd by a strong wooden railing, behind which are gathered those who "stand and wait," the unemployed of the mercantile marine. They have had their spree—poor devils—and now they will go to sea again on as low a wage as three pound ten a month, to fetch up at the end in some Shanghai stew or San Francisco hell. They have turned their backs on the seductions of the Howrah boarding-houses and the delights of Colootolla. If Fate will, "Nightingales" will know them no more for a season, and their successors may paint Collinga Bazar vermilion. But what captain will take some of these battered, shattered wrecks whose hands shake and whose eyes are red?

Enter suddenly a bearded captain, who has made his selection from the crowd on a previous day, and now wants to get his men passed. He is not fastidious in his choice. His eleven seem a tough lot for such a mild-eyed, civil-spoken man to manage. But the captain in the Shipping Office and the captain on the ship are two different things. He brings his crew up to the "Deputy Shipping's" bar, and hands in their greasy, tattered discharges. But the heart of the "Deputy Shipping" is hot within him, because, two days ago, a Howrah crimp stole a whole crew from a down-dropping ship, insomuch that the captain had to come back and whip up a new crew at one o'clock in the day. Evil will it be if the "Deputy Shipping" finds one of these bounty-jumpers in the chosen crew of the *Blenkindoon*, let us say.

The "Deputy Shipping" tells the story with heat. "I didn't know they did such things in Calcutta," says the captain. "Do such things! They'd steal the eye-teeth out of your head there, Captain." He picks up a discharge and calls for Michael Donelly, who is a loose-knit, vicious-looking Irish-American who chews. "Stand up, man, stand up!" Michael Donelly wants to lean against the desk, and the English policeman won't have it. "What was your last ship?" "*Fairy Queen.*" "When did you leave her?" "'Bout 'leven days." "Captain's name?" "Flahy." "That'll do. Next man: Jules Anderson." Jules Anderson is a Dane. His statements tally with the discharge-certificate of the United States, as the Eagle attesteth. He is passed and falls back. Slivey, the Englishman, and David, a huge plum-colored negro who ships as cook are also passed. Then comes Bassompra, a little Italian, who speaks English. "What's your last ship?" "*Ferdinand.*" "No, after that?" "German barque." Bassompra does not look happy. "When did she sail?" About three weeks ago." "What's her name?" "*Haidée.*" "You deserted from her?" "Yes, but she's left port." The "Deputy Shipping" runs rapidly through a shipping-list, throws it down with a bang. "'Twon't do. No German barque *Haidée* here for three months. How do I know you don't belong to the *Jackson's* crew? Cap'ain, I'm afraid you'll have to ship another man. He must stand over. Take the rest away and make 'em sign."

The bead-eyed Bassompra seems to have lost his chance of a voyage, and his case will be inquired into. The captain departs with his men and they sign articles for the voyage, while the "Deputy Shipping" tells strange tales of the sailorman's life. "They'll quit a good ship for the sake of a spree, and catch on again at three pound ten, and by Jove, they'll let their skippers pay 'em at ten rupees to the sovereign—poor beggars! As soon as the money's gone they'll ship, but not before. Everyone under rank of captain engages here. The competition makes first mates ship sometimes for five pounds or as low as four ten a month." (The gentleman in the boarding-house was right, you see.) . "A first mate's wages are seven ten or eight, and foreign captains ship for twelve pounds a month and bring their own small stores—everything, that is to say, except beef, peas, flour, coffee and molasses."

These things are not pleasant to listen to while the hungry-eyed men in the bad clothes lounge and scratch and loaf behind the railing. What comes to them in the end? They die, it seems, though that is not altogether strange. They die at sea in strange and horrible ways; they die, a few of them, in the Kintals, being lost and suffocated in the great sink of Calcutta; they die in strange places by the water-side, and the Hugli takes them away under the mooring chains and the buoys, and casts them up on the sands below, if the River Police have missed the capture. They sail the sea because they must live; and there is no end to their toil. Very, very few find haven of any kind, and the earth, whose ways they do not understand, is cruel to them, when they walk upon it to drink and be merry after the manner of beasts. Jack ashore is a pretty thing when he is in a book or in the blue jacket of the Navy. Mercantile Jack is not so lovely. Later on, we will see where his "sprees" lead him.

CHAPTER V.

WITH THE CALCUTTA POLICE.

> The City was of Night—perchance of Death,
> But certainly of Night."
>
> *The City of Dreadful Night.*

In the beginning, the Police were responsible. They said in a patronizing way that, merely as a matter of convenience, they would prefer to take a wanderer round the great city themselves, sooner than let him contract a broken head on his own account in the slums. They said that there were places and places where a white man, unsupported by the arm of the law, would be robbed and mobbed; and that there were other places where drunken seamen would make it very unpleasant for him. There was a night fixed for the patrol, but apologies were offered beforehand for the comparative insignificance of the tour.

"Come up to the fire look-out in the first place, and then you'll be able to see the city." This was at No. 22, Lal Bazar, which is the headquarters of the Calcutta Police, the centre of the great web of telephone wires where Justice sits all day and all night looking after one million people and a floating population of one hundred thousand. But her work shall be dealt with later on. The fire look-out is a little sentry-box on the top of the three-storied police offices. Here a native watchman waits always, ready to give warning to the brigade below if the smoke rises by day or the flames by night in any ward of the city. From this eyrie, in the warm night, one hears the heart of Calcutta beating. Northward, the city stretches away three long miles, with three more miles of suburbs beyond, to Dum-Dum and Barrackpore. The lamplit dusk on this side is full of noises and shouts and smells. Close to the Police Office, jovial mariners at the sailors' coffee-shop are roaring hymns. Southerly, the city's confused lights give place to the orderly lamp-rows of the *maidan* and Chouringhi, where the respectabilities live and the Police have very little to do. From the east goes up to the sky the clamor of Sealdah, the rumble of the trams, and the voices of all Bow Bazar chaffering and making merry. Westward are the business quarters, hushed now, the lamps of the shipping on the river, and the twinkling lights on the Howrah side. It is a wonderful sight—this Pisgah view of a huge city resting after the labors of the day. "Does the noise of traffic go on all through the hot weather?" "Of course. The hot months are the busiest in the year and money's tightest. You should see the brokers cutting about at that season. Calcutta *can't* stop, my dear sir." "What happens then?" "Nothing happens; the death-rate goes up a little. That's all!" Even in February, the weather would, up-country, be called muggy and stifling, but Calcutta is convinced that it is her cold season. The noises of the city grow perceptibly; it is the night side of Calcutta waking up and going abroad. Jack in the sailors' coffee-shop is singing joyously: "Shall we gather at the River—the beautiful, the beautiful, the River?" What an incongruity there is about his selections. However, that it amuses before it shocks the listeners, is not to be doubted. An Englishman, far from his native land is liable to become careless, and it would be remarkable if he did otherwise in ill-smelling Calcutta. There is a clatter of hoofs in the courtyard below. Some of the Mounted Police have come in from somewhere or other out of the great darkness. A clog-dance of iron hoof follows, and an Englishman's voice is heard soothing an agitated horse who seems to be standing on his hind legs. Some of the Mounted Police are going out into the great darkness. "What's on?" Walk round at Government House. The Reserve men are being formed up below. They're calling the roll." The Reserve men are all English, and big English at that. They form up and tramp out of the courtyard to line Government Place, and see that Mrs. Lollipop's brougham does not get smashed up by Sirdar Chuckerbutty Bahadur's lumbering C-spring barouche with the two raw Walers. Very military men are the Calcutta European Police in their set-up, and he who knows their composition knows some startling stories of gentlemen-rankers and the like. They are, despite the wearing climate they work in and the wearing work they do, as fine five-score of Englishmen as you shall find east of Suez.

Listen for a moment from the fire look-out to the voices of the night, and you will see why they must be so. Two thousand sailors of fifty nationalities are adrift in Calcutta every Sunday, and of these perhaps two hundred are distinctly the worse for liquor. There is a mild row going on, even now, somewhere at the back of Bow Bazar, which at nightfall fills with sailor-men who have a wonderful gift of falling foul of the native population. To keep the Queen's peace is of course only a small portion of Police duty, but it is trying. The burly president of the lock-up for European drunks—Calcutta central lock-up is worth seeing—rejoices in a sprained thumb just now, and has to do his work left-handed in consequence. But his left hand is a marvellously persuasive one, and when on duty his sleeves are turned up to the shoulder that the jovial mariner may see that there is no deception. The president's labors are handicapped in that the road of sin to the lock-up runs through a grimy little garden—the brick paths are worn deep with the tread of many drunken feet—where a man can give a great deal of trouble by sticking his toes into the ground and getting mixed up with the shrubs. "A straight run in" would be much more convenient both for the president and the drunk. Generally speaking—and here Police experience is pretty much the same all over the civilized world—a woman drunk is a good deal worse than a man drunk. She scratches and bites like a Chinaman and swears like several fiends. Strange people may be unearthed in the lock-ups. Here is a perfectly true story, not three weeks old. A visitor, an unofficial one, wandered into the native side of the spacious accommodation provided for those who have gone or done wrong. A wild-eyed Babu rose from the fixed charpoy and said in the best of English: "Good-morning, sir." "*Good*-morning; who are you, and what are you in for?" Then the Babu, in one breath: "I would have you know that I do not go to prison as a criminal but as a reformer. You've read the *Vicar of Wakefield*?" "Ye-es." "Well, *I* am the Vicar of Bengal—at least that's what I call myself." The visitor collapsed. He had not nerve enough to continue the conversation. Then said the voice of the authority: "He's down in connection with a cheating case at Serampore. May be shamming. But he'll be looked to in time."

The best place to hear about the Police is the fire

lookout. From that eyrie one can see how difficult must be the work of control over the great, growling beast of a city. By all means let us abuse the Police, but let us see what the poor wretches have to do with their three thousand natives and one hundred Englishmen. From Howrah and Bally and the other suburbs at least a hundred thousand people come in to Calcutta for the day and leave at night. Also Chandernagore is handy for the fugitive law-breaker, who can enter in the evening and get away before the noon of the next day, having marked his house and broken into it.

"But how can the prevalent offence be housebreaking in a place like this?" "Easily enough. When you've seen a little of the city you'll see. Natives sleep and lie about all over the place, and whole quarters are just so many rabbit-warrens. Wait till you see the Machua Bazar. Well, besides the petty theft and burglary, we have heavy cases of forgery and fraud, that leaves us with our wits pitted against a Bengali's. When a Bengali criminal is working a fraud of the sort he loves, he is *about* the cleverest soul you could wish for. He gives us cases a year long to unravel. Then there are the murders in the low houses—very curious things they are. You'll see the house where Sheikh Babu was murdered presently, and you'll understand. The Burra Bazar and Jora Bagan sections are the two worst ones for heavy cases; but Colootollah is the most aggravating. There's Colootollah over yonder—that patch of darkness beyond the lights. That section is full of tuppenny-ha'penny petty cases, that keep the men up all night and make 'em swear. You'll see Colootollah, and then perhaps you'll understand. Bamun Bustee is the quietest of all, and Lal Bazar and Bow Bazar, as you can see for yourself, are the rowdiest. You've no notion what the natives come to the *thannahs* for. A *naukar* will come in and want a summons against his master for refusing him half-an-hour's *chuti*. I suppose it *does* seem rather revolutionary to an up-country man, but they try to do it here. Now wait a minute, before we go down into the city and see the Fire Brigade turned out. Business is slack with them just now, but you time 'em and see." An order is given, and a bell strikes softly thrice. There is an orderly rush of men, the click of a bolt, a red fire-engine, spitting and swearing with the sparks flying from the furnace, is dragged out of its shelter. A huge brake, which holds supplementary horses, men, and hatchets, follows, and a hose-cart is the third on the list. The men push the heavy things about as though they were pith toys. Five horses appear. Two are shot into the fire-engine, two—monsters these—into the brake, and the fifth, a powerful beast, warranted to trot fourteen miles an hour, backs into the hose-cart shafts. The men clamber up, some one says softly, "All ready there," and with an angry whistle the fire-engine, followed by the other two, flies out into Lal Bazar, the sparks trailing behind. Time—1 min. 40 secs. "They'll find out it's a false alarm, and come back again in five minutes." "Why?" "Because there will be no constables on the road to give 'em the direction of the fire, and because the driver wasn't told the ward of the outbreak when he went out!" "Do you mean to say that you can from this absurd pigeon-loft locate the wards in the night-time?" "Of course: what would be the good of a look-out if the man couldn't tell where the fire was?" "But it's all pitchy black, and the lights are so confusing."

"Ha! Ha! You'll be more confused in ten minutes. You'll have lost your way as you never lost it before. You're going to go round Bow Bazar section."

"And the Lord have mercy on my soul!" Calcutta, the darker portion of it, does not look an inviting place to dive into at night.

CHAPTER VI.

THE CITY OF DREADFUL NIGHT.

"And since they cannot spend or use aright
The little time here given them in trust,
But lavish it in weary undelight
Of foolish toil, and trouble, strife and lust—
They naturally claimeth to inherit
The Everlasting Future—that their merit
May have full scope. . . . As surely is most just."
—*The City of Dreadful Night.*

The difficulty is to prevent this account from growing steadily unwholesome. But one cannot rake through a big city without encountering muck.

The Police kept their word. In five short minutes, as they had prophesied, their charge was lost as he had never been lost before. "Where are we now?" "Somewhere off the Chitpore Road, but you wouldn't understand if you were told. Follow now, and step pretty much where we step—there's a good deal of filth hereabouts."

The thick, greasy night shuts in everything. We have gone beyond the ancestral houses of the Ghoses of the Boses, beyond the lamps, the smells, and the crowd of Chitpore Road, and have come to a great wilderness of packed houses—just such mysterious, conspiring tenements as Dickens would have loved. There is no breath of breeze here, and the air is perceptibly warmer. There is little regularity in the drift, and the utmost niggardliness in the spacing of what, for want of a better name, we must call the streets. If Calcutta keeps such luxuries as Commissioners of Sewers and Paving, they die before they reach this place. The air is heavy with a faint, sour stench—the essence of long-neglected abominations—and it cannot escape from among the tall, three-storied houses. "This, my dear sir, is a *perfectly* respectable quarter as quarters go. That house at the head of the alley, with the elaborate stucco-work round the top of the door, was built long ago by a celebrated midwife. Great people used to live here once. Now it's the—Aha! Look out for that carriage." A big mail-phaeton crashes out of the darkness and, recklessly driven, disappears. The wonder is how it ever got into this maze of narrow streets, where nobody seems to be moving, and where the dull throbbing of the city's life only comes faintly and by snatches. "Now it's the what?"

"St. John's Wood of Calcutta—for the rich Babus. That 'fitton' belonged to one of them." "Well, it's not much of a place to look at?" "Don't judge by appearances. About here live the women who have beggared kings. We aren't going to let you down into unadulterated vice all at once. You must see it first with the gilding on—and mind that rotten board."

Stand at the bottom of a lift and look upwards. Then you will get both the size and the design of the tiny courtyard round which one of these big dark houses is built. The central square may be perhaps ten feet every way, but the balconies that run inside it overhang, and seem to cut away half the available space. To reach the square a man must go round many corners, down a covered-in way, and up and down two or three baffling and confused steps. There are no lamps to guide, and the janitors of the establishment seem to be compelled to sleep in the passages. The central square, the *patio* or whatever it must be called, reeks with the faint, sour smell which finds its way impartially into every room. "Now you will understand," say the Police kindly, as their charge blunders, shin-first, into a well-dark winding staircase, "that these are not the sort of places to visit alone." "Who wants to? Of all the disgusting, inaccessible dens—Holy Cupid, what's this?"

A glare of light on the stair-head, a clink of innumerable bangles, a rustle of much fine gauze, and the Dainty Iniquity stands revealed, blazing—literally blazing—with jewellery from head to foot.

Take one of the fairest miniatures that the Delhi painters draw, and multiply it by ten; throw in one of Angelica Kaufmann's best portraits, and add anything that you can think of from Beckford to Lalla Rookh, and you will still fall short of the merits of that perfect face. For an instant, even the grim, professional gravity of the Police is relaxed in the presence of the Dainty Iniquity with the gems, who so prettily invites everyone to be seated, and proffers such refreshments as she conceives the palates of the barbarians would prefer. Her Abigails are only one degree less gorgeous than she. Half a lakh, or fifty thousand pounds' worth—it is easier to credit the latter statement than the former—are disposed upon her little body. Each hand carries five jewelled rings which are connected by golden chains to a great jewelled boss of gold in the centre of the back of the hand. Ear-rings weighted with emeralds and pearls, diamond nose-rings, and how many other hundred articles make up the list of adornments. English furniture of a gorgeous and gimcrack kind, unlimited chandeliers and a collection of atrocious Continental prints—something, but not altogether, like the glazed plaques on *bon-bon* boxes—are scattered about the house, and on every landing—let us trust this is a mistake—lies, squats, or loafs a Bengali who can talk English with unholy fluency. The recurrence suggests—only suggests, mind—a grim possibility of the affectation of excessive virtue by day, tempered with the sort of unwholesome enjoyment after dusk—this loafing and lobbying and chattering and smoking, and unless the bottles lie, tippling among the foul-tongued handmaidens of the Dainty Iniquity. How many men follow this double, deleterious sort of life? The Police are discreetly dumb.

"Now *don't* go talking about 'domiciliary visits' just because this one happens to be a pretty woman. We've *got* to know these creatures. They make the rich man and the poor spend their money; and when a man can't get money for 'em honestly, he comes under *our* notice. *Now* do you see? If there was any domiciliary 'visit' about it, the whole houseful would be hidden past our finding as soon as we turned up in the courtyard. We're friends—to a certain extent." And, indeed, it seemed no difficult thing to be friends to any extent with the Dainty Iniquity who was so surpassingly different from all that experience taught of the beauty of the East. Here was the face from which a man could write *Lalla Rookhs* by the dozen, and believe every work that he wrote. Hers was the beauty that Bryon sang of when he wrote—

"Remember, if you come here alone, the chances are that you'll be clubbed, or stuck, or, anyhow, mobbed. You'll understand that this part of the world is shut to Europeans—absolutely. Mind the steps, and follow on." The vision dies out in the smells and gross darkness of the night, in evil, time-rotten brickwork, and another wilderness of shut-up houses, wherein it seems that people do continually and feebly strum stringed instruments of a plaintive and wailsome nature.

Follows, after another plunge into a passage of a

court-yard, and up a staircase, the apparition of a Fat Vice, in whom is no sort of romance, nor beauty, but unlimited coarse humor. She too is studded with jewels, and her house is even finer than the house of the other, and more infested with the extraordinary men who speak such good English and are so deferential to the Police. The Fat Vice has been a great leader of fashion in her day, and stripped a zemindar Raja to his last acre—insomuch that he ended in the House of Correction for a theft committed for her sake. Native opinion has it that she is a "monstrous well-preserved woman." On this point, as on some others, the races will agree to differ.

The scene changes suddenly as a slide in a magic lantern. Dainty Iniquity and Fat Vice slide away on a roll of streets and alleys, each more squalid than its predecessor. We are "somewhere at the back of the Machua Bazar," well in the heart of the city. There are no houses here—nothing but acres and acres, it seems, of foul wattle-and-dab huts, any one of which would be a disgrace to a frontier village. The whole arrangement is a neatly contrived germ and fire trap, reflecting great credit upon the Calcutta Municipality.

"What happens when these pigsties catch fire?" "They're built up again," say the Police, as though this were the natural order of things. "Land is immensely valuable here." All the more reason, then, to turn several Hausmanns loose into the city, with instructions to make barracks for the population that cannot find room in the huts and sleeps in the open ways, cherishing dogs and worse, much worse, in its unwashen bosom. "Here is a licensed coffee-shop. This is where your *naukers* go for amusement and to see nautches." There is a huge *chappar* shed, ingeniously ornamented with insecure kerosene lamps, and crammed with *gharriwans*, *khitmatgars*, small store-keepers and the like. Never a sign of a European. Why? "Because if an Englishman messed about here, he'd get into trouble. Men don't come here unless they're drunk or have lost their way." The *gharriwans*—they have the privilege of voting, have they not?—look peaceful enough as they squat on tables or crowd by the doors to watch the nautch that is going forward. Five pitiful draggle-tails arc huddled together on a bench under one of the lamps, while the sixth is squirming and shrieking before the impassive crowd. She sings of love as understood by the Oriental—the love that dries the heart and consumes the liver. In this place, the words that would look so well on paper, have an evil and ghastly significance. The *gharriwans* stare or sup tumblers and cups of a filthy decoction, and the *kunchenee* howls with renewed vigor in the presence of the Police. Where the Dainty Iniquity was hung with gold and gems, she is trapped with pewter and glass; and where there was heavy embroidery on the Fat Vice's dress, defaced, stamped tinsel faithfully reduplicates the pattern on the tawdry robes of the *kunchenee*. So you see, if one cares to moralize, they are sisters of the same class.

Two or three men, blessed with uneasy consciences, have quietly slipped out of the coffee-shop into the mazes of the huts beyond. The Police laugh, and those nearest in the crowd laugh applausively, as in duty bound. Perhaps the rabbits grin uneasily when the ferret lands at the bottom of the burrow and begins to clear the warren.

"The *chandoo*-shops shut up at six, so you'll have to see opium-smoking before dark some day. No, you won't, though." The detective nose sniffs, and the detective body makes for a half-opened door of a hut whence floats the fragrance of the black smoke. Those of the inhabitants who are able to stand promptly clear out—they have no love for the Police—and there remain only four men lying down and one standing up. This latter has a pet mongoose coiled round his neck. He speaks English fluently. Yes, he has no fear. It was a private smoking party and— "No business to-night—show how you smoke opium." "Aha! You want to see. Very good, I show. Hiya! you"—he kicks a man on the floor—"show how opium-smoking." The kickee grunts lazily and turns on his elbow. The mongoose, always keeping to the man's neck, erects every hair of its body like an angry cat, and chatters in its owner's ear. The lamp for the opium-pipe is the only one in the room, and lights a scene as wild as anything in the witches' revel; the mongoose acting as the familiar spirit. A voice from the ground says, in tones of infinite weariness: "You take *afim*, so"—a long, long pause, and another kick from the man possessed of the devil—the mongoose. "You take *afim*?" He takes a pellet of the black, treacly stuff on the end of a knitting-needle. "And light *afim*." He plunges the pellet into the night-light, where it swells and fumes greasily. "And then you put it in your pipe." The smoking pellet is jammed into the tiny bowl of the thick, bamboo-stemmed pipe, and all speech ceases, except the unearthly noise of the mongoose. The man on the ground is sucking at his pipe, and when the smoking pellet has ceased to smoke will be half way to *Nibhan.* "Now you go," says the man with the mongoose. "I am going smoke." The hut door closes upon a red-lit view of huddled legs and bodies, and the man with the mongoose sinking, sinking on to his knees, his head bowed forward, and the little hairy devil chattering on the nape of his neck.

After this the fetid night air seems almost cool, for the hut is as hot as a furnace. "See the *pukka chandu* shops in full blast to-morrow. Now for Colootollah. Come through the huts. There is no decoration about *this* vice."

The huts now gave place to houses very tall and spacious and very dark. But for the narrowness of the streets we might have stumbled upon Chouringhi in the dark. An hour and a half has passed, and up to this time we have not crossed our trail once. "You might knock about the city for a night and never cross the same line. Recollect Calcutta isn't one of your poky up-country cities of a lakh and a half of people." "How long does it take to know it then?" "About a lifetime, and even then some of the streets puzzle you." "How much has the head of a ward to know?" "Every house in his ward if he can, who owns it, what sort of character the inhabitants are, who are their friends, who go out and in, who loaf about the place at night, and so on and so on." "And he knows all this by night as well as by day?" "Of course. Why shouldn't he?" "No reason in the world. Only it's pitchy black just now, and I'd like to see where this alley is going to end." "Round the corner beyond that dead wall. There's a lamp there. Then you'll be able to see." A shadow flits out of a gully and disappears. "Who's that?" "Sergeant of Police just to see where we're going in case of accidents." Another shadow staggers into the darkness. "Who's *that?*" "Man from the fort or a sailor from the ships. I couldn't quite see." The Police open a shut door in a high wall, and stumble unceremoniously among a gang of women cooking their food. The floor is of beaten earth, the steps that lead into the upper stories are unspeakably grimy, and the heat is the heat of April. The women rise hastily, and the light of the bull's eye—for the Police have now lighted a lantern in regular "rounds of London" fashion—shows six bleared faces—one a half native half Chinese one, and the others Bengali. "There are no men here!" they cry. "The house is empty." Then they grin and jabber and chew *pan* and spit, and hurry up the steps into the darkness. A range of three big rooms has been knocked into one here, and there is some sort of arrangement of mats. But an average country-bred is more sumptuously accommodated in an Englishman's stable. A home horse would snort at the accommodation.

"Nice sort of place, isn't it?" say the Police, genially. "This is where the sailors get robbed and drunk." "They must be blind drunk before they come." "Na—Na! Na sailor men ee—yah!" chorus the women, catching at the one word they understand. "Arl gone!" The Police take no notice, but tramp down the big room with the mat loose-boxes. A woman is shivering in one of these. "What's the matter?" "Fever. Seek. Vary, *vary* seek." She huddles herself into a heap on the *charpoy* and groans.

A tiny, pitch-black closet opens out of the long room, and into this the Police plunge. "Hullo! What's here?" Down flashes the lantern, and a white hand with black nails comes out of the gloom. Somebody is asleep or drunk in the cot. The ring of lantern light travels slowly up and down the body. "A sailor from the ships. He's got his *dungarees* on. He'll be robbed before the morning most likely." The man is sleeping like a little child, both arms thrown over his head, and he is not unhandsome. He is shoeless, and there are huge holes in his stockings. He is a pure-blooded white, and carries the flush of innocent sleep on his cheeks.

The light is turned off, and the Police depart; while the woman in the loose-box shivers, and moans that she is "seek: vary, *vary* seek." It is not surprising.

CHAPTER VII.

DEEPER AND DEEPER STILL.

I built myself a lordly pleasure-house,
 Wherein at ease for aye to dwell;
I said :—" O Soul, make merry and carouse.
 Dear Soul—for all is well."

—*The Palace of Art.*

"And where next? I don't like Colootollah." The Police and their charge are standing in the interminable waste of houses under the starlight. "To the lowest sink of all," say the Police after the manner of Virgil when he took the Italian with the indigestion to look at the frozen sinners. "And where's that?" "Somewhere about here; but you wouldn't know if you were told." They lead and they lead and they lead, and they cease not from leading till they come to the last circle of the Inferno—a long, long, winding, quiet road. "There you are; you can see for yourself."

But there is nothing to be seen. On one side are houses—gaunt and dark, naked and devoid of furniture; on the other, low, mean stalls, lighted, and with shamelessly open doors, wherein women stand and lounge, and mutter and whisper one to another. There is a hush here, or at least the busy silence of an officer of counting-house in working hours. One look down the street is sufficient. Lead on, gentlemen of the Calcutta Police. Let us escape from the lines of open doors, the flaring lamps within, the glimpses of the tawdry toilet-tables adorned with little plaster dogs, glass balls from Christmas-trees, and—for religion must not be despised though women be fallen—pictures of the saints and statuettes of the Virgin. The street is a long one, and other streets, full of the same pitiful wares, branch off from it.

"Why are they so quiet? Why don't they make a row and sing and shout, and so on?" "Why should they, poor devils?" say the Police, and fall to telling tales of horror, of women decoyed into *palkis* and shot into this trap. Then other tales that shatter one's belief in all things and folk of good repute. "How can you Police have faith in humanity?"

"That's because you're seeing it all in a lump for the first time, and it's not nice that way. Makes a man jump rather, doesn't it? But, recollect, you've *asked* for the worst places, and you can't complain." "Who's complaining? Bring on your atrocities. Isn't that a European woman at that door?" "Yes. Mrs. D——, widow of a soldier, mother of seven children." "Nine, if you please, and good evening to you," shrills Mrs. D——, leaning against the doorpost, her arms folded on her bosom. She is a rather pretty, slightly-made Eurasian, and whatever shame she may have owned she has long since cast behind her. A shapeless Burmo-native trot, with high cheekbones and mouth like a shark, calls Mrs. D—— "Mem-Sahib." The word jars unspeakably. Her life is a matter between herself and her Maker, but in that she—the widow of a soldier of the Queen—has stooped to this common foulness in the face of the city, she has offended against the white race. The Police fail to fall in with this righteous indignation. More. They laugh at it out of the wealth of their unholy knowledge. "You're from up-country, and of course you don't understand. There are any amount of that lot in the city." Then the secret of the insolence of Calcutta is made plain. Small wonder the natives fail to respect the Sahib, seeing what they see and knowing what they know. In the good old days, the honorable the directors deported him or her who misbehaved grossly, and the white man preserved his *izzat*. He may have been a ruffian, but he was a ruffian on a large scale. He did not sink in the presence of the people. The natives are quite right to take the wall of the Sahib who has been at great pains to prove that he is of the same flesh and blood.

All this time Mrs. D—— stands on the threshold of her room and looks upon the men with unabashed eyes. If the spirit of that English solidier, who married her long ago by the forms of the English Church, be now flitting bat-wise above the roofs, how singularly pleased and proud it must be! Mrs. D—— is a lady with a story. She is not averse to telling it. "What was—ahem—the case in which you were—er—hmn—concerned, Mrs. D——?" "They said I'd poisoned my husband by putting something into his drinking water." This is interesting. How much modesty *has* this creature? Let us see. "And —ah—*did* you?" "'Twasn't proved," says Mrs.

D—— with a laugh, a pleasant, lady-like laugh that does infinite credit to her education and upbringing. Worthy Mrs. D——! It would pay a novelist —a French one let us say—to pick you out of the stews and make you talk.

The Police move forward, into a region of Mrs. D——'s. This is horrible; but they are used to it, and evidently consider indignation affectation. Everywhere are the empty houses, and the babbling women in print gowns. The clocks in the city are close upon midnight, but the Police show no signs of stopping. They plunge hither and thither, like wreckers into the surf; and each plunge brings up a sample of misery, filth and woe.

"Sheikh Babu was murdered just here," they say, pulling up in one of the most troublesome houses in the ward. It would never do to appear ignorant of the murder of Sheikh Babu. "I only wonder that more aren't killed." The houses with their breakneck staircases, their hundred corners, low roofs, hidden courtyards and winding passages, seem specially built for crime of every kind. A woman—Eurasian—rises to a sitting position on a board-charpoy and blinks sleepily at the Police. Then she throws herself down with a grunt. "What's the matter with you?" "I live in Markiss Lane and"—this with intense gravity—"I'm *so* drunk." She has a rather striking gipsy-like face, but her language might be improved.

"Come along," say the Police, "we'll head back to Bentinck Street, and put you on the road to the Great Eastern." They walk long and steadily, and the talk falls on gambling hell. "You ought to see our men rush one of 'em. They like the work—natives of course. When we've marked a hell down, we post men at the entrances and carry it. Sometimes the Chinese bite, but as a rule they fight fair. It's a pity we hadn't a hell to show you. Let's go in here—there may be something forward." "Here" appears to be in the heart of a Chinese quarter, for the pigtails—do they ever go to bed?—are scuttling about the streets. "Never go into a Chinese place alone," say the Police, and swing open a postern gate in a strong, green door. Two Chinamen appear.

"What are we going to see?" "Japanese gir—No, we aren't, by Jove! Catch that Chinaman, *quick*." The pigtail is trying to double back across a courtyard into an inner chamber; but a large hand on his shoulder spins him round and puts him in rear of the line of advancing Englishmen, who are, be it observed, making a fair amount of noise with their boots. A second door is thrown open, and the visitors advance into a large, square room blazing with gas. Here thirteen pigtails, deaf and blind to the outer world, are bending over a table. The captured Chinaman dodges uneasily in the rear of the procession. Five—ten—fifteen seconds pass, the Englishmen standing in the full light less than three paces from the absorbed gang who see nothing. Then burly Superintendent Lamb brings down his hand on his thigh with a crack like a pistol-shot and shouts: "How do, John?" Follows a frantic rush of scared Celestials, almost tumbling over each other in their anxiety to get clear. Gudgeon before the rush of the pike are nothing to John Chinaman detected in the act of gambling. One pigtail scoops up a pile of copper money, another a chinaware soup-bowl, and only a little mound of accusing cowries remains on the white matting that covers the table. In less than half a minute two facts are forcibly brought home to the visitor. First, that a pigtail is largely composed of silk, and rasps the palm of the hand as it slides through; and secondly, that the forearm of a Chinaman is surprisingly muscular and well-developed. "What's going to be done?" "Nothing. They're only three of us, and all the ringleaders would get away. Look at the doors. We've got 'em safe any time we want to catch 'em, if this little visit doesn't make 'em shift their quarters. Hi! John. No pidgin to-night. Show how you makee play. That fat youngster there is our informer."

Half the pigtails have fled into the darkness, but the remainder, assured and trebly assured that the Police really mean "no pidgin," return to the table and stand round while the croupier proceeds to manipulate the cowries, the little curved slip of bamboo and the soup-bowl. They never gamble, these innocents. They only come to look on, and smoke opium in the next room. Yet as the game progresses their eyes light up, and one by one they lose in to deposit their pice on odd or even—the number of the cowries that are covered and left uncovered by the little soup-bowl. *Mythan* is the name of the amusement, and, whatever may be its demerits, it is *clean*. The Police look on while their charge plays and oots a parchment-skinned horror—one of Swift's Struldburgs, strayed from Laputa—of the enormous sum of two annas. The return of this wealth, doubled, sets the loser beating his forehead against the table from sheer gratitude.

"*Most* immoral game this. A man might drop five whole rupees, if he began playing at sun-down and kept it up all night. Don't *you* ever play whist occasionally?"

"Now, we didn't bring you round to make fun of this department. A man can lose as much as ever he likes and he can fight as well, and if he loses all his money he steals to get more. A Chinaman is insane about gambling, and half his crime comes from it. It *must* be kept down." "And the other business. Any sort of supervision there?" "No; so long as they keep outside the penal code. Ask Dr. —— about that. It's outside our department. Here we are in Bentinck Street and you can be driven to the Great Eastern in a few minutes. Joss houses? Oh, yes. If you want more horrors, Superintendent Lamb will take you round with him to-morrow afternoon at five. Report yourself at the Bow Bazar Thanna at five minutes to. Good-night."

The Police depart, and in a few minutes the silent, well-ordered respectability of Old Council House Street, with the grim Free Kirk at the end of it, is reached. All good Calcutta has gone to bed, the last tram has passed, and the peace of the night is upon the world. Would it be wise and rational to climb the spire of that kirk, and shout after the fashion of the great Lion-slayer of Tarescon: "O true believers! Decency is a fraud and a sham. There is nothing clean or pure or wholesome under the stars, and we are all going to perdition together. Amen!" On second thoughts it would not; for the spire is slippery, the night is hot, and the Police have been specially careful to warn their charge that he must not be carried away by the sight of horrors that cannot be written or hinted at.

"Good-morning," says the Policeman tramping the pavement in front of the Great Eastern, and he nods his head pleasantly to show that he is the representative of Law and Peace and that the city of Calcutta is safe from itself for the present.

CHAPTER VIII.

CONCERNING LUCIA.

"Was a woman such a woman—cheeks so round and lips so red?
On the neck the small head buoyant like the bell flower in its bed."

Time must be filled in somehow till five this afternoon, when Superintendent Lamb will reveal more horrors. Why not, the trams aiding, go to the Old Park Street Cemetery? It is presumption, of course, because none other than the great Sir W. W. Hunter once went there, and wove from his visit certain fascinating articles for the *Englishman;* the memory of which lingers even to this day, though they were written fully two years since.

But the great Sir W. W. went in his Legislative Consular brougham and never in an unbridled tram-car which pulled up somewhere in the middle of Dhurrumtollah. "You want go Park Street? No trams going Park Street. You get out here." Calcutta tram conductors are not polite. Some day one of them will be hurt. The car shuffles unsympathetically down the street, and the evicted is stranded in Dhurrumtollah, which may be the Hammersmith Highway of Calcutta. Providence arranged this mistake, and paved the way to a Great Discovery now published for the first time. Dhurrumtollah is full of the People of India, walking in family parties and groups and confidential couples. And the people of India are neither Hindu nor Mussulman—Jew, Ethiop, Gueber or expatriated British. They are the Eurasians, and there are hundreds and hundreds of them in Dhurrumtollah now. There is Papa with a shining black hat fit for a counsellor of the Queen, and Mamma, whose silken attire is tight upon her portly figure, and The Brood made up of straw-hatted, olive-cheeked, sharp-eyed little boys, and leggy maidens wearing white, open-work stockings calculated to show dust. There are the young men who smoke bad cigars and carry themselves lordily—such as have incomes. There are also the young women with the beautiful eyes and the wonderful dresses which always fit so badly across the shoulders. And they carry prayer-books or baskets, because they are either going to mass or the market.

Without doubt, these are the people of India. They were born in it, bred in it, and will die in it. The Englishman only comes to the country, and the natives of course were there from the first, but these people have been made here, and no one has done anything for them except talk and write about them. Yet they belong, some of them, to old and honorable families, hold "houses, messuages, and tenements" in Sealdah, and are rich, a few of them. They all look prosperous and contented, and they chatter eternally in that curious dialect that no one has yet reduced to print. Beyond what little they please to reveal now and again in the newspapers, we know nothing about their life which touches so intimately the white on the one hand and the black on the other. It must be interesting—more interesting than the colorless Anglo-Indian article; but who has treated of it? There was one novel once in which the second heroine was an Eurasienne. She was a strictly subordinate character, and came to a sad end. The poet of the race, Henry Derozio—he of whom Mr. Thomas Edwards wrote a history—was bitten with Keats and Scott and Shelley, and overlooked in his search for material things that lay nearest to him. All this mass of humanity in Dhurrumtollah is unexploited and almost unknown. Wanted, therefore, a writer from among the Eurasians, who shall write so that men shall be pleased to read a story of Eurasian life; then outsiders will be interested in the People of India, and will admit that the race has possibilities.

A futile attempt to get to Park Street from Dhurrumtollah ends in the market—the Hogg Market men call it. Perhaps a knight of that name built it. It is not one-half as pretty as the Crawford Market, in Bombay but . . . it appears to be the trysting place of Young Calcutta. The natural inclination of youth is to lie abed late, and to let the seniors do all the hard work. Why, therefore, should Pyramus who has to be ruling account forms at ten, and Thisbe, who *cannot* be interested in the price of second quality beef, wander, in studiously correct raiment, round and about the stalls before the sun is well clear of the earth ? Pyramus carries a walking stick with imitation silver straps upon it, and there are cloth tops to his boots ; but his collar has been two days worn. Thisbe crowns her dark head with a blue velvet Tam-o'-Shanter ; but one of her boots lacks a button, and there is a tear in the left-hand glove. Mamma, who despises gloves, is rapidly filling a shallow basket, that the coolie-boy carries, with vegetables, potatoes, purple brinjals, and—Oh, Pryamus ! Do you ever kiss Thisbe when Mamma is not near ?—garlic—yea, *lusson* of the bazar. Mamma is generous in her views on garlic. Pyramus comes round the corner of the stall looking for nobody in particular—not he—and is elaborately polite to Mamma. Somehow, h : and Thisbe drift off together, and Mamma, very portly and very voluble, is left to chaffer and sort and select alone. In the name of the Sacred Unities do not, young people, retire to the meat-stalls to exchange confidences ! Come up to this end, where the roses are arriving in great flat baskets, where the air is heavy with the fragrance of flowers, and the young buds and greenery are littering all the floor. They won't—they prefer talking by the dead, unromantic muttons, where there are not so many buyers. How they babble! There must have been a quarrel to make up. Thisbe shakes the blue velvet Tam-o'-Shanter and says: "O yess!" scornfully. Pyramus answers: "No-a, no-a. Do-ant say thatt." Mamma's basket is full and she picks up Thisbe hastily. Pyramus departs. *He* never came here to do any marketing. He came to meet Thisbe, who in ten years will own a figure very much like Mamma's. May their ways be smooth before them, and after honest service of the Government, may Pyramus retire on Rs. 250 per mensen, into a nice little house somewhere in Monghyr or Chunar.

From love by natural sequence to death. Where *is* the Park Street Cemetery? A hundred *gharriwans* leap from their boxes and invade the market, and after a short struggle one of them uncarts his capture in a burial-ground—a ghastly new place, close to a tramway. This is not what is wanted. The living dead are here—the people whose names are not yet altogether perished and whose tombstones are tended. "Where are the *old* dead?" "Nobody goes there," says the *gharriwan.* "It is up that road." He points up a long and utterly deserted thoroughfáre, running between high walls. This is the place, and the entrance to it, with its *mallee* waiting with one brown, battered rose, its grilled door and its professional notices, bears a hideous likeness to the entrance of Simla churchyard. But, once inside, the sightseer stands in the heart of utter desolation—all the more forlorn for being swept up. Lower Park Street cuts a great graveyard in two. The guide-books will tell you when the place was opened and when it was closed. The eye is ready to swear that it is as old as Herculaneum and Pompeii. The tombs are small houses. It is as though we walked down the streets of a town, so tall are they and so closely do they stand—a town shrivelled by fire, and scarred by frost and siege. They must have been afraid of their friends rising up before the due time that they weighted them with such cruel mounds of masonry. Strong man, weak woman, or somebody's "infant son aged fifteen months"—it is all the same. For each the squat obelisk, the defaced classic temple, the cellaret of chunam, or the candle-stick of brickwork—the heavy slab, the rust-eaten railings, the whopper-jawed cherubs and the apoplectic angels. Men were rich in those days and could afford to put a hundred cubic feet of masonry into the grave of even so humble a person as "Jno. Clements, Captain of the Country Service, 1820." When the "dearly beloved" had held rank answering to that of Commissioner, the efforts are still more sumptuous and the verse . . . Well, the following speaks for itself:

"Soft on thy tomb shall fond Remembrance shed
 The warm yet unavailing tear,
And purple flowers that deck the honored dead
 Shall strew the loved and honored bier."

Failure to comply with the contract does not, let us hope, entail forfeiture of the earnest-money; or the honored dead might be grieved. The slab is out of his tomb, and leans foolishly against it ; the railings are rotted, and there are no more lasting ornaments than blisters and stains, which are the work of the weather, and not the result of the "warm yet unavailing tear." The eyes that promised to shed them have been closed any time these seventy years.

Let us go about and moralize cheaply on the tombstones, trailing the robe of pious reflection up and down the pathways of the grave. Here is a big and stately tomb sacred to "Lucia," who died in 1776 A. D., aged 23. Here also be verses which an irreverent thumb can bring to light. Thus they wrote, when their hearts were heavy in them, one hundred and sixteen years ago :—

"What needs the emblem, what the plaintive strain,
What all the arts that sculpture e'er expressed,
To tell the treasure that these walls contain?
Let those declare it most who knew her best.

"The tender pity she would oft display
Shall be with interest at her shrine returned,
Connubial love, connubial tears repay,
And Lucia loved shall still be Lucia mourned.

"Though closed the lips, though stopped the tuneful breath,
The silent, clay-cold monitress shall teach—
In all the alarming eloquence of death
With double pathos to the heart shall preach.

"Shall teach the virtuous maid, the faithful wife,
If young and fair, that young and fair was she,
Then close the useful lesson of her life,
And tell them what she is, they soon must be."

That goes well, even after all these years, does it not? and seems to bring Lucia very near, in spite of what the later generation is pleased to call the stiltedness of the old-time verse.

Who will declare the merits of Lucia—dead in her spring before there was even a *Hickey's Gazette* to chronicle the amusements of Calcutta, and publish, with scurrilous asterisks, the *liaisons* of heads of departments? What pot-bellied East Indiaman brought the "virtuous maid" up the river, and did Lucia "make her bargain," as the cant of those times went, on the first, second, or third day after her arrival? Or did she, with the others of the batch, give a spinsters' ball as a last trial—following the custom of the country? No. She was a fair Kentish maiden, sent out, at a cost of five hundred pounds, English money, under the captain's charge, to wed the man of her choice, and *he* knew Clive well, had had dealings with Omichand, and talked to men who had lived through the terrible night in the Black Hole. He was a rich man, Lucia's battered tomb proves it, and he gave Lucia all that her heart could wish. A green-painted boat to take the air in on the river of evenings. Coffree slave-boys who could play on the French horn, and even a very elegant, neat coach with a genteel rutlan roof ornamented with flowers very highly finished, ten best polished plate glasses, ornamented with a few elegant medallions enriched with mother-o'-pearl, that she might take her drive on the course as befitted a factor's wife. All these things he gave her. And when the convoys came up the river, and the guns thundered, and the servants of the Honorable the East India Company drank to the king's health, be sure that Lucia before all the other ladies in the fort had her choice of the new stuffs from England and was cordially hated in consequence. Tilly Kettle painted her picture a little before she died, and the hot-blooded young writers did duel with small swords in the fort ditch for the honor of piloting her through a minuet at the Calcutta theatre or the Punch House. But Warren Hastings danced with her instead, and the writers were confounded—every man of them. She was a toast far up the river. And she walked in the evening on the bastions of Fort-William, and said: "La! I protest!" It was there that she exchanged congratulations with all her friends on the 20th of October, when those who were alive gathered together to felicitate themselves on having come through another hot season; and the men—even the sober factor saw no wrong here—got most royally and Britishly drunk on Madeira that had twice rounded the Cape. But Lucia fell sick, and the doctor—he who went home after seven years with five lakhs and a half, and a corner of this vast graveyard to his account—said that it was a pukka or putrid fever, and the system required strengthening. So they fed Lucia on hot curries, and mulled wine worked up with spirits and fortified with spices, for nearly a week; at the end of which time she closed her eyes on the weary, weary river and the fort forever, and a gallant, with a turn for *belles lettres*, wept openly as men did then and had no shame of it, and composed the verses above set, and thought himself a neat hand at the pen—stap his vitals! But the factor was so grieved that he could write nothing at all—could only spend his money—and he counted his wealth by lakhs—on a sumptuous grave. A little later on he took comfort, and when the next batch came out—

But this has nothing whatever to do with the story of Lucia, the virtuous maid, the faithful wife. Her ghost went to Mrs. Westland's powder ball, and looked very beautiful.

PART THIRD.

CHAPTER I.

A RAILWAY SETTLEMENT.

Jamalpur is the headquarters of the E. I. Railway. This in itself is not a startling statement. The wonder begins with the exploration of Jamalpur, which is a station entirely made by, and devoted to, the use of those untiring servants of the public, the railway folk. They have towns of their own at Toondla and Assensole, a sun-dried sanitarium at Bandikui; and Howrah, Ajmir, Allahabad, Lahore and Pindi know their colonies. But Jamalpur is unadulteratedly "Railway," and he who has nothing to do with the E. I. Railway in some shape or another feels a stranger and an "interloper." Running always east and southerly, the train carries him from the torments of the north-west into the wet, woolly warmth of Bengal, where may be found the hothouse heat that has ruined the temper of the good people of Calcutta. Here the land is fat and greasy with good living, and the wealth of the bodies of innumerable dead things; and here—just above Mokameh—may be seen fields stretching, without stick, stone or bush to break the view, from the railway line to the horizon.

Up-country innocents must look at the map to learn that Jamalpur is near the top left-hand corner of the big loop that the E. I. R. throws out round Bhagalpur and part of the Bara-Banki districts. Northward of Jamalpur, as near as may be, lies the Ganges and Tirhoot, and eastward an offshoot of the volcanic Rajmehal range blocks the view.

A station which has neither Judge, Commissioner, Deputy or 'Stunt, which is devoid of law courts, ticca-gharries, District Superintendents of Police, and many other evidences of an over-cultured civilization, is a curiosity. "We administer ourselves," says Jamalpur proudly, "or we did—till we had lokil sluff brought in—and now the racket-marker administers us." This is a solemn fact. The station, which had its beginnings thirty odd years ago, used, till comparatively recent times, to control its own roads, sewage, conservancy, and the like. But, with the introduction of local self-government, it was ordained that the "inestimable boon" should be extended to a place made by, and maintained for, Europeans, and a brand new municipality was created and nominated according to the many rules of the game. In the skirmish that ensued, the club racket-marker fought his way to the front, secured a place on a board largely composed of Babus, and since that day Jamalpur's views on "local sluff" have not been fit for publication. To understand the magnitude of the insult, one must study the city—for station, in the strict sense of the word, it is not. Crotons, palms, mangoes, *mellingtonias*, teak, and bamboos adorn it, and the *ponisettia* and *bougainvillea*, the railway creeper and the *bignonia venusta* make it gay with many colors. It is laid out with military precision on the right-hand side of the line going down to Calcutta—to each house its just share of garden and green *jilmil*, its red *surki* path, its growth of trees, and its neat little wicket gate. Its general aspect, in spite of the Dutch formality, is that of an English village, such a thing as enterprising stage-managers put on the theatres at home. The hills have thrown a protecting arm round nearly three sides of it, and on the fourth it is bounded by what are locally known as the "shed;" in other words, the station, offices, and workshops of the company. The E. I. R. only exists for outsiders. Its servants speak of it reverently, angrily, despitefully, or enthusiastically as "The Company;" and they never omit the big, big C. Men must have treated the Honorable East India Company in something the same fashion ages ago. "The Company" in Jamalpur is Lord Dufferin, all the Members of Council, the Body-Guard, Sir Frederick Roberts, Mr. Westland, whose name is at the bottom of the currency notes, the Oriental Life Assurance Company, and the Bengal Government all rolled into one. At first, when a stranger enters this life, he is inclined to scoff and ask, in his ignorance: "*What* is this Company that you talk so much about?" Later on, he ceases to scoff, and his mouth opens slowly; for the Company is a "big" thing—almost big enough to satisfy an American.

Ere beginning to describe its doings, let it be written, and repeated several times hereafter, that the E. I. R. passenger carriages, and especially the second-class, are just now—horrid, being filthy and unwashen, dirty to look at, and dirty to live in. Having cast this small stone, we will examine Jamalpur. When it was laid out, in or before the Mutiny year, its designers allowed room for growth, and made the houses of one general design—some of brick, some of stone, some three, four, and six-roomed, some single men's barracks and some two-storied—all for the use of the *employes*. King's Road, Prince's Road, Queen's Road, and Victoria Road—Jamalpur is loyal—cut the breadth of the station; and Albert Road, Church Street, and Steam Road the length of it. Neither on these roads or on any of the cool-shaded smaller ones is anything unclean or unsightly to be found. There is a dreary *bustee* in the neighborhood which is said to make the most of any cholera that may be going, but Jamalpur itself is specklessly and spotlessly neat. From St. Mary's Church to the railway station, and from the buildings where they print daily about half a lakh of tickets to the ringing, roaring, rattling workshops, everything has the air of having been cleaned up at ten that very morning and put under a glass case. Also there is a holy calm about the roads—totally unlike anything in an English manufacturing town. Wheeled conveyances are few, because every man's bungalow is close to his work, and when the day has begun and the offices of the "Loco." and "Traffic" have soaked up their thousands of natives and hundreds of Europeans, you shall pass under the dappled shadows of the teak trees, hearing nothing louder than the croon of some bearer playing with a child in the verandah or the faint tinkle of a piano. This is pleasant, and produces an impression of Watteau-like refinement tempered with Arcadian simplicity. The dry, anguished howl of the "buzzer," the big steam-whistle, breaks the hush, and all Jamalpur is alive with the tramping of tiffin-seeking feet. The Company gives one hour for meals between eleven and twelve. On the stroke of noon there is another rush back to the works or the offices, and Jamalpur sleeps through the afternoon till four or half-past, and then rouses for tennis at the institute.

It is a quiet, restful place to live or die in, but not great for enterprise. Tropical or semi-tropical cities are never remarkable for excessive energy or activity. Nor do the inhabitants arrive at fortune made by the exertion of the persons possessing it. Fortunes are made in such places, but by the dull continuous labor of inferiors and natives for some supervisor or director usually foreign.

In the hot weather it splashes in the swimming bath, or reads, for it has a library of several thousand books. One of the most flourishing lodges in the Bengal jurisdiction—"St. George in the East"—lives at Jamalpur, and meets twice a month. Its members point out with justifiable pride that all the fittings were made by their own hands; and the lodge in its accoutrements and the energy of the craftsmen can compare with any in India. But the institute seems to be the central gathering place, and its half-dozen tennis-courts and neatly-laid-out grounds seem to be always full. Here, if a stranger could judge, the greater part of the flirtation of Jamalpur is carried out, and here the dashing apprentice—the apprentices are the liveliest of all—learns that there are problems harder than any he studies at the night school, and that the heart of a maiden is more inscrutable than the mechanism of a locomotive. On Tuesdays and Fridays, as a printed notification witnesseth, the volunteers parade. A and B Companies, 150 strong in all, of the E. I. R. Volunteers, are stationed here with the band. Their uniform, grey with red facings, is not lovely, but they know how to shoot and drill. They have to. The "Company" makes it a condition of service that a man must be a volunteer ; and volunteer in something more than name he must be, or some one will ask the reason why. Seeing that there are no regulars between Howrah and Dinapore, the "Company" does well in exacting this toll. Some of the old soldiers are wearied of drill, some of the youngsters don't like it, but—the way they entrain and detrain is worth seeing. They are as mobile a corps as can be desired, and perhaps ten or twelve years hence the Government may possibly be led to take a real interest in them and spend a few thousand rupees in providing them with real soldiers' kits—not uniform and rifle merely. Their ranks include all sorts and conditions of men—heads of the "loco." and "traffic," the "Company" is no great respecter of rank—clerks in the "audit," boys from mercantile firms at home, fighting with the intricacies of time, fare and freight tables; guards who have grown grey in the service of the Company; mail and passenger drivers with nerves of cast-iron, who can shoot through a long afternoon without losing temper or flurring; light-built East Indians; Tyne-side men, slow of speech and uncommonly strong in the arm; lathy apprentices who have not yet "filled out;" fitters, turners, foremen, full assistant and sub-assistant station-masters, and a host of others. In the hands of the younger men the regulation Martini-Henri naturally goes off the line occasionally on a *shikar* expedition.

There is a twelve-hundred yards' range running down one side of the station, and the condition of the grass by the firing butts tells its own tale. Scattered in the ranks of the volunteers are a fair number of old soldiers, for the Company has a weakness for recruiting from the army for its guards who may, in time, become station-masters. A good man from the army, with his papers all correct and certificates from his commanding officer, may, after depositing twenty pounds to pay his home passage, in the event of his services being dispensed with, enter the Company's service on something less than one hundred rupees a month and rise in time to four hundred as a station-master. A railway bungalow—and they are as substantially built as the engines—cannot cost him more than one-ninth of the pay of his grade, and the Provident Fund provides for his latter end.

Think for a moment of the number of men that a line running from Howrah to Delhi must use, and you will realize what an enormous amount of patronage the Company holds in its hands. Naturally a father who has worked for the line expects the line to do something for the son; and the line is not backward in meeting his wishes where possible. The sons of old servants may be taken on at fifteen years of age, or thereabouts, as apprentices in the "shops," receiving twenty rupees in the first and fifty in the last year of the indentures. Then they come on the books as full "men" on perhaps Rs. 65 a month, and the road is open to them in many ways. They may become foremen of departments on Rs. 500 a month, or drivers earning with overtime Rs. 370; or if they have been brought into the audit or the traffic, they may control innumerable Babus and draw several hundreds of rupees monthly; or, at eighteen or nineteen, they may be ticket-collectors, working up to the grade of guard, etc. Every rank of the huge, human hive has a desire to see its sons placed properly, and the native workmen, about three thousand, in the locomotive department only, are, said one man, "making a family affair of it altogether. You see all those men turning brass and looking after the machinery? They've all got relatives, and a lot of 'em own land out Monghyr-way close to us. They bring on their sons as soon as they are old enough to do anything, and the Company rather encourages it. You see the father is in a way responsible for his son, and he'll teach him all he knows, and in that way the Company has a hold on them all. You've no notion how sharp a native is when he's working on his own hook. All the district round here, right up to Monghyr, is more or less dependent on the railway."

The Babus in the traffic department, in the stores, issue department, in all the departments where men sit through the long, long Indian day among ledgers, and check and pencil and deal in figures and items and rupees, may be counted by hundreds. Imagine the struggle among them to locate their sons in comfortable cane-bottomed chairs, in front of a big pewter inkstand and stacks of paper! The Babus make beautiful accountants, and if we could only see it, a merciful Providence has made the Babu for figures and detail. Without him on the Bengal side, the dividends of any company would be eaten up by the expenses of English or country-bred clerks. The Babu is a great man, and, to respect him, you must see five score or so of him in a room a hundred yards long bending over ledgers, ledgers, and yet more ledgers—silent as the Sphinx and busy as a bee. He is the lubricant of the great machinery of the Company whose ways and works cannot be dealt with in a single scrawl.

CHAPTER II.

THE MIGHTY SHOPS.

A study of this Republic of Jamalpur is not easy. The railway folk, like the army and civilian castes, have their own language and life, which an outsider cannot hope to understand. For instance, when Jamalpur refers to itself as being "on the long siding," a lengthy explanation is necessary before the visitor grasps the fact that the whole of the two hundred and thirty odd miles of the loop from Luckeeserai to Kanu-Junction *via* Bhagalpur is thus contemptuously treated. Jamalpur insists that it is out of the world, and makes this an excuse for being proud of itself and all its institutions. But in one thing it is badly, disgracefully provided. At a moderate estimate there must be about two hundred Europeans with their families in this place. They can, and do, get their small supplies from Calcutta, but they are dependent on the tender mercies of the bazar for their meat, which seems to be hawked from door to door. Also, there is a Raja who owns or has an interest in the land on which the station stands, and he is averse to cow-killing. For these reasons, Jamalpur is not too well supplied with good meat, and what it wants is a decent meat-market with cleanly controlled slaughtering arrangements. The "Company," who gives grants to the schools and builds the institute and throws the shadow of its protection all over the place, might help this scheme forward.

The heart of Jamalpur is the "shops," and here a visitor will see more things in an hour than he can understand in a year. Steam Street very appropriately leads to the forty or fifty acres that the "shops" cover, and to the busy silence of the loco. superintendent's office, where a man must put down his name and his business on a slip of paper before he can penetrate into the Temple of Vulcan. About three thousand five hundred men are in the "shops," and, ten minutes after the day's work has begun, the assistant superintendent knows exactly how many are "in." The heads of departments—silent, heavy-handed men, captains of five hundred or more—have their names fairly printed on a board which is exactly like a pool-marker. They "star a life" when they come in, and their few names alone represent salaries to the extent of six thousand a month. They are men worth hearing deferentially. They hail from Manchester and the Clyde, and the great iron-works of the North, and pleasant as cold water in a thirsty land is it to hear again the full Northumbrian burr or the long-drawn Yorkshire "aye." Under their great gravity of demeanor—a man who is in charge of a few lakhs' worth of plant cannot afford to be riotously mirthful—lurks melody and humor. They can sing like north-countrymen, and in their hours of ease go back to the speech of the iron countries they have left behind, when "Ab o' th' yate" and all "Ben Briarly's" shrewd wit shakes the warm air of Bengal with deep-chested laughter. Hear "Ruglan' Toon," with a chorus as true as the fall of trip-hammers, and fancy that you are back again in the smoky, rattling, ringing North.

But this is the "unofficial" side. Let us go forward through the gates under the mango trees, and set foot at once in sheds which have as little to do with mangoes as a locomotive with Lakshmi. The "buzzer" howls, for it is nearly tiffin time. There is a rush from every quarter of the shops, a cloud of flying natives, and a procession of more sedately pacing Englishmen, and in three short minutes you are left absolutely alone among arrested wheels and belts, pulleys, cranks, and cranes—in a silence only broken by the soft sigh of a far-away steam-valve or the cooing of pigeons. You are, by favor freely granted, at liberty to wander anywhere you please through the deserted works. Walk into a huge, brick-built, tin-roofed stable, capable of holding twenty-four locomotives under treatment, and see what must be done to the Iron Horse once in every three years if he is to do his work well. On reflection, Iron Horse is wrong. An engine is a she—as distinctly feminine as a ship or a mine. Here stands the *Echo*, her wheels off, resting on blocks, her underside machinery taken out, and her side scrawled with mysterious hieroglyphics in chalk. An enormous green-painted iron marness-rack bears her piston and eccentric rods, and a neatly-painted board shows that such and such Englishmen are the fitter, assistant and apprentice engaged in editing the *Echo*. An engine seen from the platform and an engine viewed from underneath are two very different things. The one is as unimpressive as a *ticca-gharri*; the other as imposing as a man-of-war in the yard.

In this manner is an engine treated for navicular, laminitis, backsinew, or whatever it is that engines most suffer from. No. 607, we will say, goes wrong at Dinapore, Assensole, Buxar, or whatever it may be, after three years' work. The place she came from is stencilled on the boiler, and the foreman examines her. Then he fills in a hospital sheet, which bears one hundred and eighty printed heads under which an engine can come into the shops. No. 607 needs repair in only one hundred and eighteen particulars, ranging from mud-hole flanges and blower-cocks to lead-plugs, and platform brackets which have shaken loose. This certificate the foreman signs, and it is framed near the engine for the benefit of the three Europeans and the eight or nine natives who have to mend No. 607. To the ignorant the superhuman wisdom of the examiner seems only equalled by the audacity of the two men and the boy who are to undertake what is frivolously called the "job." No. 607 is in a sorely mangled condition, but 403 is much worse. She is reduced to a shell—is a very lean woman of an engine, bearing only her funnel, the iron frame and the saddle that supports the boiler. All the pretty little instruction primers say that an engine takes to pieces like a watch, but it is not good to see an engine so treated. Better had a man believe that "they light the fire under the water, y'know, and that makes the water steam, and that gets into those piston things, and that drives the train.

Four-and-twenty engines in every stage of decomposition stand in one huge shop. A travelling crane runs overhead, and the men have hauled up one end of a bright vermilion loco. The effect is the silence of a scornful stare—just such a look as a colonel's portly wife gives through her *pince-nez* at the audacious subaltern. Engines are the "liveliest" things that man ever made. They glare through their spectacle-plates, they tilt their noses contemptuously, and when their insides are gone they adorn themselves with red lead and leer like decayed beauties; and in the Jamalpur works there is no escape from them. The shops can hold fifty without pressure, and on occasion as many again. Everywhere there are engines, and everywhere brass domes lie about on the ground like huge helmets in a pantomime. The silence is the weirdest touch of all. Some sprightly soul—an apprentice be sure—has daubed in red lead on the end of an iron tool box a caricature of some friend who is evidently a riveter. The picture has all the interest of an Egyptian cartouche, for it shows that men have been here, and that the engines do not have it all their own way.

And so, out in the open, away from the three great sheds between and under more engines, till we strike a wilderness of lines all converging to one turn-table. Here be elephant stalls ranged round a half-circle, and in each stall stands one engine, and each engine stares at the turn-table. A stolid and disconcerting company is this ring of eyes monsters;

324, 432, and 8 are shining like Bon Marche toys. They are ready for their turn of duty, and are as spruce as hansoms. Lacquered chocolate, picked out with black, red and white, is their dress, and delicate lemon graces the ceilings of the cabs. The driver should be a gentleman in evening dress with white kid gloves, and there should be gold-headed champagne bottles in the spick and span tenders. Huckleberry Finn says of a timber raft: "It amounted to something being captain of that raft." Thrice enviable is the man who, drawing Rs. 220 a month, is allowed to make Rs. 150 overtime out of locos. Nos. 324, 432 or 8. Fifty yards beyond this gorgeous trinity are ten to twelve engines who have put in to Jamalpur to bait. They are alive, their fires are lighted, and they are swearing and purring and growling one at another as they stand alone—all alone. Here is evidently one of the newest type—No. 25, a giant who has just brought the mail in and waits to be cleaned up preparatory to going out afresh.

The tiffin hour has ended. The buzzer blows, and with a roar, a rattle and a clang the shops take up their toil. The hubbub that followed on the prince's kiss to the sleeping beauty was not so loud or sudden. Experience, with a foot-rule in his pocket, authority in his port, and a merry twinkle in his eye, comes up and catches Ignorance walking gingerly round No. 25. "That's one of the best we have," says Experience, "a four-wheeled coupled bogie they call her. She's by Dobbs. She's done her hundred and fifty miles to-day; and she'll run in to Rampore

Haut this afternoon; then she'll rest a day and be cleaned up. Roughly, she does her three hundred miles in the four-and-twenty hours. She's a beauty. She's out from home, but we can build our own engines—all except the wheels. We're building ten locos. now, and we've got a dozen boilers ready if you care to look at them. How long does a loco. last? That's just as may be. She will do as much as her driver lets her. Some men play the mischief with a loco. and some handle 'em properly. Our drivers prefer Hawthorne's old four-wheel coupled engines because they give the least bother. There is one in that shed, and it's a good 'un to travel. But 80,000 miles generally sees the gloss off an engine, and she goes into the shops to be overhauled and re-fitted and re-planed, and a lot of things that you wouldn't understand if I told you about them. No. 1, the first loco. on the line, is running still, but very little of the original engine must be left by this time. That one there, called the *Fawn*, came out in the Mutiny year. She's by Slaughter and Grunning, and she's built for speed in front of a light load. French-looking sort of thing, isn't she? That's because her cylinders are on a tilt. We used her for the mail once, but the mail has grown heavier and heavier, and now we use six-wheel coupled eighteen inch, inside cylinder, 45-ton locos. to shift thousand-ton trains. *No!* All locos. aren't alike. It isn't merely pulling a lever. The company likes its drivers to know their locos., and a man will keep his Hawthorne for two or three years. The more mileage he gets out of her before she has to be overhauled the better man he is. It pays to let a man have his fancy engine. The Company knows that. Other lines don't. There's the ——. They run the life out of the men and the locos. together. They'll run an engine into the cleaning shed where-ever it may be, and then another driver jumps on and runs her back again, and so on till they've run the inside out of her. The drivers don't care. 'Tisn't *their* engine? The other man always said to have damaged her, and so the —— get their stock into a sweet state. 'Come in with a slide bar about red hot, and everything else to match. A man must take an interest in his loco., and that means she must belong to him. Some locos. won't do anything, even if you coax and humor them. I don't *think* there are any unlucky ones now, but some years ago No. 31 wasn't popular. The drivers went sick or took leave when they were told off for her. She killed her driver on the Jubbulpore line, she left the rails at Kajra, she did something or other at Rampur Haut, and Lord knows what she didn't do or try to do in other places! All the drivers fought shy of her, and in the end she disappeared. They said she was condemned, but I shouldn't wonder if the Company changed her number quietly, and changed the luck at the same time. You see, the Government Inspector comes and looks at our stock now and again, and when an engine's condemned he puts his dhobi mark on her, and she's broken up. Well, No. 31 was condemned, but there was a whisper that they only shifted her number, and ran her out again. When the drivers didn't know there were no accidents.

I don't think we've got an unlucky one running now. Some are different from others, but there are no man-eaters. Yes, a driver of the mail *is* somebody. He can make Rs. 370 a month if he's a covenanted man. We get a lot of our drivers in the country, and we don't import from England as much as we did. Stands to reason that, now there's more competition both among lines and in the labor market, the Company can't afford to be as generous as it used to be. It doesn't trap a man though. It's this way with the drivers. A native driver gets about Rs. 20 a month, and in his way he's supposed to be good enough for branch work and shunting and such. Well, an English driver'll get from Rs. 80 to Rs. 220, and overtime. The English driver knows what the native gets, and in time they tell the driver that the native'll improve. The driver has that to think of. You see? That's competition! A driver, one day with another, does his hundred miles a day. Say a man leaves Buxar at 2 p. m. he gets to Allahabad at 7 p. m. That's 163 miles. He rests at Allahabad till 8 : 20 next morning, when he goes back to Buxar, and rests till about 2 p. m. the next day. Then goes to Mokameh, reaches Mokameh at 7 p. m., stays till 4 next morning, and gets back to Buxar at 9 : 20 a. m. Then it all begins over again. He has got about three thousand pounds' worth of the Company's property to look after under his own hand, and the Lord knows how much value in the train behind him. Oh, he's got quite enough to think of when he's on his engine."

Experience returns to the engine-sheds, now full

of clamor, and enlarges on the beauties of sick locomotives. The fitters and the assistants and the apprentices are hammering and punching and gauging, and otherwise technically disporting themselves round their enormous patients, and their language, as caught in snatches, is beautifully unintelligible.

But one flying sentence goes straight to the heart. It is the cry of humanity over the task of life, done into unrefined English. An apprentice, grimed to his eyebrows, his cloth cap well on the back of his curly head and his hands deep in his pockets, is sitting on the edge of a tool-box ruefully regarding the very much disorganized engine whose slave is he. A handsome boy, this apprentice, and well made. He whistles softly between his teeth and his brow puckers. Then he addresses the engine, saying, half in expostulation and half in depair: "Oh, you condemned old female dog!" He puts the sentence more crisply—much more crisply—and Ignorance chuckles sympathetically.

Ignorance also is puzzled over these engines.

CHAPTER III.

AT VULCAN'S FORGE.

In the wilderness of the railway shops—and machinery that planes and shaves, and bevels and stamps, and punches and hoists and nips—the first idea that occurs to an outsider, when he has seen the men who people the place, is that it must be the birth-place of inventions—a pasture-ground of fat patents. If a writing-man, who plays with shadows and dresses dolls that others may laugh at their antics, draws help and comfort and new methods of working old ideas from the stored shelves of a library, how, in the name of Commonsense, his god, can a doing-man, whose mind is set upon things that snatch a few moments from flying Time or put power into weak hands, refrain from going forward and adding new inventions to the hundreds among which he daily moves?

Appealed to on this subject, Experience, who had served the E. I. R. loyally for many years, held his peace. "We don't go in much for patents; but," he added, with a praiseworthy attempt to turn the conversation, "we can build you any mortal thing you like. We've got the *Bradford Leslie* for the Sahibgunge ferry. Come and see the brass-work for her bows. It's in the casting-shed."

It would have been cruel to have pressed Experience further, and Ignorance, to foredate matters a little, went about to discover why Experience shied off this question, and why the men of Jamalpur had not each and all invented and patented something. He won his information in the end, but did not come from Jamalpur. *That* must be clearly understood. It was found anywhere you please between Howrah and Hoti Mardan ; and here it is that all the world may admire a prudent and far-sighted Board of Directors. Once upon a time, as everyone in the profession knows, two men invented the D. and O. sleeper—cast iron, of five pieces, very serviceable. The men were in the Company's employ, and their masters said : "Your brains are ours. Hand us over those sleepers." Being of pay and position, D. and O. made some sort of resistance and got a royalty or a bonus. At any rate, the Company had to pay for its sleepers. But thereafter, and the condition exists to this day, they caused it to be written in each servant's covenant, that if by chance he invented aught, his invention was to belong to the Company. Providence has mercifully arranged that no man or syndicate of men can buy the "holy spirit of man" outright without suffering in some way or another just as much as the purchase. America fully, and Germany in part, recognizes this law. The E. I. Railway's breach of it is thoroughly English. They say, or it is said of them that they say : "We are afraid of our men, who belong to us waking and sleeping, wasting their time on trying to invent."

Is it wholly impossible, then, for men of mechanical experience and large sympathies to check the mere patent-hunter and bring forward the man with an idea? Is there no supervision in the "shops," or have the men who play tennis and billiards at the institute not a minute which they can rightly call their very own? Would it ruin the richest Company in India to lend their model shop and their lathes to half-a-dozen, or, for the matter of that, half-a-hundred, abortive experiments? A Massachusetts organ factory, a Racine buggy shop, an Oregon lumber yard would laugh at the notion. An American toy-maker might swindle an *employe* after the invention, but he would in his own interests help the man to "see what comes of the thing." Surely a wealthy, a powerful and, as all Jamalpur bears witness, a considerate Company might cut that clause out of the covenant and await the issue. There would be quite enough jealousy between man and man, grade and grade, to keep down all the keenest souls; and, with due respect to the steam-hammer and the rolling-mill, we have not yet made machinery perfect. The "shops" are not likely to spawn unmanageable Stephensons or grasping Brunels; but in the minor turns of mechanical thought that find concrete expressions in links, axle-boxes, joint-packings, valves and spring-stirrups something might—something would—be done were the practical prohibition removed. Will a North countryman give you anything but warm hospitality for nothing? Or if you claim from him overtime service as a right, will he fall to work zealously? "Onything but t' brass," is his motto, and his ideas are his "brass."

Gentlemen in authority, if this should meet your august eyes, spare it a minute's thought, and, clearing away the floridity, get to the heart of the mistake and see if it cannot be rationally put right. Above all, remember that Jamalpur supplied no information. It was as mute as an oyster. There is no one within your jurisdiction to—ahem—"drop upon."

Let us, after this excursion into the offices, return to the shops and only ask Experience such questions as he can without disloyalty answer.

"We used once," says he, leading to the foundry, "to sell our old rails and import new ones. Even when we used 'em for roof beams and so on, we had more than we knew what to do with. Now we have got rolling-mills, and we use the rails to make tie-bars for the D. and O. sleepers and all sorts of things. We turn out five hundred D. and O. sleepers a day. Altogether, we use about seventy-five tons of our own iron a month here. Iron in Calcutta costs about five-eight a hundredweight; ours costs between three-four and three-eight, and on that item alone we save three thousand a month. Don't ask me how many miles of rails we own. There are fifteen hundred miles of line, and you can make your own calculation. All those things like babies' graves, down in that shed, are the moulds of the D. and O. sleepers. We test them by dropping three hundredweight and three hundred quarters of iron on top of them from a height of seven feet, or eleven sometimes. They don't often smash. We have a notion here that our iron is as good as the home stuff."

A sleek, white and brindled pariah thrusts himself into the conversation. His home appears to be on the warm ashes of the bolt-maker. This is a horrible machine, which chews red-hot iron bars and spits them out perfect bolts. Its manners are disgusting, and it gobbles over its food.

"Hi, Jack!" says Experience, stroking the interloper, "you've been trying to break your leg again. That's the dog of the works. At least he makes believe that the works belong to him. He'll follow any one of us about the shops as far as the gate, but never a step further. You can see he's first-class condition. The boys give him his ticket, and, one of these days, he'll try to get on to the Company's books as a regular worker. He's too clever to live." Jack heads the procession as far as the walls of the rolling-shed and then returns to his machinery room. He waddles with fatness and despises strangers.

"How would you like to be hot-potted there?" says Experience, who has read and who is enthusiastic over *She*, as he points to the great furnaces whence the slag is being dragged out by hooks. "Here is the old material going into the furnace in that big iron bucket. Look at the scraps of iron. There's an old D. and O. sleeper, there's a lot of clips from a cylinder, there's a lot of snipped-up rails, there's a driving-wheel block, there's an old hook, and a sprinkling of boiler-plates and rivets."

The bucket is tipped into the furnace with a thunderous roar and the slag below pours forth more quickly. "An engine," says Experience reflectively, "can run over herself so to say. After she's broken up she is made into sleepers for the line. You'll see how she's broken up later." A few paces further on, semi-nude demons are capering over strips of glowing hot iron which are put into a mill as rails and emerge as thin, shapely tie-bars. The natives wear rough sandals and some pretence of aprons, but the greater part of them is "all face." "As I said before," says Experience, "a native's cuteness when he's working on ticket is something startling. Beyond occasionally hanging on to a red-hot bar too long and so letting their pincers be drawn through the mills, these men take precious good care not to go wrong. Our machinery is fenced and guard-railed as much as possible, and these men don't get caught up by the belting. In the first place, they're careful—the father warns the son and so on—and in the second, there's nothing about 'em for the belting to catch on unless the man shoves his hand in. Oh, a native's no fool! He knows that it doesn't do to be foolish when he's dealing with a crane or a driving-wheel. You're looking at all those chopped rails? We make our iron as they blend baccy. We mix up all sorts to get the required quality. Those rails have just been chopped by this tobacco-cutter thing." Experience bends down and sets a vicious-looking, parrot-headed beam to work. There is a quiver—a snap—and a dull smash and a heavy 76-pound rail is nipped in two like a stick of barley-sugar.

Elsewhere, a bull-nosed hydraulic cutter is rail cutting as if it enjoyed the fun. In another shed stand the steam-hammers; the unemployed ones murmuring and muttering to themselves, as is the uncanny custom of all steam-souled machinery. Experience, with his hand on a long lever, makes one of the monsters perform: and though Ignorance knows that a man designed and men do continually build steam hammers, the effect is as though Experience were maddening a chained beast. The massive block slides down the guides, only to pause hungrily an inch above the anvil, or restlessly throb through a foot and a half of space, each motion being controlled by an almost imperceptible handling of the levers. "When these things are newly overhauled, you can regulate your blow to within an eighth of an inch," says Experience. "We had a foreman here once who could work 'em beautifully. He had the touch. One day a visitor, no end of a swell in a tall, white hat, came round the works, and our foreman borrowed the hat and brought the hammer down just enough to press the knap and no more. 'How wonderful!' said the visitor, putting his hand carelessly upon this lever rod here." Experience suits the action to the word and the hammer thunders on the anvil. "Well you can guess for yourself. Next minute there wasn't enough left of that tall, white hat to make a postage-stamp of. Steam-hammers aren't things to play with. Now we'll go over to the stores and see what happens to the old stock."

Experience leads the way to the Golgotha of Jamalpur. A great tripod, whence depends a pulley, chain, and hook, hangs over a circular fence, strong as an elephant stockade. Inside the stockade is a pit some ten feet deep and twelve or fourteen in diameter. The logs that shore its sides are scarred and bruised and dented and splintered in horrible fashion : even the timbers of the stockade bear the marks of manglement, and at the bottom of the pit lie two enormous iron balls, each nearly a ton's weight, and each bearing a handle. One look at the tripod and chain above and a rent cylinder below explains everything. A row of hopelessly decayed engines and tenders are the "subjects" of this grim dissecting-room. "You see," says Experience, "they hook on one of these balls to that chain, and haul it up by the winch in that fenced shed. Then they drop it on whatever is to be broken up, and—well, they dropped it upon that cylinder, and you can see for yourself what happened. Now, it has often struck me that Rider Haggard might use this place for a sort of variety entertainment, you know. No need to put a man in the pit. Just keep him inside the stockade when the ball fell, and let him dodge the splinters. A shell would be a joke to it. We break up old cannons here. There's the breach of one of them, but some are so curious I've saved them and mounted 'em yonder. They look neat on the red gravel by that fountain—don't they ?"

Whatever apparent disorder there might have been in the works, the store department is as clean as a new pin, and stupefying in its naval order. Copper plates, bar, angle, and rod iron, duplicate cranks and slide bars, the piston rods of the *Bradford Leslie* steamer, engine grease, files and hammer-heads—every conceivable article, from leather laces of beltings to head-lamps, necessary for the due and proper working of a long line, is stocked, stacked, piled, and put away in appropriate compartments. In the midst of it all, neck deep in ledgers and indent forms, stands the many-handed Babu, the steam of the engine whose power extends from Howruh to Ghaziabad.

One small set of pigeon-holes contains the bulk of the daily correspondence. It is noticeable that "Sir Bradford Leslie" has a pigeon-hole all to himself. A surreptitious grab at one paper shows that a sergeant-instructor of volunteers, four huudred miles away, has had something done to his kitchen table. And this department knows all about it? *Wah! Wah!* One can only gape vacantly. The E. I. R. is a great chief. When it cracks its whip, we stand on our hind legs, and walk round the ring backwards. Jamalpur does not say this, but that is the feeling in the air.

The Company does everything, and *knows everything*. The gallant apprentice may be a wild youth with an earnest desire to go occasionally "upon the bend." But three times a week, between 7 and 8 p. m., he must attend the night-school and sit at the feet of M. Bonnaud, who teaches him mechanics and statics so thoroughly that even the awful Government Inspector is pleased. And when there is no night-school the Company will by no means wash its hands of its men out of working-hours. No man can be violently restrained from going to the bad if he insists upon it, but in the service of the Company a man has every warning; his escapades are known, and a judiciously-arranged transfer sometimes keeps a good fellow clear of the down-grade, No one can flatter himself that in the multitude he is overlooked, or believe that between 4 p. m. and 9 a. m. he is at liberty to misdemean himself. Sooner or later, but generally sooner, his goings-on are known, and he is reminded that "Britons never shall be slaves"—to things that destroy good work as well as souls. Maybe the Company acts only in its own interest, but the result is good.

Best and prettiest of the many good and pretty things in Jamalpur is the institute of a Saturday when the Volunteer Band is playing and the tennis courts are full and the babydom of Jamalpur—fat, sturdy children—frolic round tbe band-stand. The people dance—but big as the institute is, it is getting too small for their dances—they act, they play billiards, they study their newspapers, they play cards and everything else, and they flirt in a sumptuous building, and in the hot weather the gallant apprentice ducks his friend in the big swimming-bath. Decidedly the railway folk make their lives pleasant.

Let us go down southward to the big Giridih collieries and see the coal that feeds the furnace that smelts the iron that makes the sleeper that bears the loco. that pulls the carriage that holds the freight that comes from the country that is made richer by the Great Company Bahadur, the East Indian Railway.

PART FOURTH.

CHAPTER I.

ON THE SURFACE.

Southward, always southward and easterly, runs the Calcutta Mail from Luckeeserai, till she reaches Madapur in the Sonthal Parganas. From Madapur a train, largely made up of coal-trucks, heads westward into the Hazaribagh district and towards Giridih. A week would not have exhausted "Jamalpur and its environs," as the guide-books say. But since time drives and man must e'en be driven, the weird, echoing bund in the hills above Jamalpur, where the owls hoot at night and hyenas come down to laugh over the grave of "Qullem Roberts, who died from the effects of an encounter with a tiger near this place, A. D. 1864," goes undescribed. Nor is it possible to deal with Monghyr, the headquarters of the district, where one sees for the first time the age of old Bengal in the sleepy, creepy station, built in a time-eaten fort, which runs out into the Ganges, and is full of quaint houses, with fat-legged balustrades on the roofs. Pensioners certainly, and probably a score of ghosts, live in Monghyr. All the country seems haunted. Is there not at Pir Bahar a lonely house on a bluff, the grave of a young lady, who, thirty years ago, rode her horse down the *khud* and perished? Has not Monghyr a haunted house in which tradition says skeptics have seen much more than they could account for? And is it not notorious throughout the countryside that the seven miles of road between Jamalpur and Monghyr are nightly paraded by tramping battalions of spectres, phantoms of an old-time army massacred, who but Sir W. W. Hunter knows how long ago? The common voice attests all these things, and an eerie cemetery packed with blackened, lichened, candle-extinguished tomb-stones persuades the listener to believe all that he hears. Bengal is second—or third is it?—in order of seniority among the Provinces, and like an old nurse, she tells many witch-tales.

But ghosts have nothing to do with collieries, and that ever-present "Company," the E. I. R., has more or less made Giridih—principally more. "Before the E. I. R. came," say the people, "we had one meal a day. Now we have two." Stomachs do not tell fibs, whatever mouths may say. That "Company," in the course of business, throws about five lakhs a year into the Hazaribah district in the form of wages alone, and Giridih Bazar has to supply the wants of twelve thousand men, women and children. But we have now the authority of a number of high-souled and intelligent native prints that the Sahib of all grades spends his time in "sucking the blood out of the country," and "flying to England to spend his ill-gotten gains." It is curious to watch a Sahib engaged in this operation. He—but no matter. His way shall be dealt with later on.

Giridih is perfectly mad—quite insane! Geologically, the big, thick books show that the country is in the metamorphic higher grounds that rise out of the alluvial flats of Lower Bengal between the Osri and the Barakar rivers. Translated, this sentence means that you can twist your ankle on pieces of pure white, pinky and yellowish granite, slip over weather-worn sandstone, grievously cut your boots over flakes of trap, and throw hornblende pebbles at the dogs. Never was such a place for stone-throwing as Giridih. The general aspect of the country is falsely park-like, because it swells and sings in a score of grass-covered undulations, and is adorned with plantation-like *sal* jungle. There are low hills on every side, and twelve miles away bearing south the blue bulk of the holy hills of Parasnath, greatest of the Jain Tirthankars, overlooks the world. In Bengal they consider four thousand five hundred feet good enough for a Dagshai or Kasauli, and once upon a time tried to put troops on Parasnath. There was a scarcity of water, and Thomas of those days found the silence and seclusion prey upon his spirits. Since twenty years, therefore, Parasnath has been abandoned by Her Majesty's Army.

As to Giridih itself, the last few miles of train bring up the reek of the "Black Country." Memory depends on smell. A noseless man is devoid of sentiment, just as a noseless woman, in this country, must be devoid of honor. That first breath of the coal should be the breath of the murky, clouded tract between Yeadon and Dale—or Barnsley, rough and hospitable Barnsley—or Dewsbury and Batley and the Derby Canal, on a Sunday afternoon when the wheels are still and the young men and maidens walk stolidly in pairs. Unfortunately, it is nothing more than Giridih—seven thousand miles away from home and blessed with a warm and genial sunshine, soon to turn into something very much worse. The insanity of the place is visible at the station door. A G. B. T. cart once married a bathing-machine, and they called the child *tum-tum*. You who in flannel and Cawnpore harness drive bamboo-carts about up-country roads, remember that a Giridih *tum-tum* is painfully pushed by four men, and must be entered crawling on all-fours, head first. So strange are the ways of Bengal.

They drive mad horses in Giridih—animals that become hysterical as soon as the dusk falls and the countryside blazes with the fires of the great coke ovens. If you expostulate tearfully, they produce another horse, a raw, red fiend whose ear has to be screwed round and round, and round and round, in a twitch before she will by any manner of means consent to start. Also, the roads carry neat little eighteen inch trenches at their sides, admirably adapted to hold the flying wheel. Skirling about this savage land in the dark, the white population beguile the time by rapturously recounting past accidents, insisting throughout on the super-equine "steadiness" of their cattle. Deep and broad and wide is their jovial hospitality; but somebody—the Tirhoot planters for choice—ought to start a mission to teach the men of Giridih what to drive. They know how, or they would be severally and separately and many times dead, but they do not, they do not indeed, know that animals who stand on one hind leg and beckon with all the rest, or try to pikstick in harness, are not trap-horses worthy of endearing names, but things to be pole-axed. Their feelings are hurt when you say this. "Sit tight," say the men of Giridih ; "we're insured ! We can't be hurt."

And now with grey hairs, dry mouth, and chattering teeth to the collieries. The E. I. R. estate, bought or leased in perpetuity from the Serampore Raja, may be about four miles long and between one and two miles across. It is in two pieces, the Serampore field being separated from Karharbari (or Kurhurballi or Kabarbari) field by the property of the Bengal Coal Company. The Raneegunge Coal Association lies to the east of all other workings. So we have three companies at work on about eleven square miles of land.

There is no such thing as getting a full view of the whole place. A short walk over a grassy down gives on to an outcrop of very dirty sandstone, which in the excessive innocence of their hearts most visitors will naturally take to be the coal lying neatly on the surface. Up to this sandstone the path seems to be made of crushed sugar, so white and shiny is the quartz. Over the brow of the down comes in sight the old familiar pit-head wheel, spinning for the dear life, and the eye loses itself in a maze of pumping sheds, red-tiled, mud-walled miners' huts, dotted all over the landscape and railway lines that seem to run on every kind of gradient. There are lines that dip into valleys and disappear round the shoulders of slopes, and lines that career on the tops of rises and disappear over the brow of the slopes. Along these lines whistle and pant metre-gauge engines, some with trucks at their tail and others rattling back to the pit-bank with the absurd air of a boy late for school that an unemployed engine always assumes. There are six engines in all, and as it is easiest to walk along the lines one sees a good deal of them. They bear not altogether unfamiliar names. Here, for instance, passes the "Cockburn" whistling down a grade with thirty tons of coal at her heels; while the "Whitly" and the "Olpherts" are waiting for their complement of trucks. Now a Mr. T. F. Cockburn was superintendent of these mines nearly thirty years ago, in the days before the chord lines from Kanu to Luckeeserai was built, and all the coal was carted to the latter place: and surely Mr. Olpherts was an engineer who helped to think out a new sleeper. What may these things mean?

"Apotheosis of the manager," is the reply. "Christen the engines after the managers. You'll find Cockburn, Dunn, Whitly, Abbott, Olpherts and Saise knocking about the place. Sounds funny, doesn't it? Doesn't sound so funny, when one of these idiots does his best to derail Saise, though, by putting a line down anyhow. Look at that line! Laid out in knots—by Jove!" To the unprofessional eye the rails seem all correct; but there must be something wrong, because "one of those idiots" is asked why in the name of all he considers sacred he does not ram the ballast properly.

"What would happen if you threw an engine off the line?" "Can't say that I know exactly. You see, our business is to keep them *on*, and we do that. Here's rather a curiosity. You see that pointsman! They say he's an old mutineer, and when he relaxes he boasts of the Sahibs he has killed. He's glad enough to eat the Company's salt now." Such a withered old face was the face of the pointsman at No. 11 point! The information suggested a host of questions, and the answers were these: "You won't be able to understand till you've been down into a mine. We work our men in two ways: some by direct payment—*sirkari*—under our own hand, and some by contractors. The contractor undertakes to deliver us the coal, supplying his own men, tools and props. He's responsible for the safety of his men, and of course the Company knows and sees his work. Just fancy, among these five thousand people, what sort of effect the *khuber* of an accident would produce! It would go all through the Sonthal Parganas. We have any amount of Sonthal besides Mahomedans and Hindus of every possible caste, down to those Musahers who eat pig. They don't require much administering in the civilian sense of the word. On Sundays, as a rule, if any man has had his daughter eloped with, or anything of that kind, he generally comes up to the manager's bungalow to get the matter put straight. If a man is disabled through accident he knows that as long as he's in the hospital he gets full wages, and the

Company pays for the food of any of his women-folk who come to look after him. One of course: not the whole clan. That makes our service popular with the people—poor beggars. Don't you believe that a native is a fool. You can train him to everything except responsibility. There's a rule in the workings that if there is any dangerous work, no—we haven't choke damps, I will show you when we get down—no gang must work without an Englishman to look after them. A native wouldn't be wise enough to understand what the danger was, or where it came in. Even if he did, he'd shirk the responsibility. We can't afford to risk a single life. All our output is just as much as the Company want—about a thousand tons per working day. Three hundred thousand in the year. We could turn out more? Yes—a little. Well, yes, twice as much. I won't go on, because you wouldn't believe me. There's the coal under us, and we work it at any depth from following up an outcrop down to six hundred feet. That is our deepest shaft. We have no necessity to go deeper. At home the mines are sometimes fifteen hundred feet down. Well, the thickness of this coal here varies from anything you please to anything you please. There's enough of it to last your time and one or two hundred years longer. Perhaps even longer than that. Look at that stuff. That's big coal from the pit."

It was aristocratic-looking coal, just like the picked lumps that are stacked in baskets of coal agencies at home with the printed legend atop "only 23*s* a ton." But there was no picking in this case. The great piled banks were all "equal to samples," and beyond them lay piles of small, broken, "smithy" coal. "The Company doesn't sell to the public. This small, broken coal is an exception. That is sold, but the big stuff is for the engines and the shops. It doesn't cost much to get out, as you say; but our men can earn as much as twelve rupees a month. Very often when they've earned enough to go on with they retire from the concern till they've spent their money and then come on again. It's piece-work and they are improvident. If some of them only lived like other natives they would have enough to buy land and cows with. When there's a press of work they make a good deal by overtime, but they don't seem to keep it. You should see Giridih Bazar on a Sunday if you want to know where the money goes. About ten thousand rupees change hands once a week there. If you want to get at the number of people who are indirectly dependent or profit by the E. I. R. you'll have to conduct a census of your own. After Sunday is over the men generally lie off on Monday and take it easy on Tuesday. Then they work hard for the next four days and make it up. Of course there's nothing in the wide world to prevent a man from resigning and going away to wherever he came from—behind those hills if he's a Sonthal. He loses his employment, that's all. And they have their own point of honor. A man hates to be told by his friends that he has been guilty of *nimakharami*. And now we'll go to breakfast. You shall be "pitted" to-morrow to any depth you like."

CHAPTER II.

IN THE DEPTHS.

"Pitted to any extent you please." The only difficulty was for Joseph to choose his pit. Giridih was full of them. There was an arch in the side of a little hill, a blackened brick arch leading into thick night. A stationary engine was hauling a procession of coal-laden trucks—"tubs" is the technical word—out of its depths. The tubs were neither pretty nor clean. "We are going down in those when they are emptied. Put on your helmet, and *keep* it on and keep your head down." The trucks were unloaded into the wagons of the metre-gauge colliery line in this wise. Drawn out by the engine along the line, they were pulled on to a platform of smooth iron, dexterously swung round by black demons in attendance, and slid on to what is technically termed a "tippler." This is a most crafty arrangement, partaking of the nature of a drop and a safety-stirrup. The tub goes forward until it is brought up by the curved ends of the metals it travels on, and sticks in a sort of gigantic stirrup. Then, gravely and solemnly, it overbalances itself, turns through half a circle, and shoots its load into the big truck below. Some of the "tipplers" are fixed on travelling platforms and can be moved down the whole length of a waiting coal-train. The

Ratel—is it not?—is the eccentric beast in the Zoo who runs round his cage and turns head-over-heels at a given place. These absurd tubs are Ratels, and the gravity of their self-arranged somersaults is very comic.

But there is nothing mirth-provoking in going down a coal-mine—even though it be only a shallow incline running to one hundred and forty feet vertical below the earth. "Get into the tub and lie down. Hang it, no! This is not a railway carriage: you can't see the country out of the windows. *Lie down* in the dust and don't lift your head. Let her go!"

The tubs strain on the wire rope and slide down fourteen hundred feet of incline, at first through a chastened gloom, and then through darkness. An absurd sentence from a trial report rings in the head:—"About this time prisoner expressed a desire for the consolations of religion." A hand with a reeking flare-lamp hangs over the edge of the tub, and there is a glimpse of a blackened *solah topee* near it, for those accustomed to the pits have a merry trick of going down sitting or crouching on the coupling of the rear tub. The noise is deafening, and the roof is very close indeed. The tubs bump, and the occupant crouches lovingly in the coal dust. What would happen if the train went off the line? The desire for the "consolations of religion" grows keener and keener as the air grows closer and closer. The tubs stop in darkness spangled, not lifted, by the light of the flare-lamps which many black devils carry. Underneath and on both sides there is the greasy blackness of the coal, and, above, a roof of grey sandstone, smooth as the flow of a river at evening. "Now, remember that if you don't keep your *topee* on, you'll get your head broken, because you will forget to stoop. If you hear any tubs coming up behind you step off to one side. There's a tramway under your feet, and be careful not to trip over it."

The miner has a gait as peculiarly his own as Tommy's measured paces or the blue jacket's roll. Big men who slouch in the light of day become almost things of beauty underground. Their foot is on their native heather; and the slouch is a very necessary act of homage to the great earth, which if a man observe not, he shall without doubt have his *solah topee*—bless the man who invented pith hats!—grievously cut and dented, and himself dowered with an aching head.

The road turns and winds and the roof becomes lower, but those accursed tubs still rattle by on the tramways. The roof throws back their noises, and when all the place is full of a grumbling and a growling, how under earth is one to know whence danger will turn up next? Also, the air is choking, and brings about, to the unacclimatized, a singing in the ears, a hotness of the eyeballs, and a jumping of the heart. "That's because the pressure here is different from the pressure up above. It'll wear off in a minute. *We* don't notice it. Wait till you get down a four-hundred-foot pit. *Then* your ears will begin to sing, if you like." Most people know the One Night of each hot weather—that still, clouded night just before the rain breaks, when there seems to be no more breathable air under the bowl of the pitiless skies, and all the weight of the silent, dark house lies on the chest of the sleep-hunter. This is the feeling in a coal-mine—only more so—much more so, for the darkness is the "gross darkness of the inner sepulchre." It is hard to see which is the black coal and which the passage driven through it. From far away, down the side galleries, comes the regular beat of the pick—thick and muffled as the beat of the laboring heart. "Six men to a gang, and they aren't allowed to work alone. They make six-foot drives through the coal—two and sometimes three men working together. The rest clear away the stuff and load it into the tubs. We have no props in this gallery because we have a roof as good as a ceiling. The coal lies under the sandstone here. It's beautiful sandstone." It *was* beautiful sandstone—as hard as a billiard table and devoid of any nasty little bumps and jags which cut into the hat.

There was a roaring down one road—the roaring of infernal fires. This is not a pleasant thing to hear in the dark. It is too suggestive. "That's our ventilating shaft. Can't you feel the air getting brisker? Come and look."

Imagine a great iron-bound crate of burning coal, hanging over a gulf of darkness faintly showing the brickwork of the base of a chimney. "We're at the bottom of the shaft. That fire makes a draught that sucks up the foul air from the bottom of the pit. There's another down-draw shaft in another part of the mine where the clean air comes in. We aren't going to set the mines on fire. There's an earth and *kutcha* brick floor at the bottom of the pit ; the crate hangs over. It isn't so deep as you think." Then a devil—a naked devil—came in with a pitchfork and fed the spouting flames. This was perfectly in keeping with the landscape, but it was not pretty. "That's only a little shaft. We've got one, an oval, eighteen feet by twelve, and four hundred and fifty feet deep. They aren't sunk like wells. Our sandstones are stronger than any bricks. We brick through the twenty feet of surface soil, but we can sink straight through the sandstone, knowing that the sinkings will stand. Now we'll go to the place where they are taking out the coal."

More trucks, more muffled noises, more darkness made visible, and more devils—male and female—coming out of darkness and vanishing. Then a picture to be remembered. A great Hall of Eblis, twenty feet from inky-black floor to grey roof, upheld by huge pillars of shining coal and filled with flitting and passing devils. On a shattered pillar near the roof stood a naked man, his flesh olive-colored in the light of the lamps, hewing down a mass of coal that still clove to the roof. Behind him was the wall of darkness, and when the lamps shifted he disappeared like a ghost. The devils were shouting directions, and the man howled in reply, resting on his pick and wiping the sweat from his brow. When he smote the coal crushed and slid and rumbled from the darkness into the darkness, and the devils cried *shabash!* The man stood erect like a bronze statue, he twisted and bent himself like a Japanese grotesque, and anon threw himself on his side after the manner of the dying gladiator. Then spoke the still small voice of fact: "A first-class workman if he would only stick to it. But as soon as he makes a little money he lies of and spends it. That's the last of a pillar that we've knocked out. See here. These pillars of coal are square, about thirty feet each way. As you can see, we make the pillar first by cutting out all the coal between. Then we drive a square tunnel, about seven feet wide, through and across the pillar, propping it with baulks. There's one fresh cut."

Two tunnels crossing at right angles had been driven through a pillar which in its under-cut condition seemed like the rough draft of a statue for an elephant. "When the pillar stands only on four legs we chip away one leg at a time from a square to an hour-glass shape, and then either the whole of the pillar crashes down from the roof or else a quarter or a half. If the coal lies against the sandstones it carries away clear, but in some places it brings down stone and rubbish with it. The chipped-away legs of the pillars are called stooks." "Who has to make the last cut that breaks a leg through?" "Oh! Englishmen of all sorts. We can't trust natives for the job unless it's very easy. The natives take kindly to the pillar work though. They are paid just as much for their coal as though they had hewed it out of the solid. Of course we take very good care to see that the roof doesn't come in on us. You would never understand how and why we prop our roofs with those piles of sleepers. Anyway, you can see that we cannot take out a whole line of pillars. We work 'em *en echelon*, and those big beams you see running from floor to roof are our indicators. They show when the roof is going to give. Oh! dear no, there's no dramatic effect about it. No splash, you know. Our roofs give plenty of warning by cracking and then *baito* slowly. The parts of the work that we have cleared out and allowed to fall in are called goafs'. You're on the edge of a goaf' now. All that darkness there marks the limit of the mine. We have worked that out piece-meal, and the props are gone and the place is down. The roof of any pillar-working is tested every morning by tapping—pretty hard tapping."

"Hi yi! yi!" shout all the devils in chorus, and the Hall of Eblis is full of rolling sound. The olive man has brought down an *avalanche* of coal. "It is a sight to see the whole of one of the pillars come away. They make an awful noise. It would startle you out of your wits. Some of 'em are ninety feet square. But there's not an atom of risk."

("Not an atom of risk." Oh, genial and courteous host, when you turned up next day blacker than any sweep that ever swept, with a neat, half-inch gash on your forehead—won by cutting a "stook" and getting caught by a bounding coal-knob—how long and earnestly did you endeavor to show that "stook-cutting" was an employment as harmless and unexciting as wool-samplering?)

"If you knew about mining, you'd see that our ways are rather primitive, but they're cheap, and they're safe as houses. Doms and Bauris, Kols and Beldars don't understand refinements in mining. They'd startle an English pit where there was fire-damp. Do you know it's a solemn fact that if you drop a Davy lamp or snatch it quickly you can blow a whole English pit inside out with all the miners? Good for us that we don't know what fire-damp is here. We can use the flare-lamps."

After the first feeling of awe and wonder is worn out, a mine becomes monotonous. How could a mine be anything but monotonous. Mile after mile of blackness stretching before the eyes as far as sight will carry, which is not saying much, even when one has been some time accustomed to the lack of light. There is only the humming, palpitating darkness, the rumble of the tubs and the endless procession of galleries to arrest the attention. And one pit to the uninitiated is as like to another as two peas. Tell a miner this and he laughs—slowly and softly. To him the pits have each distinct personalities, and each must be dealt with a different way. A descent from the pit-bank, and not from the mouth of an incline, is sickening—channel-passage sickening. Over pulley-wheels, mounted on shearlegs thirty, forty, or fifty feet high, passes the wire rope that is fastened to the "cages"—the two lifts on which the empty coal tubs go down and the loaded ones come up. A cage either has wooden guides at the four corners of the shaft or grips wire guide-ropes to steady it as it is let down. An engine drives the drum on which the wire-rope hauling line is coiled.

Very curious is a pit-bank when the work is in full swing. A hammer close to the winding engine strikes one, the driver places his foot on the lever: there is a roar far down the shaft, and an iron-railed platform with the loaded tub on it flies up and settles with a clang on four catches. The tub is run out into a "tippler" and discharges itself into a coal-truck. By the time it is run back empty into the second cage, a loaded truck is made ready at the bottom of the shaft, and as the empty truck sinks the full rises.

The hammer strikes three. The "winder" by the engine pulls a lever thrice, no empty tub is put into the cage, and the speed of the rise is not so great. There springs up a miner. He is a man, if we could get through the coal dust, and on his account special precautions are taken, and woe betide the pit-men who neglect them. All these things are lovely to look at. But the actual descent is not so good. If you swing a child vehemently, the little innocent is likely to complain that he feels as though his "tummy were left in the air." Now this is the exact sensation of dropping into a pit. The hangman adjusts the white cap. That is to say, you cram your hat down and go—drop away from the day and every-one you ever loved, *and* your "tummy." That comes down later. You arrive destitute of any inside, and are told for your comfort that in some of the English mines you can go down two thousand feet at the rate of sixty miles an hour. Two hundred feet at a considerably slower rate is enough—quite enough. Try it once or twice, and see what the air is like.

The return journey is said to possess an element of risk. For this reason. If the "winder" of the engine at the top stopped to think, or hunted for a flea, or got a fit, or was choked by a fly, his engine would continue to wind and wind until the cage was hauled up to the pulley-wheels thirty feet in the air, where it would have three courses open to it. It might jam, break the wire rope and fall back unbridled into the pit, or part into several pieces, or be hauled with one tremendous bound right over the pulley-wheels and come down a bundle of shattered ribs. In any case the occupant would not be in a position to describe the precise nature of the accident. But a native "winder" knows these things, and thinks of them every time the three taps come to his ears. For him "over-winding" would mean loss of post and pay. Therefore he does not overwind. He generally has a keen rivalry with a fellow-winder at another pit-bank, and lays himself out to see if he cannot bring more tons of coal to the bank than his *bhai*.

CHAPTER III.

THE PERILS OF THE PITS.

An engineer, who has built a bridge, can strike you nearly dead with professional facts; the captain of a seventy horse power Ganges river-steamer can, in one hour, tell legends about the Sandheads and the James and Mary shoal sufficient to fill half a *Pioneer*, but a couple of days spent on, above, and in a coal mine yields more mixed information than two engineers and three captains. It is hopeless to pretend to understand it all.

When your host says: "Ah, such an one is a thundering good fault-reader!" you smile hazily, and by way of keeping up the conversation, adventure on the statement that fault-reading and palmistry are very popular amusements. Then men laugh consumedly, and enter into explanations.

Everyone knows that coal strata, in common with women, horses, and official superiors, have "faults" caused by some colic of the earth in the days when things were settling into their places. A coal seam is suddenly sliced off as a pencil is cut through with one slanting blow of the penknife, and one-half is either pushed up or pushed down any number of feet. The miners work the seam till they come to this break-off, and then call for an expert to "read the fault." It is sometimes very hard to discover whether the sliced-off beam has gone up or down. Theoretically, the end of the broken piece should show the direction. Practically its indications are not always clear. Then a good "fault-reader," who must more than know geology, is a useful man, and is much prized, for the Giridih fields are full of faults and "dykes." Tongues of what was once molten lava thrust themselves sheer into the coal, and the disgusted miner finds that for about twenty feet on each side of the tongue all the coal has been burnt away.

The head of the mine is supposed to foresee these things and ever so many more. He can tell you, without looking at the map, what is the geological formation of any thousand square miles of India ; he knows as much about brickwork and the building of houses, arches, and shafts as an average P. W. D. man ; he has not only to know the intestines of a pumping or winding engine, but must be able to take them to pieces with his own hands, indicate on the spot such parts as need repair, and make drawings of anything that requires renewal ; he knows how to lay out and build railways with a grade of one in twenty-seven ; he has to carry in his head all the signals and points between and over which his locomotive engines work ; he has to be an electrician capable of controlling the apparatus that fires the dynamite charges in the pits, and must thoroughly understand boring operations with thousand-foot drills. Over and above this, he must know by name, at least, one thousand of the men on the works, and must fluently speak the vernaculars of the low castes. If he has Sonthali, which is more elaborate than Greek, so much the better for him. He must know how to handle men of all grades, and, while himself holding aloof, must possess sufficient grip of the men's private lives to be able to see at once the merits of a charge of attempted abduction preferred by a clucking, croaking Kol against a fluent English-speaking Brahmin. For he is literally the Light of Justice, and to him the injured husband or the wrathful father looks for redress. He must be on the spot and take all responsibility when any specially risky job is under way in the pit, and he can claim no single hour of the day or the night for his own. From eight in the morning till one in the afternoon he is coated with coal-dust and oil. From one till eight in the evening he has office work. After eight o'clock he is free to attend to anything that he may be wanted for.

This is a soberly-drawn picture of a life that *Sahibs* on the mines actually enjoy. They are spared all private socio-official worry, for the Company, in its mixture of State and private interest, is as perfectly cold-blooded and devoid of bias as any great, grinding Department of the Empire. If certain things be done, well and good. If certain things be not done the defaulter goes, and his place is filled by another. The conditions of service are graven on stone. There may be generosity: there undoubtedly is justice, but above all there is freedom within broad limits. No irrepressible shareholder cripples the executive arm with suggestions and restrictions, and no private piques turn men's blood to gall within them. Therefore men work like horses and are happy.

When he can snatch a free hour, the grimy, sweating, cardigan-jacketed, ammunition-booted, pick-bearing ruffian turns into a well-kept English gentleman, who plays a good game of billiards, and has a batch of new books from England every week. The change is sudden, but in Giridih nothing is startling. It is right and natural that a man should be alternately Valentine and Orson, specially Orson. It is right and natural to drive—always behind a mad horse—away and away towards the lonely hills till the flaming coke ovens become glow-worms on the dark horizon, and in the wilderness to find a lovely English maiden teaching squat, filthy Sonthal girls how to become Christians. Nothing is strange in Giridih, and the stories of the pits, the raffle of conversation that a man picks up as he passes, are quite in keeping with the place. Thanks to the law, which enacts that an Englishman must look after the native miners, and if any be killed, he and he alone has to explain satisfactorily that the accident was not due to preventable causes, the death-roll is kept astoundingly low. In one "bad" half-year six men out of the five thousand were killed, in another four, and in another none at all. Given "butcher bills" as small as these, it is not astonishing that the men in charge do their best to cut them down at any cost of time and sleep. As has been said before, a big accident would scare off the workers, for, in spite of the age of the mines—nearly thirty years—the hereditary pitman has not yet been evolved. But to small accidents the men are orientally apathetic. Be pleased to read of a death among the five thousand.

A gang has been ordered to cut clay for the luting of the coke furnaces. The clay is piled in a huge bank in the open sunlight above ground. A coolie hacks and hacks till he has hewn out a small cave with twenty feet of clay above him. Why should he trouble to climb up the bank and bring down the eave of the cave? It is easier to cut in. The Sirdar of the gang is watching round the shoulder of the bank. The coolie cuts lazily as he stands: Sunday is very near, and he will get gloriously drunk in Giridih Bazar with his week's earnings. He digs his own grave stroke by stroke, for he has not sense enough to see that undercut clay is dangerous. He is a Sonthal from the hills. There is a smash and a dull thud, and his grave has shut down upon him in an *avalanche* of heavy-caked clay.

The Sirdar calls to the Babu of the Ovens, and with the promptitude of his race the Babu loses his head. He runs puffily, without giving orders, anywhere, everywhere. Finally he runs to the *Sahib's* house. The *Sahib* is at the other end of the collieries. He runs back. The *Sahib* has gone home to wash. Then his indiscretion strikes him. He should have sent runners—fleet-footed boys from the coal-screening gangs. He sends them and they fly. One catches the *Sahib* just changed after his bath. "There is a man dead at such a place"—he gasps, omitting to say whether it is a surface or a pit accident. On goes the grimy pit kit, and in three minutes the *Sahib's* dogcart is flying to the place indicated.

They have dug out the Sonthal. His head is smashed in, spine and breastbone are broken, and the gang Sirdar, bowing double, throws the blame of the accident on the poor, shapeless, battered dead. "I had warned him, but he would not listen! *Twice* I warned him! These men are witnesses."

The Babu is shaking like a jelly. "Oh, sar, I have never seen a man killed before! Look at that eye, sar! I should have sent runners. I ran everywhere. I ran to your house. You were not in. I was running for hours. It was not my fault! It was the fault of the gang Sirdar." He wrings his hands and gurgles. The best of accountants, but the poorest of coroners is he. No need to ask how the accident happened. No need to listen to the Sirdar and his "witnesses." The Sonthal had been a fool, but it was the Sirdar's business to protect him against his own folly. "Has he any people here?"

"Yes, his *rukni*, his kept-woman, and his sister's brother-in-law. His home is far-off."

The sister's brother-in-law breaks through the crowd howling for vengeance on the Sirdar. He will send for the police, he will have the price of his *bhai's* blood full tale. The windmill arms and the angry eyes fall, for the *Sahib* is making the report of the death.

"Will this Sirkar give me *pensin?* I am his wife," a woman clamors, stamping her pewter-ankleted feet. "He was killed in your service. Where is his *pensin?* I am his wife." "You lie! You're his *rukni*. Keep quiet! Go! The *pensin* comes to *us*." The sister's brother-in-law is not a refined man, but the *rukni* is his match. They are silenced. The Sahib takes the report, and the body is borne away. Before to-morrow's sun rises the Sirdar may find himself a simple "surface-coolie," earning nine pice a day; and, in a week some Sonthal woman behind the hills may discover that she is entitled to draw monthly great wealth from the coffers of the *Sirkar*. But this will not happen if the sister's brother-in-law can prevent it. He goes off swearing at the *rukni*.

But, in the meantime, what have the rest of the dead man's gang been doing? They have, if you please, abating not one stroke, dug out all the clay, and would have it verified. They have seen their comrade die. He is dead. *Bus!* Will the Sirdar take the tale of clay? And yet, were twenty men to be crushed by their own carelessness in the pit, these impassive workers would scatter like panic-stricken horses.

But, turning from this sketch, let us set in order some of the stories of the pits. These are quaint tales. The miner-folk laugh when they tell them. In some of the mines the coal is blasted out by the dynamite which is fired by electricity from a battery on the surface. Two men place the charges, and then signal to be drawn up in the cage which hangs in the pit-eye. On one occasion two natives were entrusted with the job. They performed their parts beautifully till the end, when the vaster idiot of the two scrambled into the cage, gave signal, and was hauled up before his friend could enter.

Thirty or forty yards up the shaft all possible danger for those in the cage was over, and the charge was accordingly exploded. Then it occurred to the man in the cage that his friend stood a very good chance of being by this time riven to pieces and choked.

But the friend was wise in his generation. He had missed the cage, but found a coal-tub—one of the little iron trucks—and turning this upside down, had crawled into it. His account of the explosion has never been published. When the charge went off, his shelter was battered in so much, that men had to hack him out, for the tub had made, as it were, a tinned sardine of its occupant. He was absolutely uninjured, but his feeling were lacerated. On reaching the pit-bank his first words were: "I do not desire to go down the pit with *that* man any more." His wish had been already gratified for "that man" had fled. Later on, the story goes, when "that man" found that the guilt of murder was not at his door, he returned, and was made a surface-coolie, and his *bhai-band* jeered at him as they passed to their better-paid occupation.

Occasionally there are mild cyclones in the pits. An old working, perhaps a mile away, will collapse : a whole gallery sinking in bodily. Then the displaced air rushes through the inhabited mine, and, to quote their own expression, blows the pitmen about "like dry leaves." Few things are more amusing than the spectacle of a burly Tyneside foreman who, failing to dodge round a corner in time, is "put down" by the wind, sitting fashion, on a knobby lump of coal.

But most impressive of all is a tale they tell of a fire in a pit many years ago. The coal caught—light. They had to send earth and bricks down the shaft and build great dams across the galleries to choke the fire. Imagine the scene, a few hundred feet underground, with the air growing hotter and hotter each moment, and the carbonic acid gas trickling through the dams. After a time the rough dams gaped, and the gas poured in afresh, and the Englishmen went down and leeped the cracks between roof and dam-sill with anything they could get. Coolies fainted, and had to be taken away, but no one died, and behind the kutcha dams they built great masonry ones, and bested that fire; though for a long time afterwards, whenever they pumped water into it, the steam would puff out from crevices in the ground above.

It is a queer life that they lead, these men of the coal-fields, and a "big" life to boot. To describe one-half of their labors would need a week at the least, and would be incomplete then. "If you want to see anything," they say, "you should go over to the Baragunda copper-mines ; you should look at the Barakar ironworks ; you should see our boring operations five miles away ; you should see how we sink pits ; you should, above all, see Giridih Bazar on a Sunday. Why, you haven't seen anything. There's no end of a Sonthal Mission hereabouts. All the little dev—dears have gone on a picnic. Wait till they come back, and see 'em learning to learn."

Alas ! one cannot wait. At the most one can but thrust an impertinent pen skin-deep into matters only properly understood by specialists.

CHAPTER IV.

IN AN OPIUM FACTORY.

On the banks of the Ganges, forty miles below Benares as the crow flies, stands the Ghazipur Factory, an opium mint as it were, whence issue the precious cakes that are to replenish the coffers of the Indian Government. The busy season is setting in, for with April the opium comes in from districts after having run the gauntlet of the district officers of the Opium Department, who will pass it as fit for use. Then the really serious work begins under a roasting sun. The opium arrives by *challans*, regiments of one hundred jars, each holding one maund and each packed in a basket and sealed atop. The district officer submits forms—never was such a place for forms as the Ghazipur Factory—showing the quality and weight of each pot, and with the jars come a ziladar responsible for the safe carriage of the *challans*, their delivery and their virginity. If any pots are broken or tampered with an unfortunate individual called the import officer, and appointed to work like a horse from dawn till dewy eve, must examine the ziladar in charge of the *challan* and reduce his statement to writing. Fancy getting any native to explain how a *matka* has been smashed. But the perfect flower is about as valuable as silver.

Then all the pots have to be weighed, and the weights—Calcutta Mint, if you please—and the beams must be daily tested. The weight of each pot is recorded on the pot, in a book, and goodness knows where else, and everyone has to sign certificates that the weighing is correct. *Nota bene.* The pots have been weighed once in the district and once in the factory. Therefore a certain number of them are taken at random and weighed afresh before they are opened. This is only the beginning of the long series of checks. All sorts of inquiries are made aboutlight pots, and then the testing begins. Every single, serially-numbered pot has to be tested for quality. A native called the *purkhea* drives his fist into the opium, rubs and smells it, and calls out the class for the benefit of the opium examiner. A sample picked between finger and thumb is thrown into a jar, and if the opium examiner thinks the *purkhea* has said sooth, the class of the jar is marked in chalk, and everything is entered in a book. Every ten samples are put in a locked box with duplicated keys, and sent over to the laboratory for assay. With the tenth boxful—and this marks the end of the *challan* of a hundred jars—the Englishman in charge of the testing signs the test paper, and enters the name of the native tester and sends it over to the laboratory. For convenience sake, it may be as well to say that, unless distinctly stated to the contrary, every single thing in Ghazipur is locked, and every operation is conducted under more than police supervision.

In the laboratory each set of ten samples is thoroughly mixed by hand, a quarter ounce lump is then tested for starch adulteration by iodine which turns the decoction blue, and, if necessary, for gum adulteration by alcohol which makes the decoction filmy. If adulteration be shown, all the ten pots of that set are tested separately. When the sinful pot is discoverd, all the opium is tested in four-pound lumps. Over and above this test, three samples of one hundred grains each are taken from the *jummakaroed* set of ten samples, dried on a steam table and then weighed for consistence. The result is written down in a ten-columned form in the assay register, and by the mean result are those ten pots paid for. This, after everything has been done in duplicate and counter-signed, completes the test and assay. If a district officer has classed the opium in a glaringly wrong way, he is thus caught and reminded of his error. No one trusts anyone in Ghazipur. They are always weighing, testing and assaying.

Before the opium can be used it must be "alligated" in big vats. The pots are emptied into these, and special care is taken that none of the drug sticks to the hands of the coolies. Opium has a special knack of doing this, and therefore coolies are searched at most inopportune moments. There are a good many Mahomedans in Ghazipur, and they would all like a little opium. The pots after emptying are smashed up and scraped, and heaved down the steep river bank of the factory, where they help to keep the Ganges in its place, so many are they, and the little earthen bowls in which the opium cakes are made. People are forbidden to wander about the river front of the factory in search of remnants of opium on the strands. There are no remnants, but people will not credit this. After vatting, as has been said, the big vats, holding from one to three thousand maunds, are probed with test rods, and the samples are treated just like the samples of the *challans*, everybody writing everything in duplicate and signing it. Having secured the mean consistence of each vat, the requisite quantity of each blend—Calcutta Mint scales again, and an unlimited quantity of supervision—is weighed out, thrown into an alligation vat, of 250 maunds, and worked up by the feet of coolies, who hang on to ropes and drag their legs painfully through the probe. Try to wade in mud of 70° consistency, and see what it is like.

This completes the working of the opium. It is now ready to be made into cakes after a final assay. Man has done nothing to improve it since it streaked the capsule of the poppy—this mysterious drug. Perhaps half a hundred sinners have tried to adulterate it and been paid out accordingly, but that has been the utmost. April, May and June are the months for receiving and manufacturing opium, and in the winter months comes the packing and the despatch.

At the beginning of the cold weather Ghazipur holds locked up a trifle, say, of three and a half millions sterling in opium. Now, there may be only a paltry three-quarters of a million on hand, and that is going out at the rate of one Viceroy's salary for two and a half years per diem. For such a flea-bite it seems absurd to prohibit smoking in the factory or to stud the place with tanks and steam fire-engines. Really, Ghazipur is unnecessarily timid. A long time ago some one threatened to cast down a tree sacred to Mahadeo. In a very few days, just as soon as Mahadeo got news of the insult, a fire broke out and damaged thousands of pounds' worth of opium.

But all this time we have not gone through the factory. There are ranges and ranges of gigantic godowns, huge barns that can hold over half-a-million pounds' worth of opium. There are acres of bricked floor, regiments on regiments of chests; and yet more godowns and more godowns. The heart of the whole is the laboratory which is full of the sick faint smell of a *chandu-kh na*. This makes Ghazipur indignant. "That's the smell of opium. We don't need *chandu* here. You don't know what real opium smells like. *Chandu-khana* indeed! That's refined opium under treatment for morphia, and *cocaine* and perhaps *narcoine*." "Very well, let's see some of the real opium made for the China market." "We shan't be making any for another six weeks at earliest; but we can show you one cake made, and you must imagine two hundred and fifty men making 'em as hard as they can up to one every four minutes." A *Sirdar* of cake-makers is called, and appears with a miniature *dhobi's* washing board on which he sits, a little square box of dark wood, a tin cup, an earthen bowl, and a mass of poppy petal *chupattis*. A larger earthen bowl holds a mass of what looks like bad Cape tobacco. "What's that?" "Trash—dried poppy leaves, not petals, broken up and used for packing cakes in. You'll see presently." The cake-maker sits down and receives a lump of opium, weighed out, of one seer seven chittacks and a half, neither more nor less. "That's pure opium of seventy consistence." Every allowance is weighed. "What are they weighing that brown water for?" "That's *lewa*—thin opium at fifty consistence. It's the paste. He gets four chittacks and a half." "And do they weigh the *chupattis*?" "Of course. Five chittacks of *chupattis*—about sixteen *chupattis* of all three kinds." This is overwhelming. This *sirdar* takes a brass hemispherical cup and wets it with a rag. Then he tears a *chupatti* across so that it fits into the cup without a wrinkle, and pastes it with the thin opium, the *lewa.* After this his actions become incomprehensible, but there is evidently a deep method in them. *Chupatti* after *chupatti* is torn across, dressed with *lewa* and pressed down into the cup, the fringes hanging over the edge of the bowl. He takes half *chupattis* and fixes them skilfully, picking now first-class and now second-class ones. Everything is gummed into everything else with the *lewa*, and he presses all down by twisting his wrists inside the bowl. "He is making the *gattia* now." *Gattia* means a tight coat at any rate, so there is some ray of enlightenment. Torn *chupatti* follows torn *chupatti*, till the bowl is lined half-an-inch deep with them, and they all glisten with the greasy *lewa.* He now takes up an ungummed *chupatti* and fits in carefully all round. The opium is dropped tenderly upon this, and a curious washing motion of the hand follows. The opium is drawn up into a cone as one by one the *sirdar* picks up the overlapping portions of the *chupattis* that hung outside the bowl and plasters them against the drug. He makes a clever waist-belt while he keeps all the flags in place, and so strengthens the midriff of the lump. He tucks in the top of the cone with his thumbs, brings the fringe of *chupattis* over to close the opening, and pastes fresh leaves upon all. The cone has now taken a spherical shape, and he gives it the finishing touch by gumming a large chupatti, one of the "moon" kind, set aside from the first, on the top, so deftly that no wrinkle is visible. The cake is now complete, and all the Celestials of the middle kingdom shall not be able to disprove that it weighs two seers one and three-quarter chittacks, with a play of half a chittack for the personal equation.

The Sirdar takes it up and rubs it in the bran-like poppy trash in the big bowl, so that two-thirds of it are powdered with the trash and one-third is fair and shiny *chupatti.* "That is the difference between a Ghazipur and a Patna cake. Our cakes have always an unpowdered head. The Patna ones are rolled in trash all over. You can tell them anywhere by that mark. Now we'll cut this one open and you can see how a section looks." One half of an inch as nearly as may be is the thickness of the *chupatti* shell all round the cake, and even in this short time so firmly has the *lewa* set that any attempt at 'undering the skins of *chupatti* is followed by the renaing of the poppy petals that compose the *chupatti.* "You've seen in detail what a cake is made of—that is to say, pure opium 70 consistence, poppy-petal pancakes, *lewa*, of 52'50 consistence, and a powdering of poppy-trash." "But why are you so particular about the shell?" "Because of the China market. The Chinaman likes every inch of the stuff we send him, and uses it. He boils the shell and gets out every grain of the *lewa* used to gum it together. He smokes that after he has dried it. Roughly speaking, the value of the cake we've just cut open is two pound ten. All the time it is in our hands we have to look after it and check it, and treat it as though it were gold. It mustn't have too much moisture in it, or it will swell and crack, and if it is too dry John Chinaman won't have it. He values his opium for qualities just the opposite of those in Smyrna opium. Smyrna opium gives as much as ten per cent. of morphia, and is nearly solid—90 consistence. Our opium does not give more than three or three and a half per cent. of morphia on the average, and, as you know it is only 70 or in Patna 75 consistence. That is the drug the Chinaman likes. He can get the maximum of extract out of it by soaking it in hot water, and he likes the flavor. He knows it is absolutely pure too, and it comes to him in good condition." "But has nobody found out any patent way of making these cakes and putting skins on them by machinery?" Not *yet*. Poppy to poppy. There's nothing better. Here are a couple of cakes made in 1849, when they tried experiments in wrapping them in paper and cloth. You can see that they are beautifully wrapped and sewn like cricket balls, but it would take about half-an-hour to make such cakes, and we could not be sure of keeping the aroma in them. Nothing like poppy plant for poppy drug."

And this is the way the drug, which yields such a splendid income to the Indian Government, is prepared. To tell how it is thereafter kept in store, packed for export, put upon the market at certain fixed periods, and shipped away, for John Chinaman's consumption chiefly, would be a tame story. The interest lies in the actual manufacture and manipulation of the cakes, and we have seen how this is done in the busy factory at Ghazipur.

THE END.